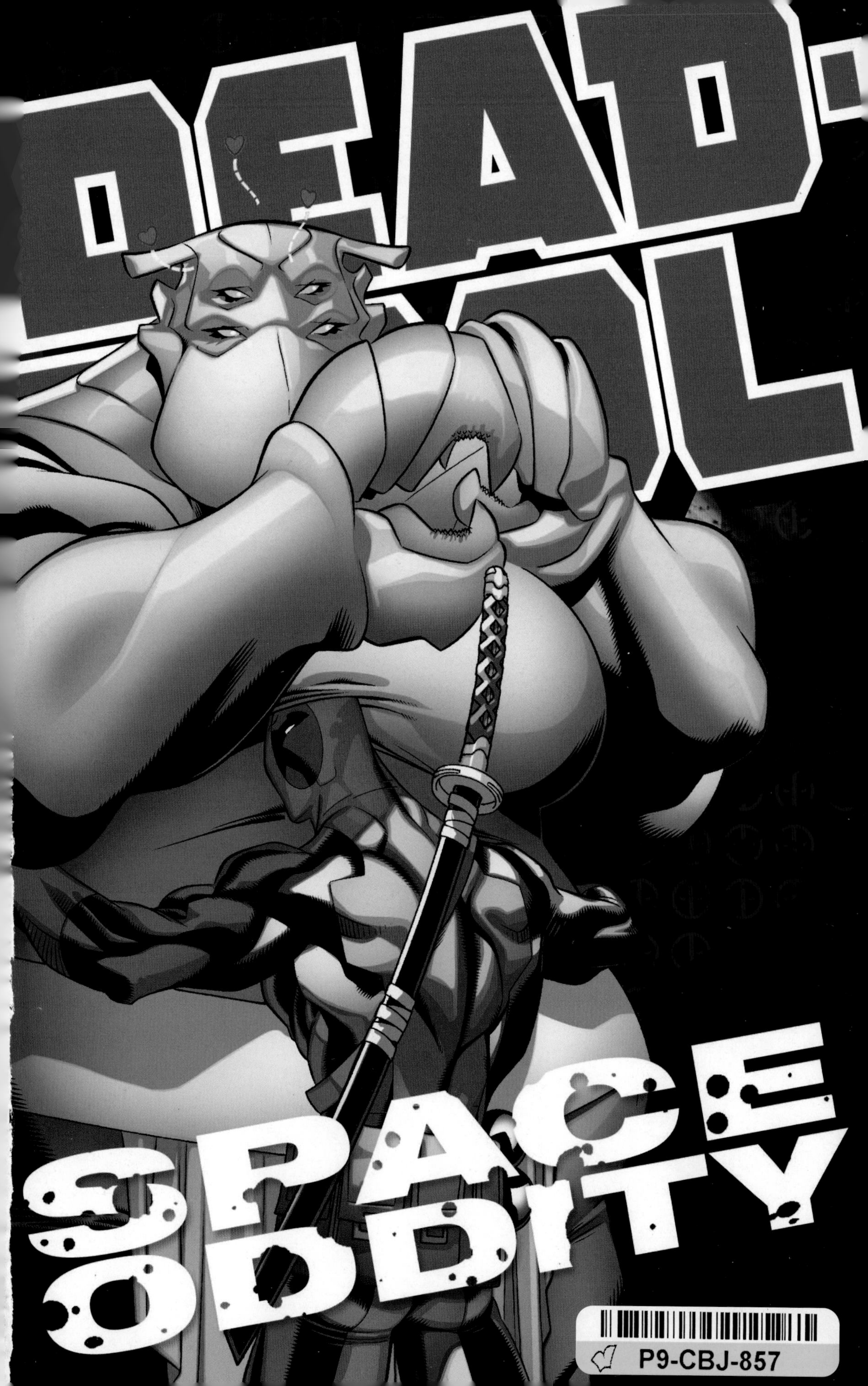
DEAD-
SPACE
ODDITY
P9-CBJ-857

DEADPOOL
SPACE ODDITY

WRITER: **DANIEL WAY**

PENCILS: **SHELDON VELLA** (ISSUE #32), **CARLO BARBERI** (ISSUES #33-35)
& **BONG DAZO** (ISSUE #33.1)

INKS: **SHELDON VELLA** (ISSUE #32), **WALDEN WONG** (ISSUES #33-35)
& **JOE PIMENTEL** (ISSUE #33.1)

COLORS: **SHELDON VELLA** (ISSUE #32), **MARTE GRACIA** (ISSUE #33)
& **ANDRES MOSSA** (ISSUES #33.1 & 34-35)

LETTERS: **VIRTUAL CALLIGRAPHY'S JOE SABINO**

COVER ARTIST: **DAVE JOHNSON**

EDITORS: **JODY LEHEUP** & **JORDAN D. WHITE**

CONSULTING EDITOR: **AXEL ALONSO**

COLLECTION EDITOR: **CORY LEVINE**
EDITORIAL ASSISTANTS: **JAMES EMMETT** & **JOE HOCHSTEIN**
ASSISTANT EDITORS: **MATT MASDEU, ALEX STARBUCK** & **NELSON RIBEIRO**
EDITORS, SPECIAL PROJECTS: **JENNIFER GRÜNWALD** & **MARK D. BEAZLEY**
SENIOR EDITOR, SPECIAL PROJECTS: **JEFF YOUNGQUIST**
SENIOR VICE PRESIDENT OF SALES: **DAVID GABRIEL**
SVP OF BRAND PLANNING & COMMUNICATIONS: **MICHAEL PASCIULLO**
BOOK DESIGN: **RODOLFO MURAGUCHI**

EDITOR IN CHIEF: **AXEL ALONSO** • CHIEF CREATIVE OFFICER: **JOE QUESADA**
PUBLISHER: **DAN BUCKLEY** • EXECUTIVE PRODUCER: **ALAN FINE**

DEADPOOL VOL. 7: SPACE ODDITY. Contains material originally published in magazine form as DEADPOOL #32-35 and #33.1. First printing 2011. Hardcover ISBN# 978-0-7851-5137-1. Softcover ISBN# 978-0-7851-5138-8. Published by MARVEL WORLDWIDE, INC., a subsidiary of MARVEL ENTERTAINMENT, LLC. OFFICE OF PUBLICATION: 135 West 50th Street, New York, NY 10020. Copyright © 2011 Marvel Characters, Inc. All rights reserved. Hardcover: $19.99 per copy in the U.S. and $21.99 in Canada (GST #R127032852). Softcover: $15.99 per copy in the U.S. and $17.99 in Canada (GST #R127032852). Canadian Agreement #40668537. All characters featured in this issue and the distinctive names and likenesses thereof, and all related indicia are trademarks of Marvel Characters, Inc. No similarity between any of the names, characters, persons, and/or institutions in this magazine with those of any living or dead person or institution is intended, and any such similarity which may exist is purely coincidental. **Printed in the U.S.A.** ALAN FINE, EVP - Office of the President, Marvel Worldwide, Inc. and EVP & CMO Marvel Characters B.V.; DAN BUCKLEY, Publisher & President - Print, Animation & Digital Divisions; JOE QUESADA, Chief Creative Officer; JIM SOKOLOWSKI, Chief Operating Officer; DAVID BOGART, SVP of Business Affairs & Talent Management; TOM BREVOORT, SVP of Publishing; C.B. CEBULSKI, SVP of Creator & Content Development; DAVID GABRIEL, SVP of Publishing Sales & Circulation; MICHAEL PASCIULLO, SVP of Brand Planning & Communications; JIM O'KEEFE, VP of Operations & Logistics; DAN CARR, Executive Director of Publishing Technology; JUSTIN F. GABRIE, Director of Publishing & Editorial Operations; SUSAN CRESPI, Editorial Operations Manager; ALEX MORALES, Publishing Operations Manager; STAN LEE, Chairman Emeritus. For information regarding advertising in Marvel Comics or on Marvel.com, please contact John Dokes, SVP Integrated Sales and Marketing, at jdokes@marvel.com. For Marvel subscription inquiries, please call 800-217-9158. **Manufactured between 5/2/2011 and 5/30/2011 (hardcover), and 5/2/2011 and 10/31/2011 (softcover), by R.R. DONNELLEY, INC., SALEM, VA, USA.**

10 9 8 7 6 5 4 3 2 1

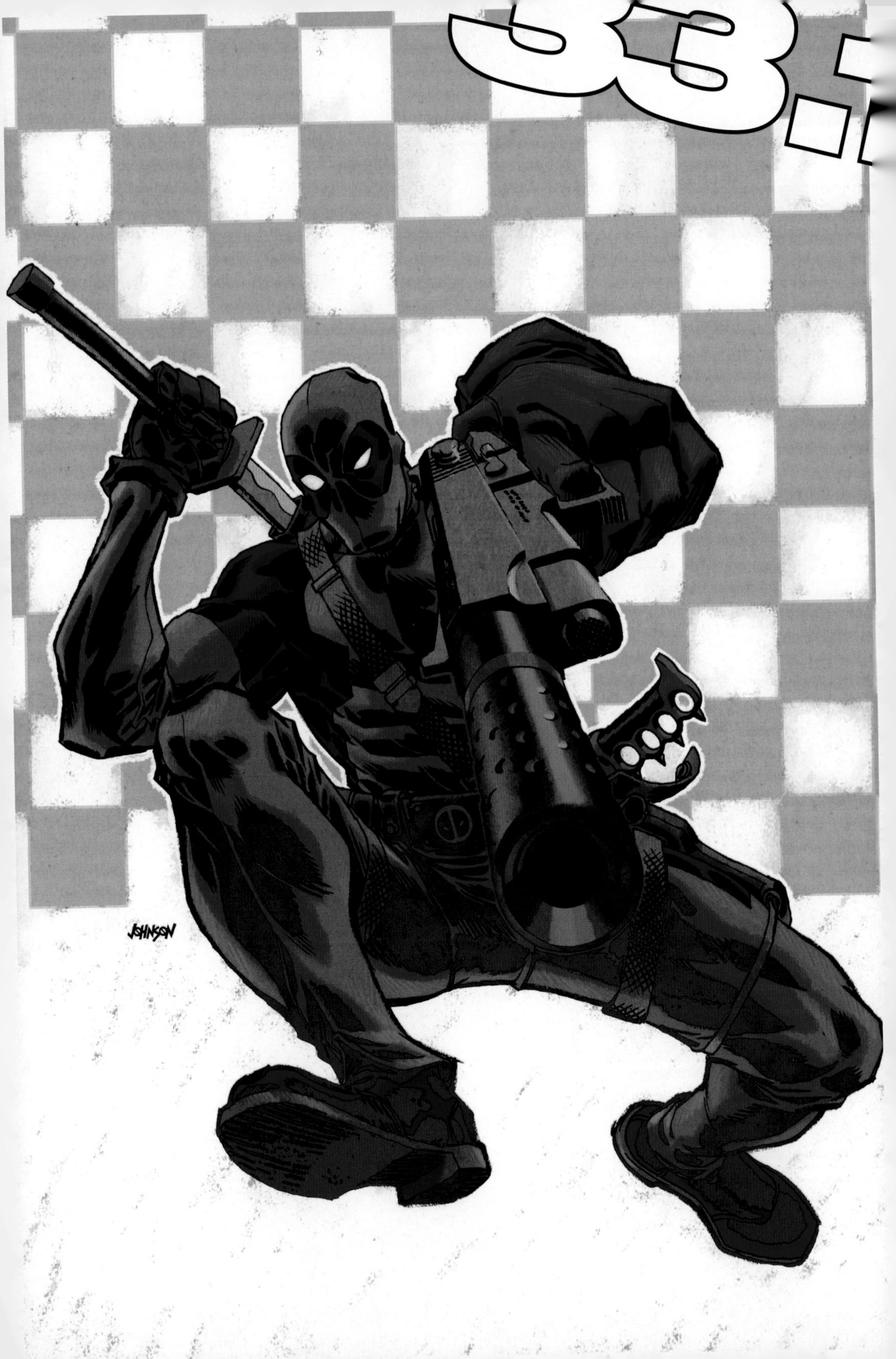
33.
JOHNSON

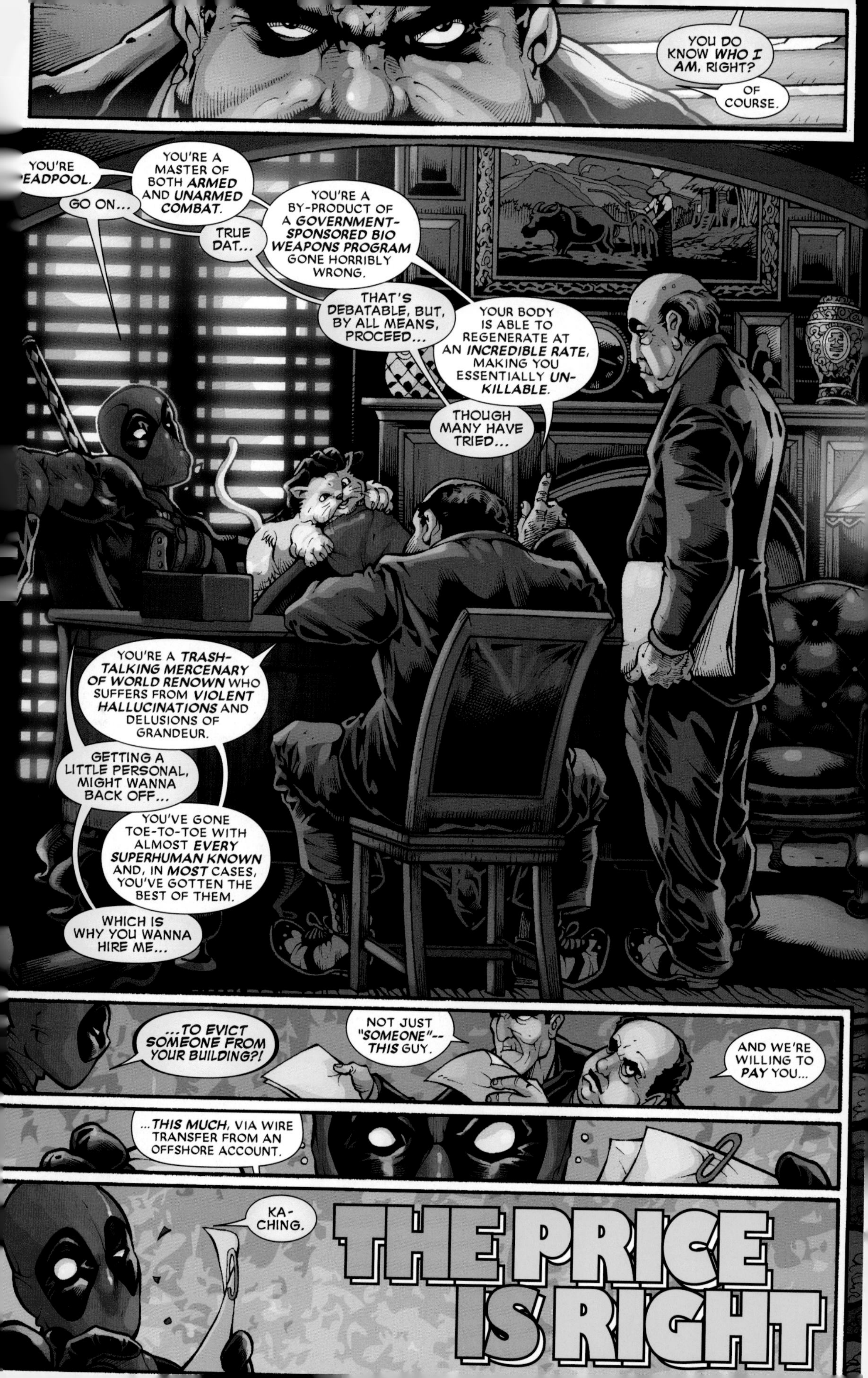

YOU DO KNOW WHO I AM, RIGHT?
OF COURSE.
YOU'RE DEADPOOL.
GO ON...
YOU'RE A MASTER OF BOTH ARMED AND UNARMED COMBAT.
TRUE DAT...
YOU'RE A BY-PRODUCT OF A GOVERNMENT-SPONSORED BIO WEAPONS PROGRAM GONE HORRIBLY WRONG.
THAT'S DEBATABLE, BUT, BY ALL MEANS, PROCEED...
YOUR BODY IS ABLE TO REGENERATE AT AN INCREDIBLE RATE, MAKING YOU ESSENTIALLY UN-KILLABLE.
THOUGH MANY HAVE TRIED...
YOU'RE A TRASH-TALKING MERCENARY OF WORLD RENOWN WHO SUFFERS FROM VIOLENT HALLUCINATIONS AND DELUSIONS OF GRANDEUR.
GETTING A LITTLE PERSONAL, MIGHT WANNA BACK OFF...
YOU'VE GONE TOE-TO-TOE WITH ALMOST EVERY SUPERHUMAN KNOWN AND, IN MOST CASES, YOU'VE GOTTEN THE BEST OF THEM.
WHICH IS WHY YOU WANNA HIRE ME...
...TO EVICT SOMEONE FROM YOUR BUILDING?!
NOT JUST "SOMEONE"-- THIS GUY.
AND WE'RE WILLING TO PAY YOU...
...THIS MUCH, VIA WIRE TRANSFER FROM AN OFFSHORE ACCOUNT.
KA-CHING.
THE PRICE IS RIGHT

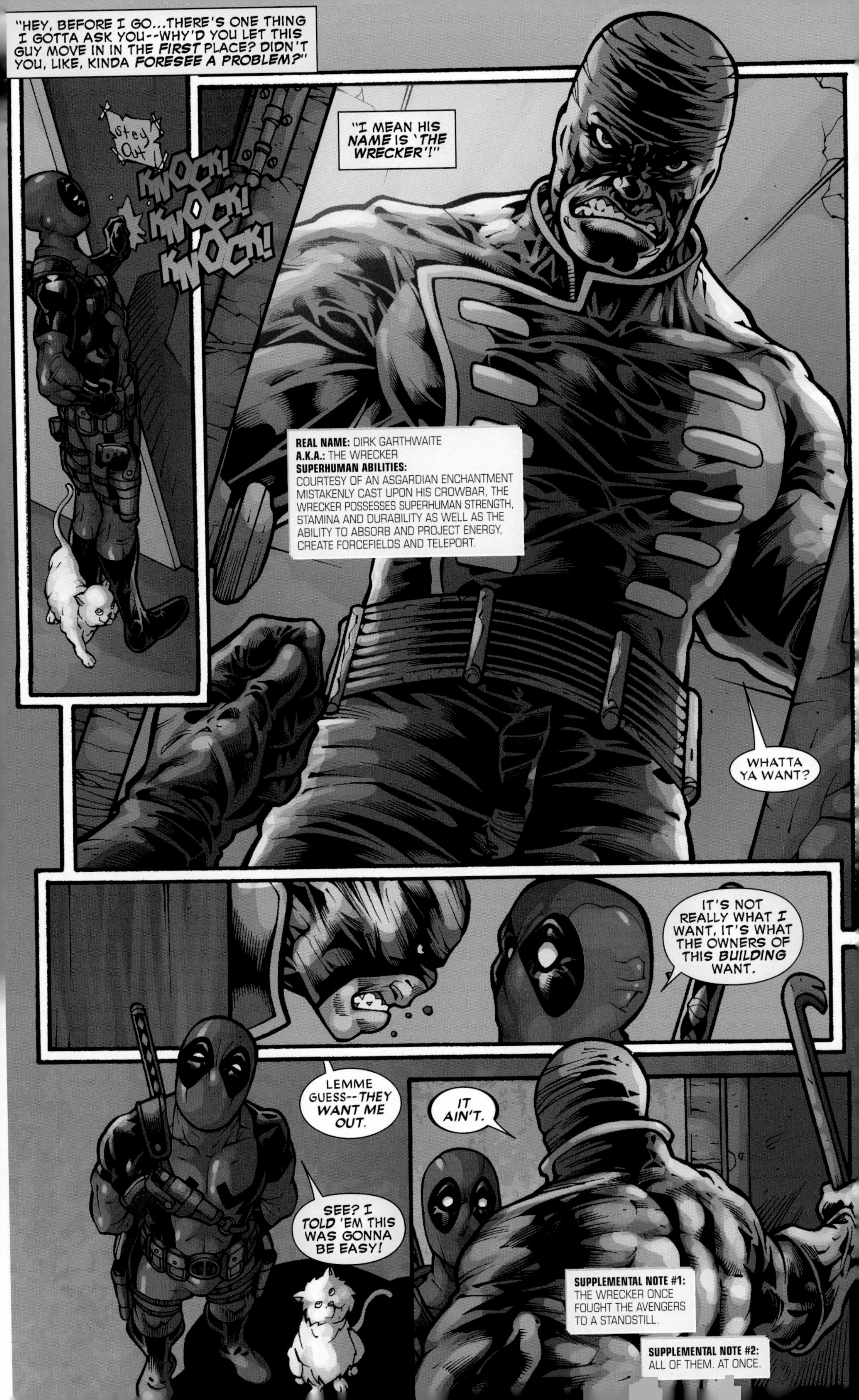
"HEY, BEFORE I GO...THERE'S ONE THING I GOTTA ASK YOU--WHY'D YOU LET THIS GUY MOVE IN IN THE FIRST PLACE? DIDN'T YOU, LIKE, KINDA FORESEE A PROBLEM?"
Stay Out
KNOCK! KNOCK! KNOCK!
"I MEAN HIS NAME IS 'THE WRECKER'!"
REAL NAME: DIRK GARTHWAITE
A.K.A.: THE WRECKER
SUPERHUMAN ABILITIES:
COURTESY OF AN ASGARDIAN ENCHANTMENT MISTAKENLY CAST UPON HIS CROWBAR, THE WRECKER POSSESSES SUPERHUMAN STRENGTH, STAMINA AND DURABILITY AS WELL AS THE ABILITY TO ABSORB AND PROJECT ENERGY, CREATE FORCEFIELDS AND TELEPORT.
WHATTA YA WANT?
IT'S NOT REALLY WHAT I WANT, IT'S WHAT THE OWNERS OF THIS BUILDING WANT.
LEMME GUESS--THEY WANT ME OUT.
IT AIN'T.
SEE? I TOLD 'EM THIS WAS GONNA BE EASY!
SUPPLEMENTAL NOTE #1:
THE WRECKER ONCE FOUGHT THE AVENGERS TO A STANDSTILL.
SUPPLEMENTAL NOTE #2:
ALL OF THEM. AT ONCE.

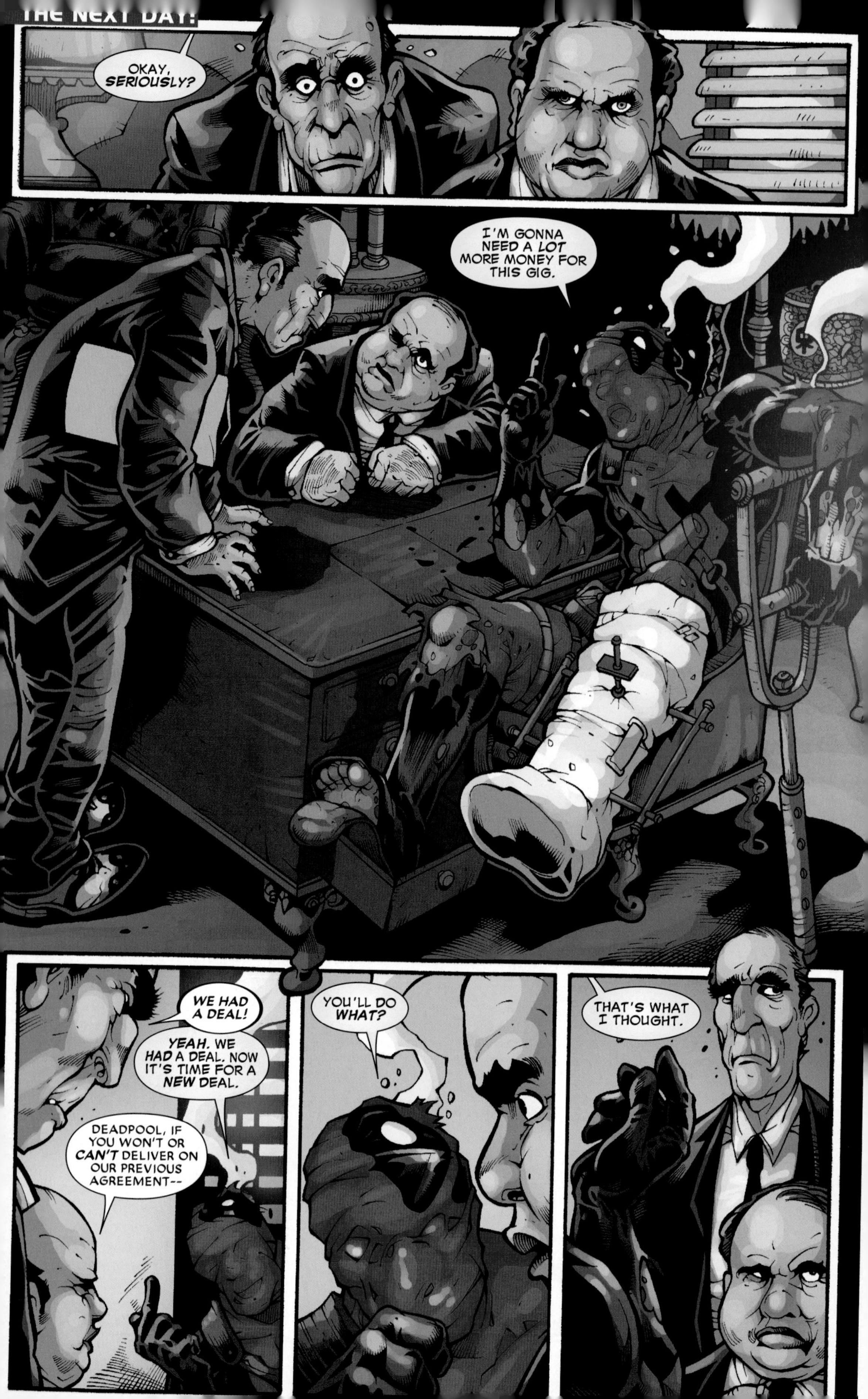
THE NEXT DAY:
OKAY, SERIOUSLY?
I'M GONNA NEED A LOT MORE MONEY FOR THIS GIG.
WE HAD A DEAL!
YEAH. WE HAD A DEAL. NOW IT'S TIME FOR A NEW DEAL.
DEADPOOL, IF YOU WON'T OR CAN'T DELIVER ON OUR PREVIOUS AGREEMENT--
YOU'LL DO WHAT?
THAT'S WHAT I THOUGHT.

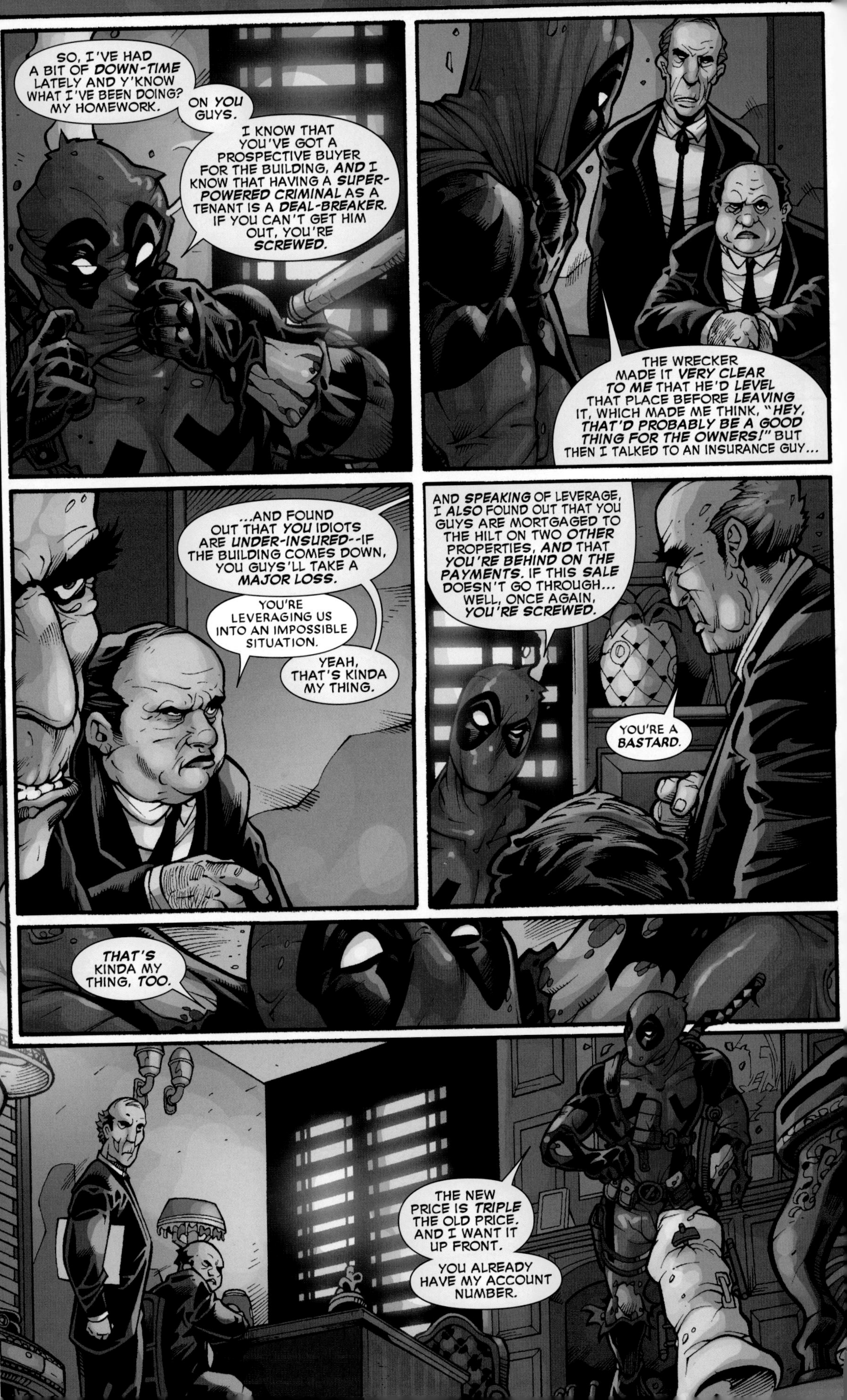
SO, I'VE HAD A BIT OF *DOWN-TIME* LATELY AND Y'KNOW WHAT I'VE BEEN DOING? MY HOMEWORK.
ON *YOU* GUYS.
I KNOW THAT YOU'VE GOT A PROSPECTIVE BUYER FOR THE BUILDING, *AND* I KNOW THAT HAVING A *SUPER-POWERED CRIMINAL* AS A TENANT IS A *DEAL-BREAKER*. IF YOU CAN'T GET HIM OUT, YOU'RE *SCREWED*.
THE WRECKER MADE IT *VERY CLEAR TO ME* THAT HE'D LEVEL THAT PLACE BEFORE *LEAVING* IT, WHICH MADE ME THINK, "*HEY, THAT'D PROBABLY BE A GOOD THING FOR THE OWNERS!*" BUT THEN I TALKED TO AN INSURANCE GUY...
...AND FOUND OUT THAT *YOU* IDIOTS ARE *UNDER-INSURED*--IF THE BUILDING COMES DOWN, YOU GUYS'LL TAKE A *MAJOR LOSS*.
YOU'RE LEVERAGING US INTO AN IMPOSSIBLE SITUATION.
YEAH, THAT'S KINDA MY THING.
AND *SPEAKING* OF LEVERAGE, I *ALSO* FOUND OUT THAT YOU GUYS ARE MORTGAGED TO THE HILT ON TWO *OTHER* PROPERTIES, *AND* THAT *YOU'RE BEHIND ON THE PAYMENTS*. IF THIS *SALE* DOESN'T GO THROUGH... WELL, ONCE AGAIN, *YOU'RE SCREWED*.
YOU'RE A *BASTARD*.
THAT'S KINDA MY THING, *TOO*.
THE NEW PRICE IS *TRIPLE* THE OLD PRICE. AND I WANT IT UP FRONT.
YOU ALREADY HAVE MY ACCOUNT NUMBER.

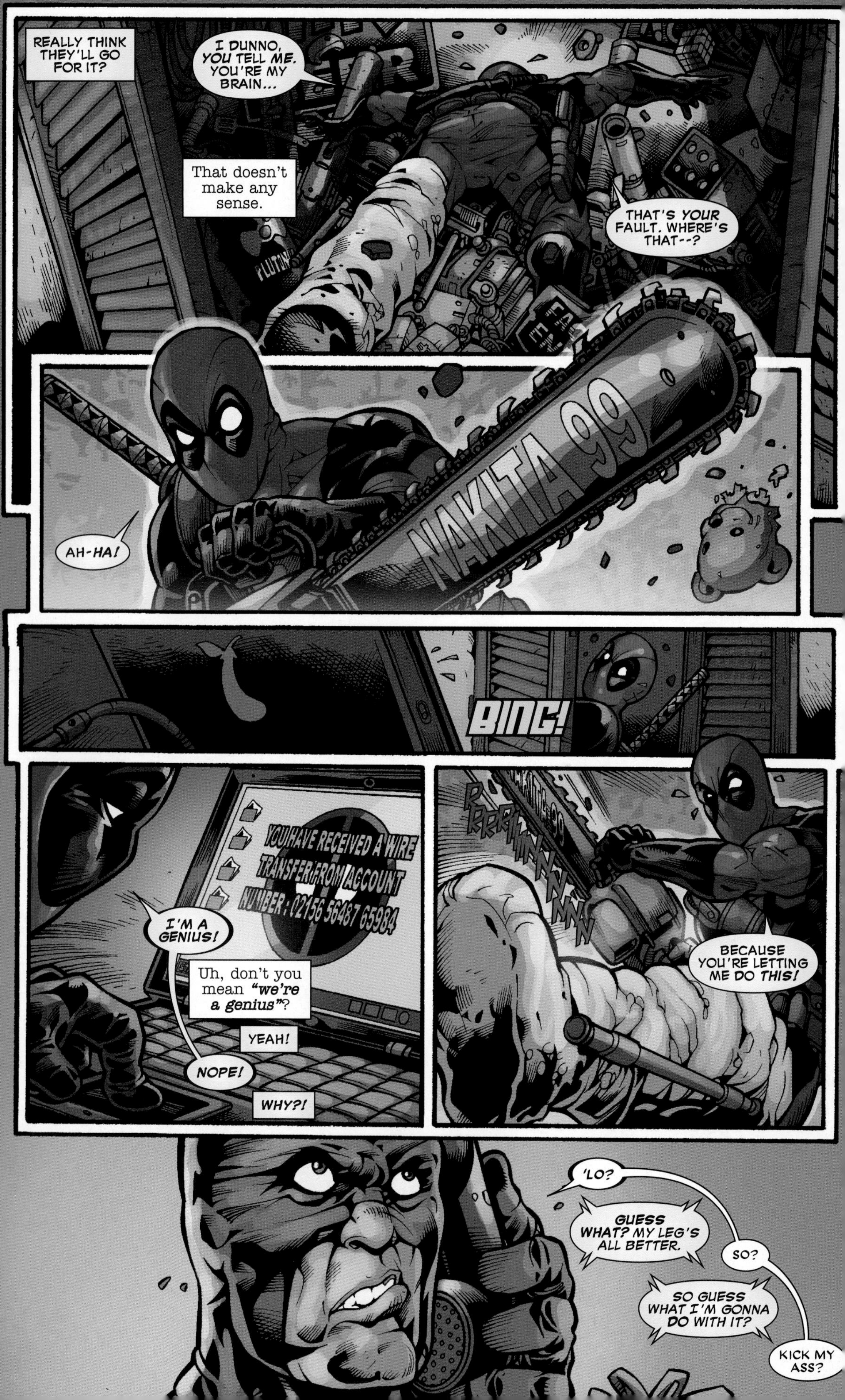

REALLY THINK THEY'LL GO FOR IT?
I DUNNO, YOU TELL ME. YOU'RE MY BRAIN...
That doesn't make any sense.
THAT'S YOUR FAULT. WHERE'S THAT--?
AH-HA!
NAKITA 99
BING!
YOU HAVE RECEIVED A WIRE TRANSFER FROM ACCOUNT NUMBER : 02156 56487 65984
I'M A GENIUS!
Uh, don't you mean "we're a genius"?
YEAH!
NOPE!
WHY?!
RRRRAWWNNNNNNNNN
BECAUSE YOU'RE LETTING ME DO THIS!
'LO?
GUESS WHAT? MY LEG'S ALL BETTER.
SO?
SO GUESS WHAT I'M GONNA DO WITH IT?
KICK MY ASS?

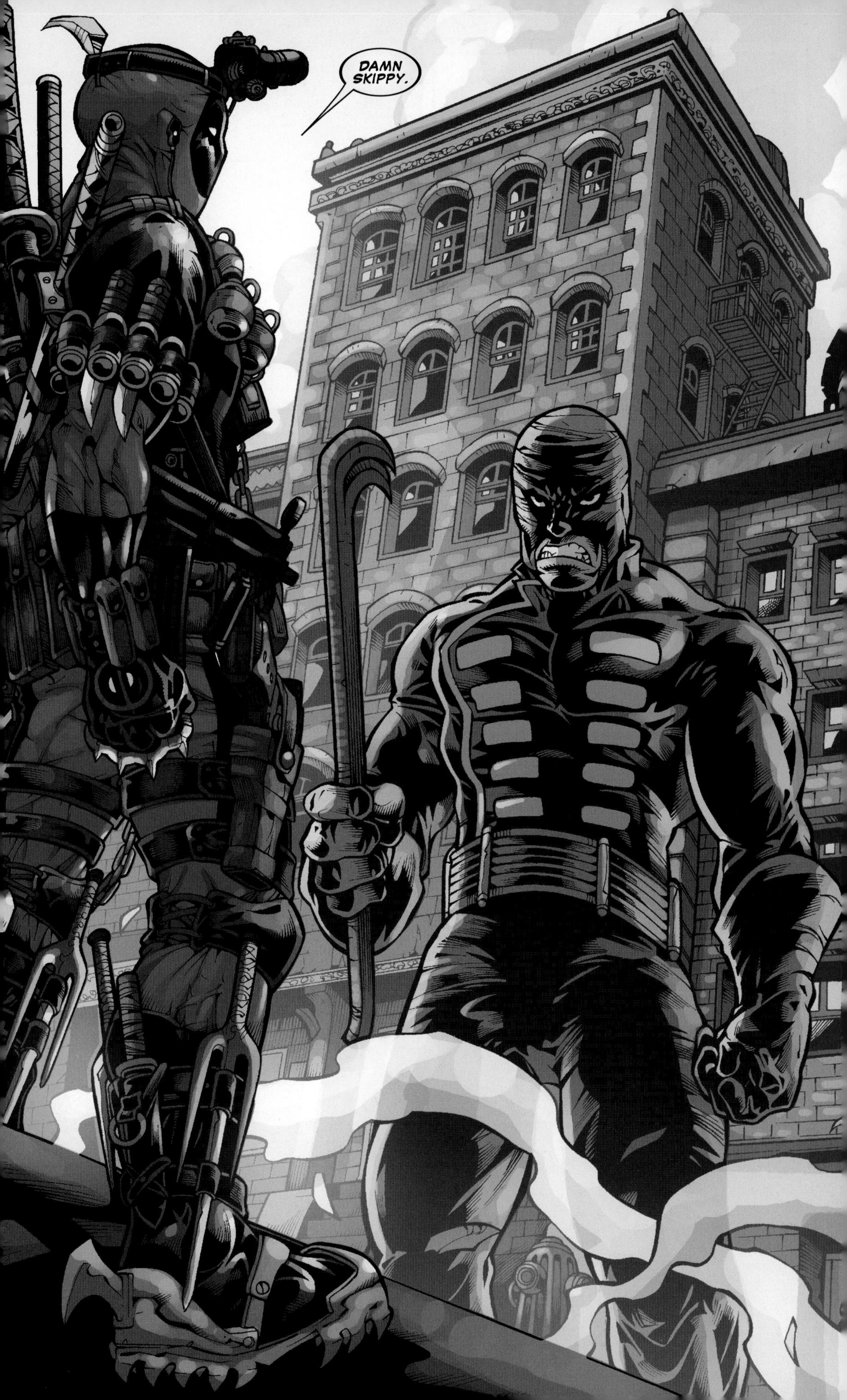
DAMN SKIPPY.

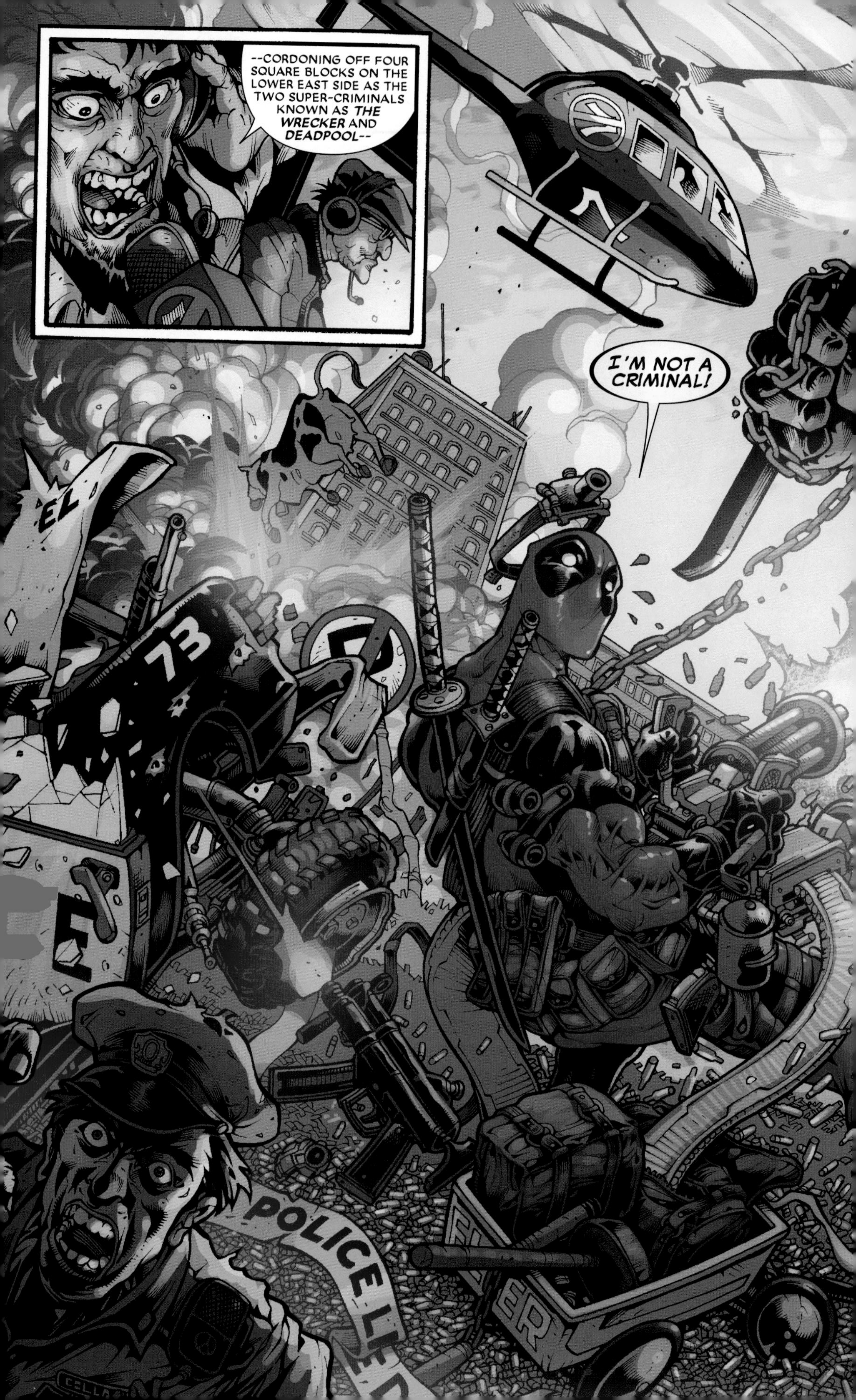
--CORDONING OFF FOUR SQUARE BLOCKS ON THE LOWER EAST SIDE AS THE TWO SUPER-CRIMINALS KNOWN AS THE WRECKER AND DEADPOOL--
I'M NOT A CRIMINAL!
73
POLICE

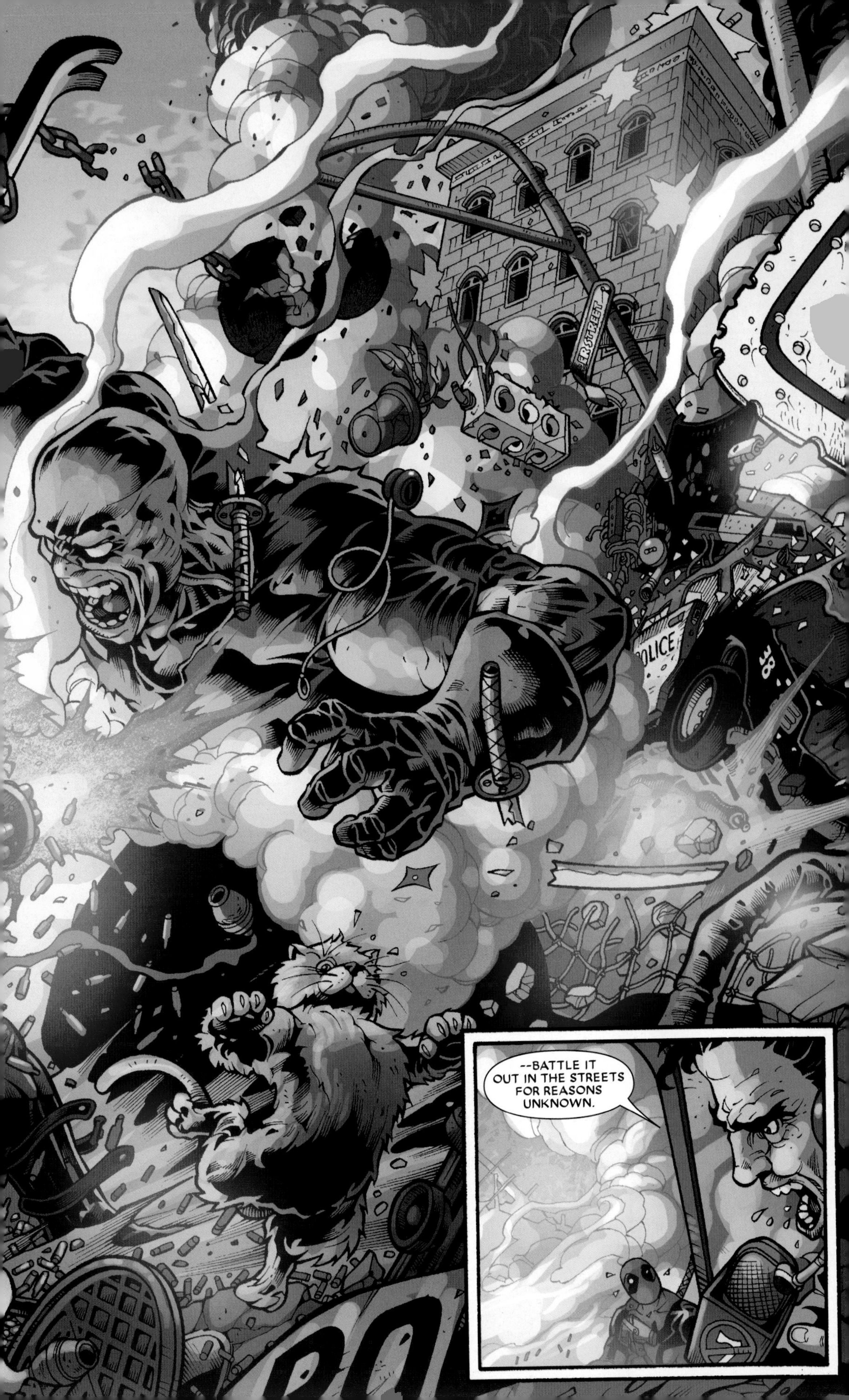
--BATTLE IT OUT IN THE STREETS FOR REASONS UNKNOWN.
POLICE
38

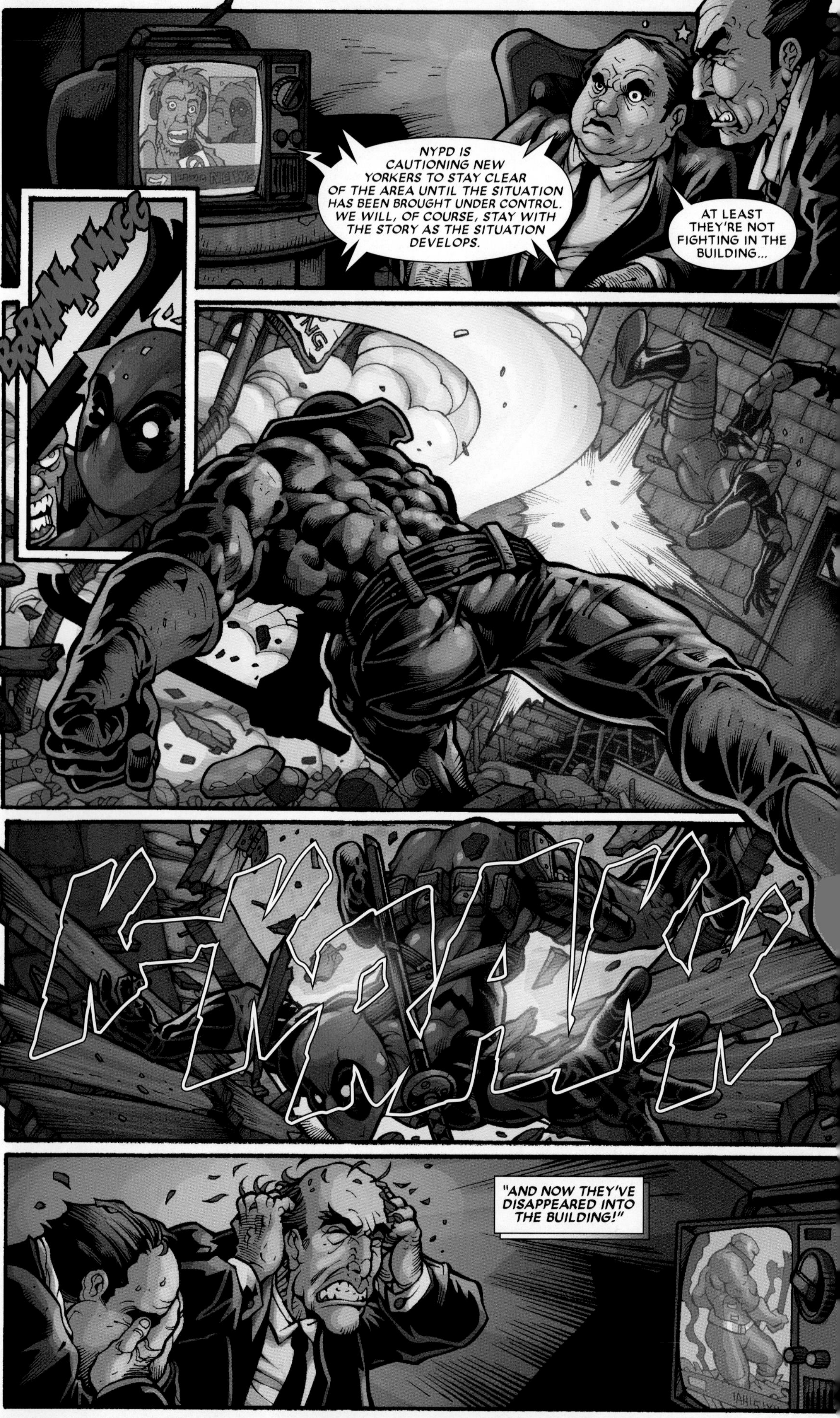

NYPD IS CAUTIONING NEW YORKERS TO STAY CLEAR OF THE AREA UNTIL THE SITUATION HAS BEEN BROUGHT UNDER CONTROL. WE WILL, OF COURSE, STAY WITH THE STORY AS THE SITUATION DEVELOPS.
AT LEAST THEY'RE NOT FIGHTING IN THE BUILDING...
BRRAKAKKG
"AND NOW THEY'VE DISAPPEARED INTO THE BUILDING!"

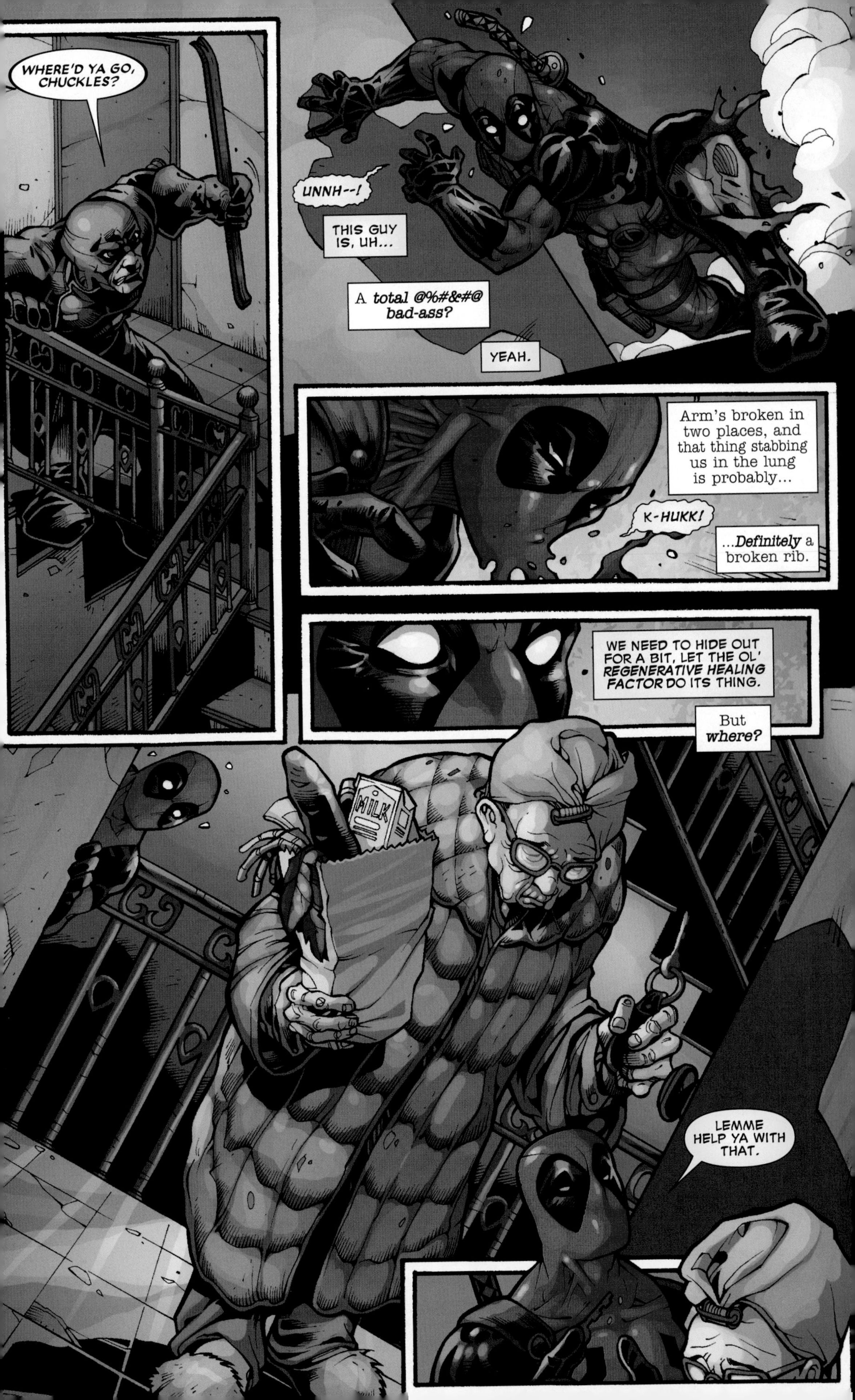
WHERE'D YA GO, CHUCKLES?
UNNH--!
THIS GUY IS, UH...
A total @%#&#@ bad-ass?
YEAH.
Arm's broken in two places, and that thing stabbing us in the lung is probably...
K-HUKK!
...Definitely a broken rib.
WE NEED TO HIDE OUT FOR A BIT, LET THE OL' REGENERATIVE HEALING FACTOR DO ITS THING.
But where?
MILK
LEMME HELP YA WITH THAT.

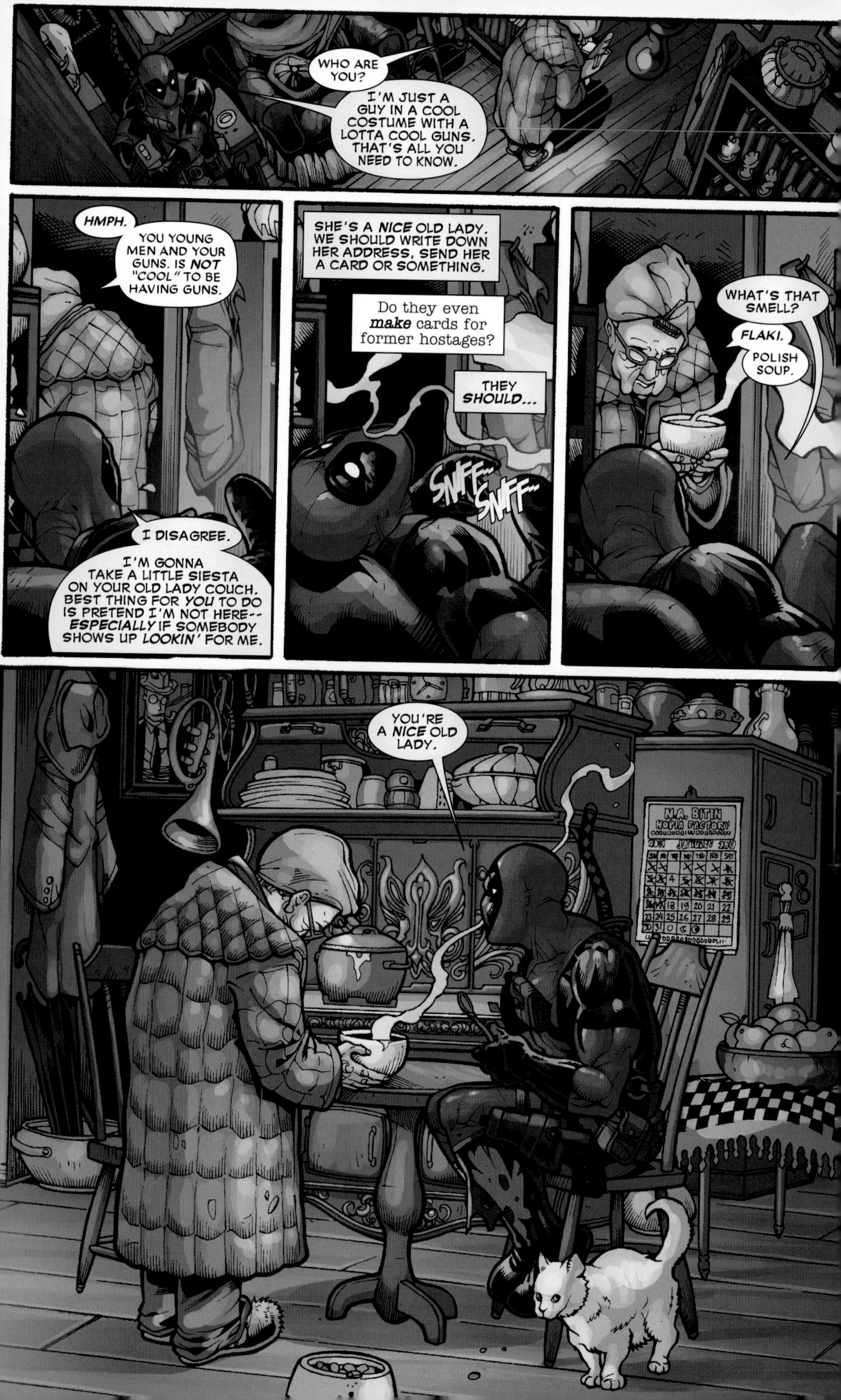

WHO ARE YOU?
I'M JUST A GUY IN A COOL COSTUME WITH A LOTTA COOL GUNS. THAT'S ALL YOU NEED TO KNOW.
HMPH.
YOU YOUNG MEN AND YOUR GUNS. IS NOT "COOL" TO BE HAVING GUNS.
I DISAGREE.
I'M GONNA TAKE A LITTLE SIESTA ON YOUR OLD LADY COUCH. BEST THING FOR YOU TO DO IS PRETEND I'M NOT HERE-- ESPECIALLY IF SOMEBODY SHOWS UP LOOKIN' FOR ME.
SHE'S A NICE OLD LADY. WE SHOULD WRITE DOWN HER ADDRESS, SEND HER A CARD OR SOMETHING.
Do they even make cards for former hostages?
THEY SHOULD...
SNIFF-- SNIFF--
WHAT'S THAT SMELL?
FLAKI.
POLISH SOUP.
YOU'RE A NICE OLD LADY.

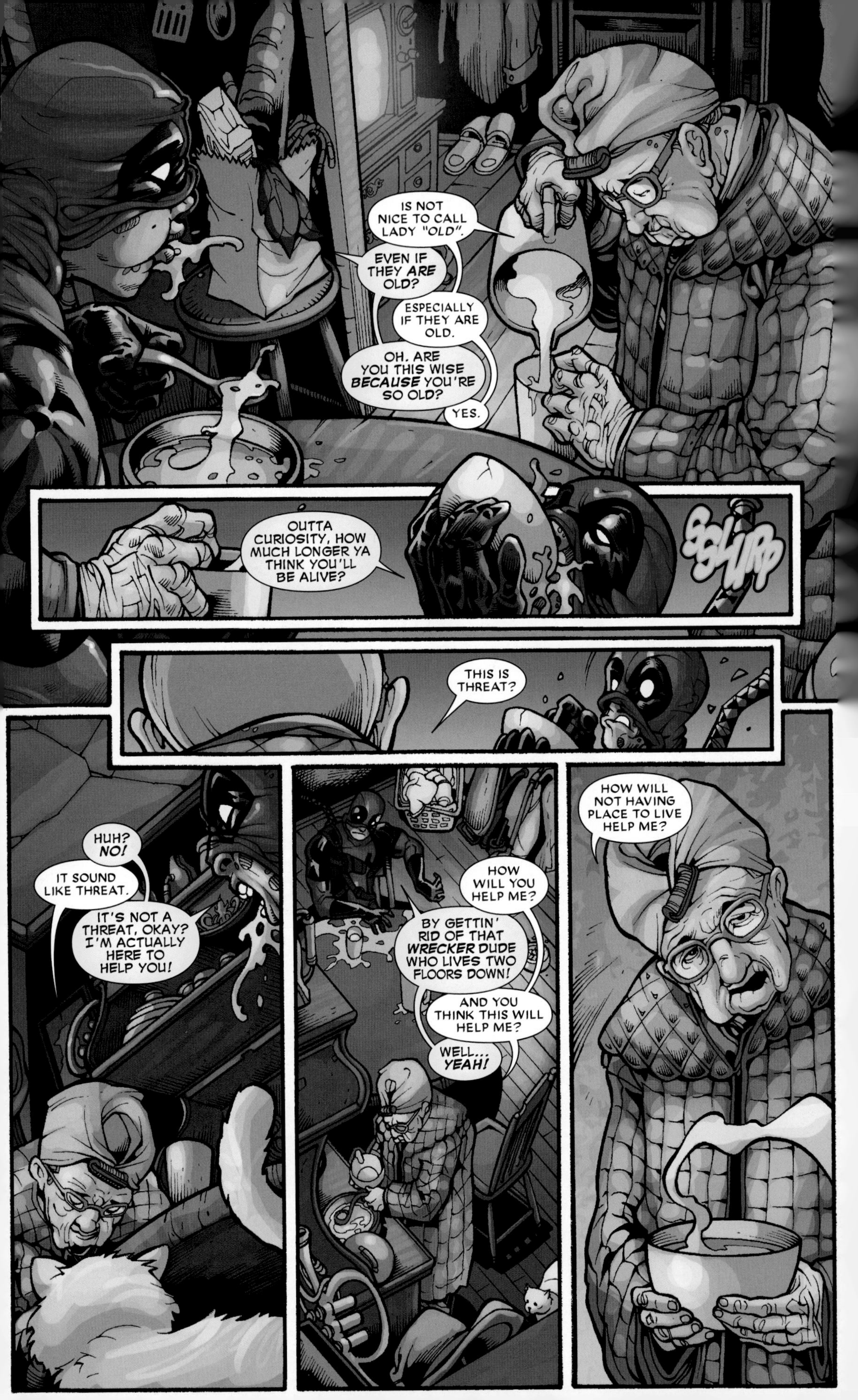
IS NOT NICE TO CALL LADY "OLD".
EVEN IF THEY ARE OLD?
ESPECIALLY IF THEY ARE OLD.
OH. ARE YOU THIS WISE BECAUSE YOU'RE SO OLD?
YES.
OUTTA CURIOSITY, HOW MUCH LONGER YA THINK YOU'LL BE ALIVE?
SSLURP
THIS IS THREAT?
HUH? NO!
IT SOUND LIKE THREAT.
IT'S NOT A THREAT, OKAY? I'M ACTUALLY HERE TO HELP YOU!
HOW WILL YOU HELP ME?
BY GETTIN' RID OF THAT WRECKER DUDE WHO LIVES TWO FLOORS DOWN!
AND YOU THINK THIS WILL HELP ME?
WELL... YEAH!
HOW WILL NOT HAVING PLACE TO LIVE HELP ME?

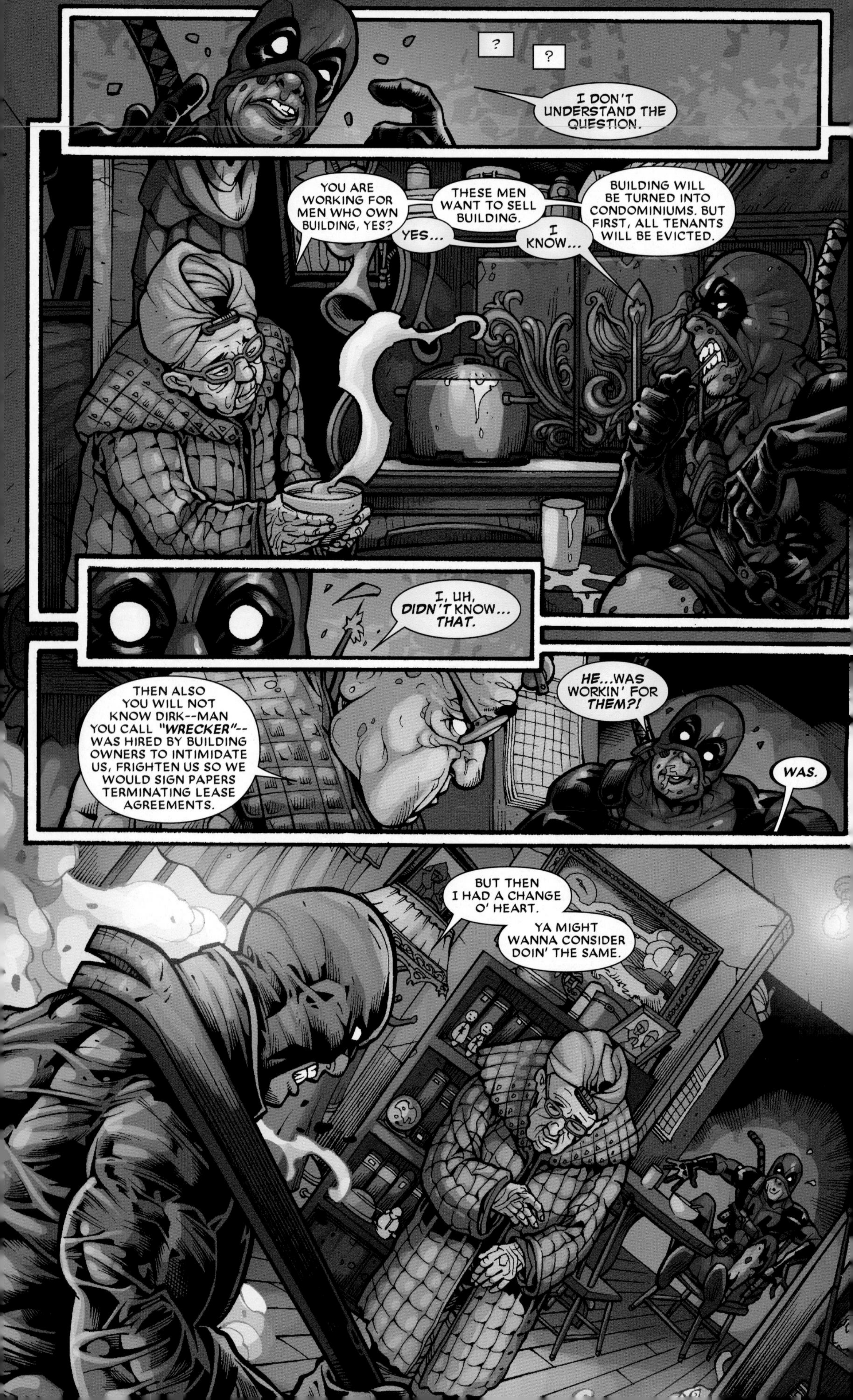

?
?
I DON'T UNDERSTAND THE QUESTION.
YOU ARE WORKING FOR MEN WHO OWN BUILDING, YES?
YES...
THESE MEN WANT TO SELL BUILDING.
I KNOW...
BUILDING WILL BE TURNED INTO CONDOMINIUMS. BUT FIRST, ALL TENANTS WILL BE EVICTED.
I, UH, DIDN'T KNOW... THAT.
THEN ALSO YOU WILL NOT KNOW DIRK--MAN YOU CALL "WRECKER"--WAS HIRED BY BUILDING OWNERS TO INTIMIDATE US, FRIGHTEN US SO WE WOULD SIGN PAPERS TERMINATING LEASE AGREEMENTS.
HE...WAS WORKIN' FOR THEM?!
WAS.
BUT THEN I HAD A CHANGE O' HEART.
YA MIGHT WANNA CONSIDER DOIN' THE SAME.

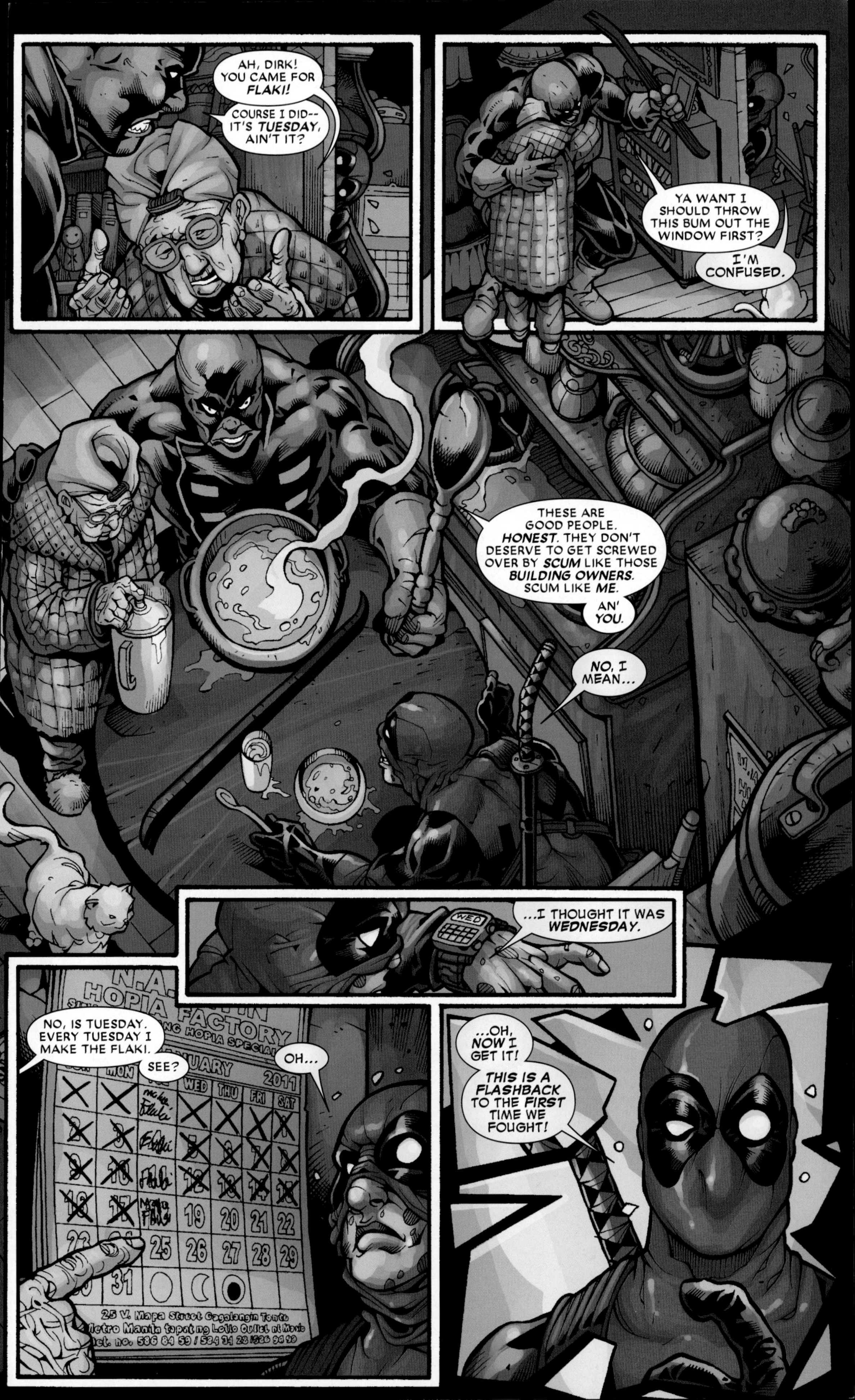

AH, DIRK! YOU CAME FOR FLAKI!
COURSE I DID-- IT'S TUESDAY, AIN'T IT?
YA WANT I SHOULD THROW THIS BUM OUT THE WINDOW FIRST?
I'M CONFUSED.
THESE ARE GOOD PEOPLE. HONEST. THEY DON'T DESERVE TO GET SCREWED OVER BY SCUM LIKE THOSE BUILDING OWNERS. SCUM LIKE ME.
AN' YOU.
NO, I MEAN...
WED
...I THOUGHT IT WAS WEDNESDAY.
NO, IS TUESDAY. EVERY TUESDAY I MAKE THE FLAKI.
SEE?
HOPIA FACTORY
JANUARY 2011
MON WED THU FRI SAT
19 20 21 22
25 26 27 28 29
31
25 V. Mapa Street
OH...
...OH, NOW I GET IT!
THIS IS A FLASHBACK TO THE FIRST TIME WE FOUGHT!

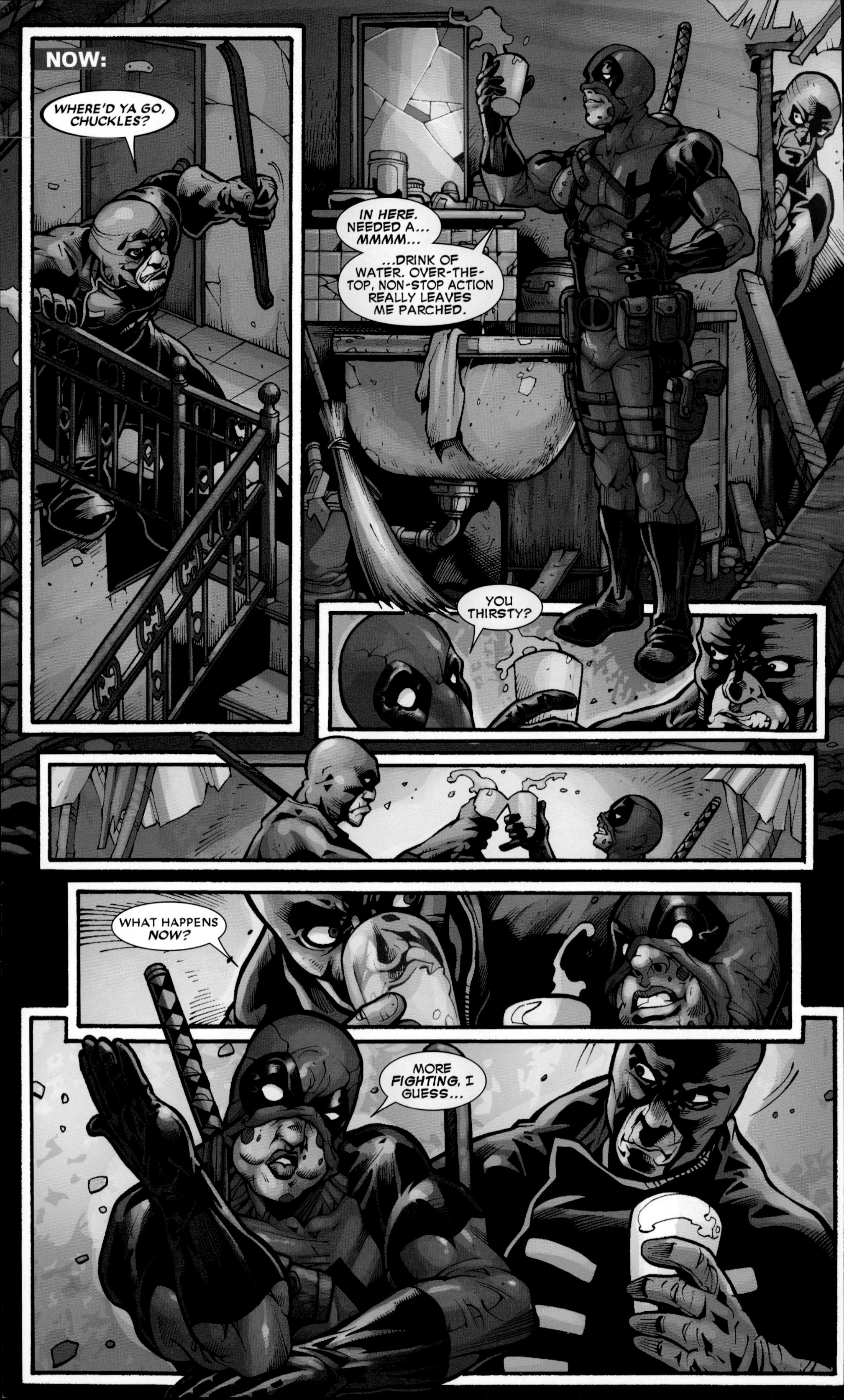
NOW:
WHERE'D YA GO, CHUCKLES?
IN HERE. NEEDED A... MMMM...
...DRINK OF WATER. OVER-THE-TOP, NON-STOP ACTION REALLY LEAVES ME PARCHED.
YOU THIRSTY?
WHAT HAPPENS NOW?
MORE FIGHTING, I GUESS...

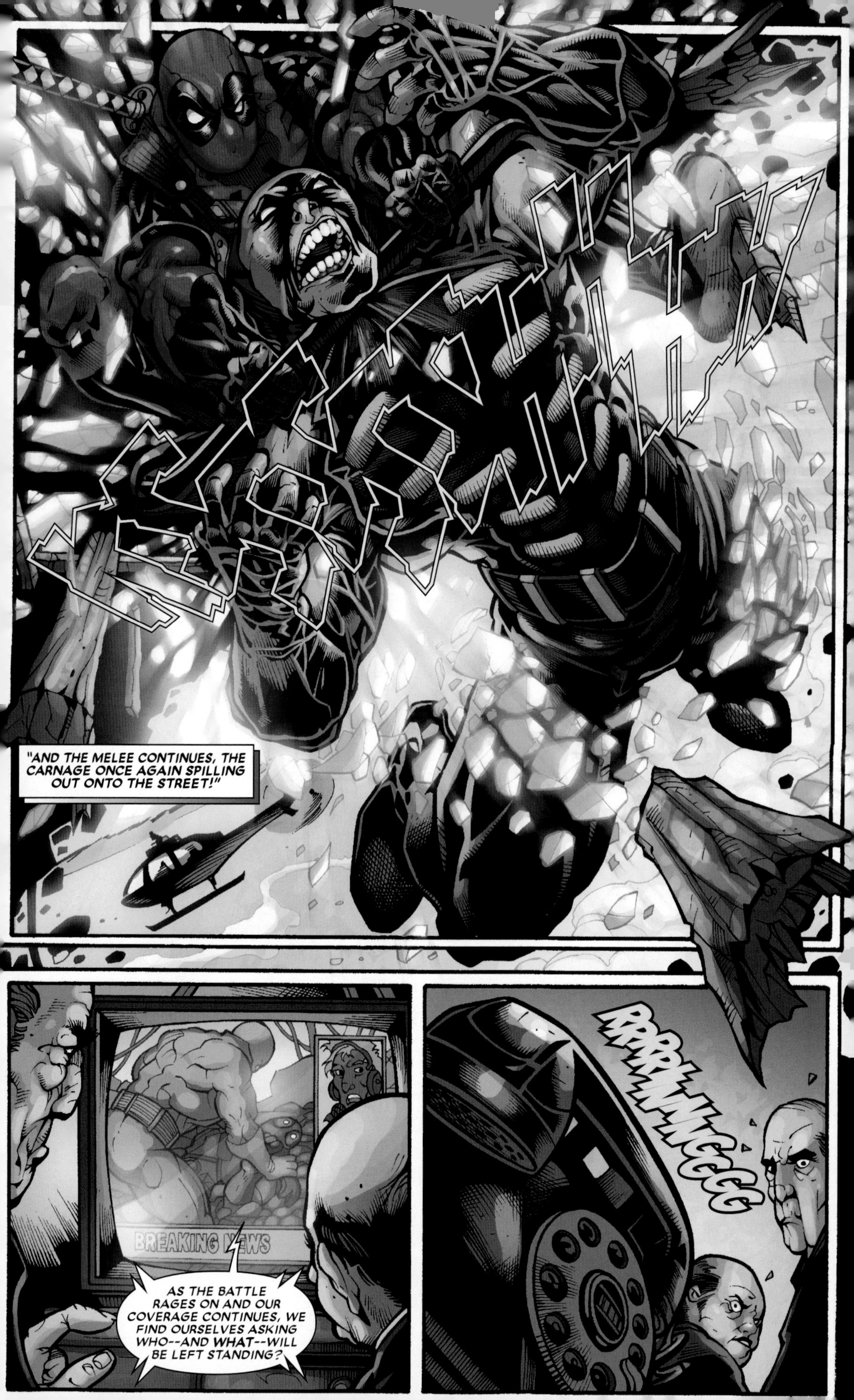
"AND THE MELEE CONTINUES, THE CARNAGE ONCE AGAIN SPILLING OUT ONTO THE STREET!"
BREAKING NEWS
AS THE BATTLE RAGES ON AND OUR COVERAGE CONTINUES, WE FIND OURSELVES ASKING WHO--AND WHAT--WILL BE LEFT STANDING?
RRRRIIINNNGGG

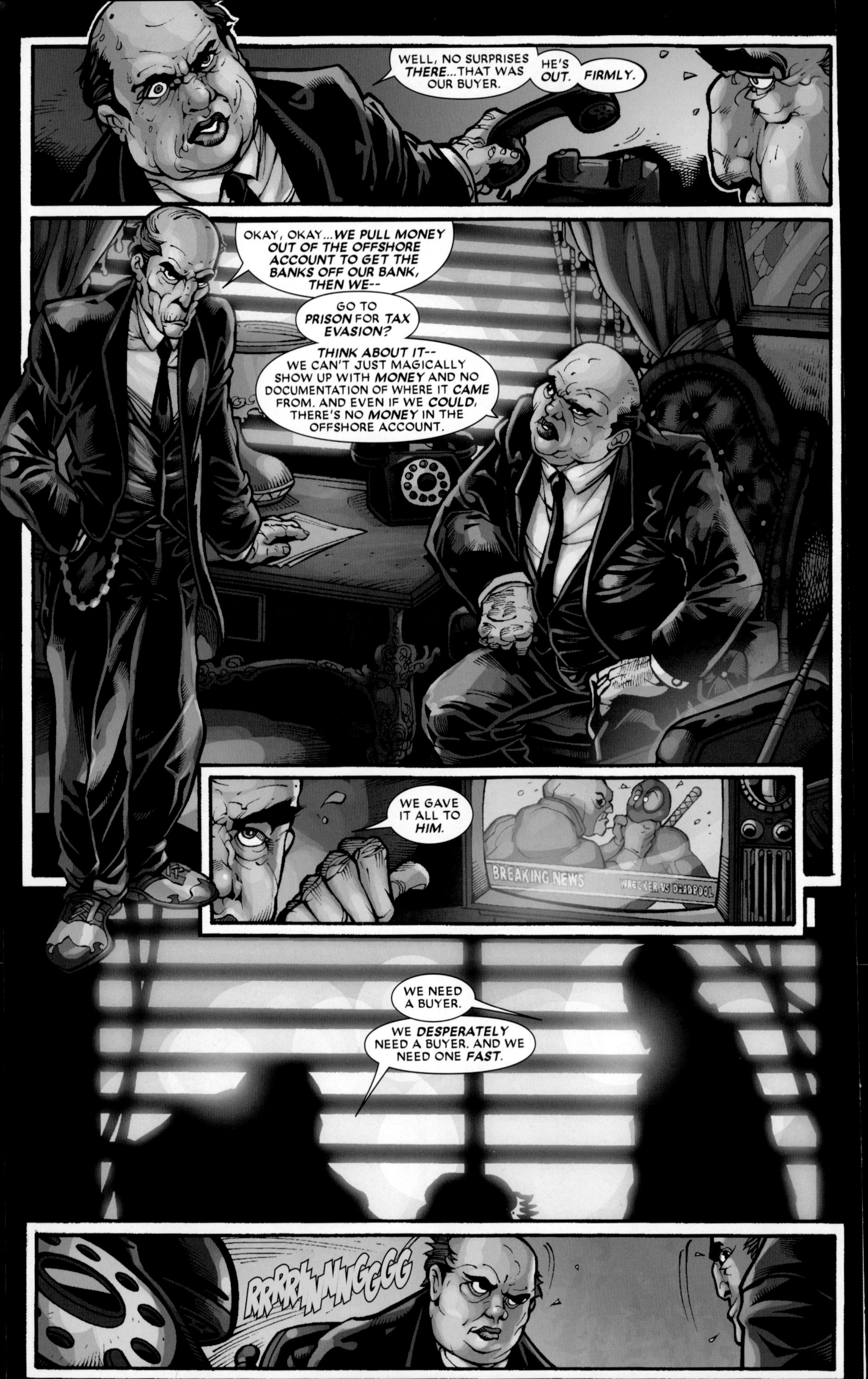

WELL, NO SURPRISES THERE...THAT WAS OUR BUYER.
HE'S OUT.
FIRMLY.
OKAY, OKAY...WE PULL MONEY OUT OF THE OFFSHORE ACCOUNT TO GET THE BANKS OFF OUR BANK, THEN WE--
GO TO PRISON FOR TAX EVASION?
THINK ABOUT IT-- WE CAN'T JUST MAGICALLY SHOW UP WITH MONEY AND NO DOCUMENTATION OF WHERE IT CAME FROM. AND EVEN IF WE COULD, THERE'S NO MONEY IN THE OFFSHORE ACCOUNT.
WE GAVE IT ALL TO HIM.
BREAKING NEWS
WRECKER VS DEADPOOL
WE NEED A BUYER.
WE DESPERATELY NEED A BUYER. AND WE NEED ONE FAST.
RRRRINNNGGGG

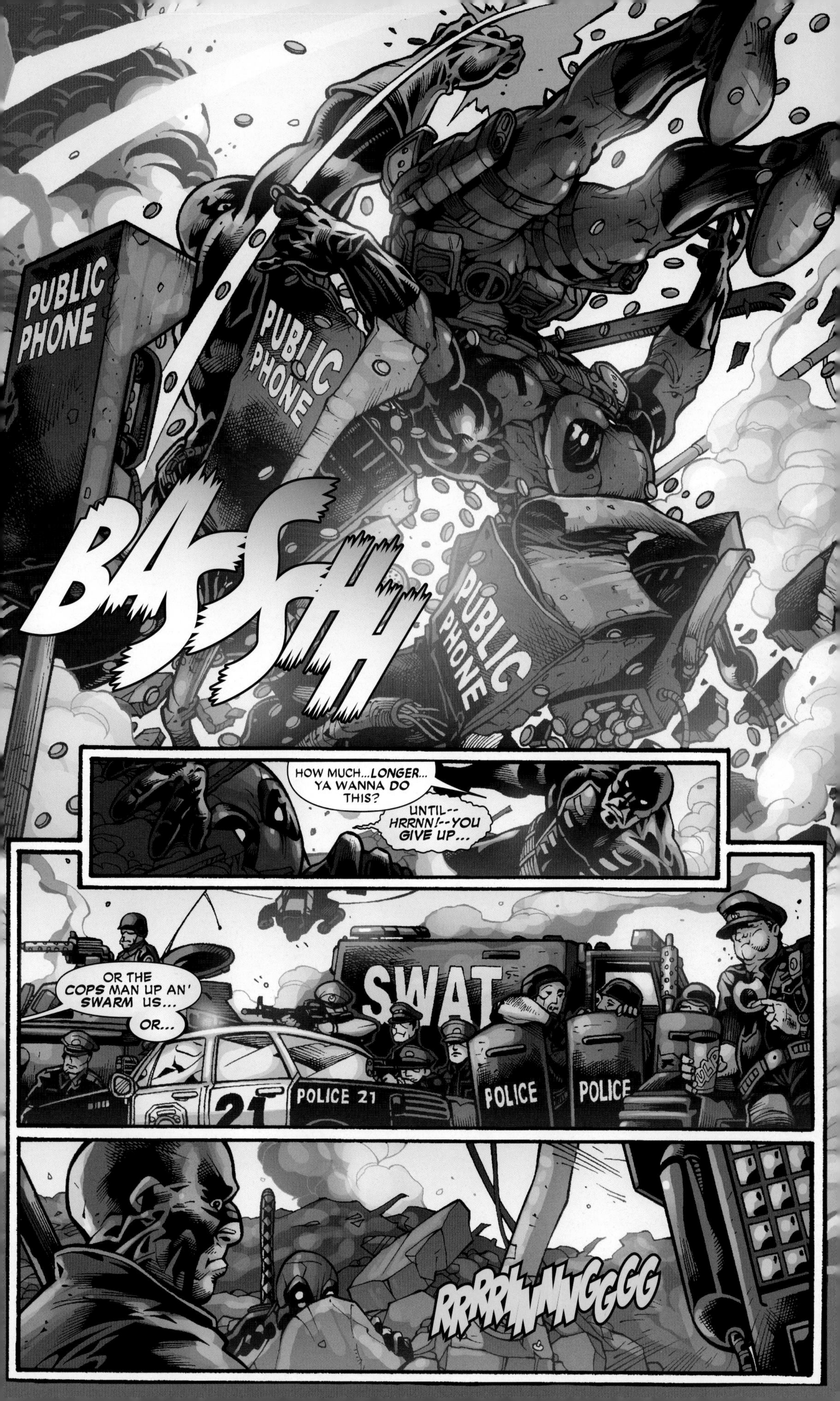
PUBLIC PHONE
PUBLIC PHONE
BASH
PUBLIC PHONE
HOW MUCH...LONGER... YA WANNA DO THIS?
UNTIL-- HRRNN!--YOU GIVE UP...
SWAT
OR THE COPS MAN UP AN' SWARM US... OR...
POLICE 21
21
POLICE
POLICE
RRRRINNNGGGG

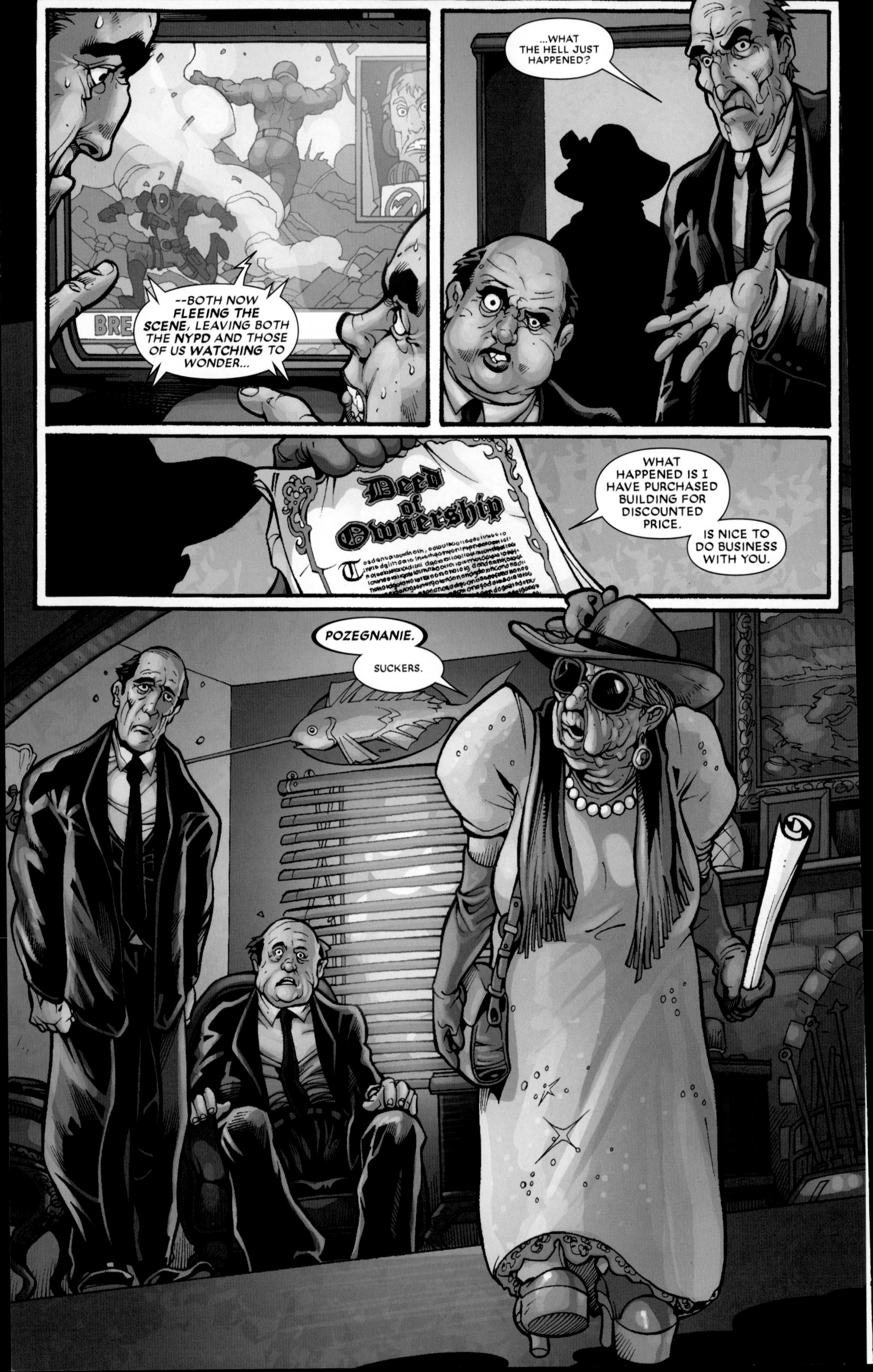
BRE
--BOTH NOW FLEEING THE SCENE, LEAVING BOTH THE NYPD AND THOSE OF US WATCHING TO WONDER...
...WHAT THE HELL JUST HAPPENED?
Deed of Ownership
WHAT HAPPENED IS I HAVE PURCHASED BUILDING FOR DISCOUNTED PRICE.
IS NICE TO DO BUSINESS WITH YOU.
POZEGNANIE.
SUCKERS.

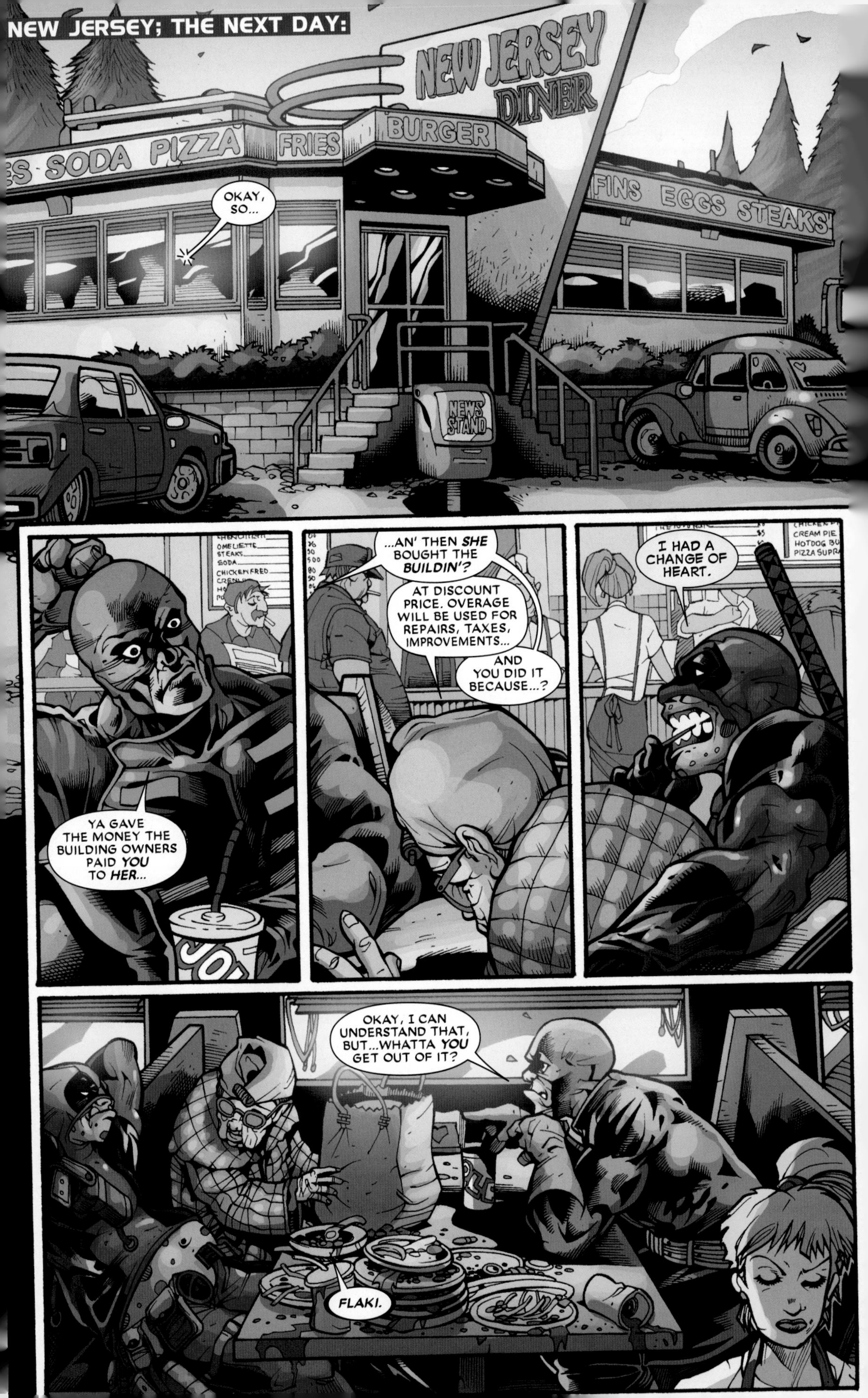
NEW JERSEY; THE NEXT DAY:
NEW JERSEY DINER
SODA PIZZA FRIES BURGER
FINS EGGS STEAKS
OKAY, SO...
NEWS STAND
YA GAVE THE MONEY THE BUILDING OWNERS PAID YOU TO HER...
...AN' THEN SHE BOUGHT THE BUILDIN'?
AT DISCOUNT PRICE. OVERAGE WILL BE USED FOR REPAIRS, TAXES, IMPROVEMENTS...
AND YOU DID IT BECAUSE...?
I HAD A CHANGE OF HEART.
OKAY, I CAN UNDERSTAND THAT, BUT...WHATTA YOU GET OUT OF IT?
FLAKI.

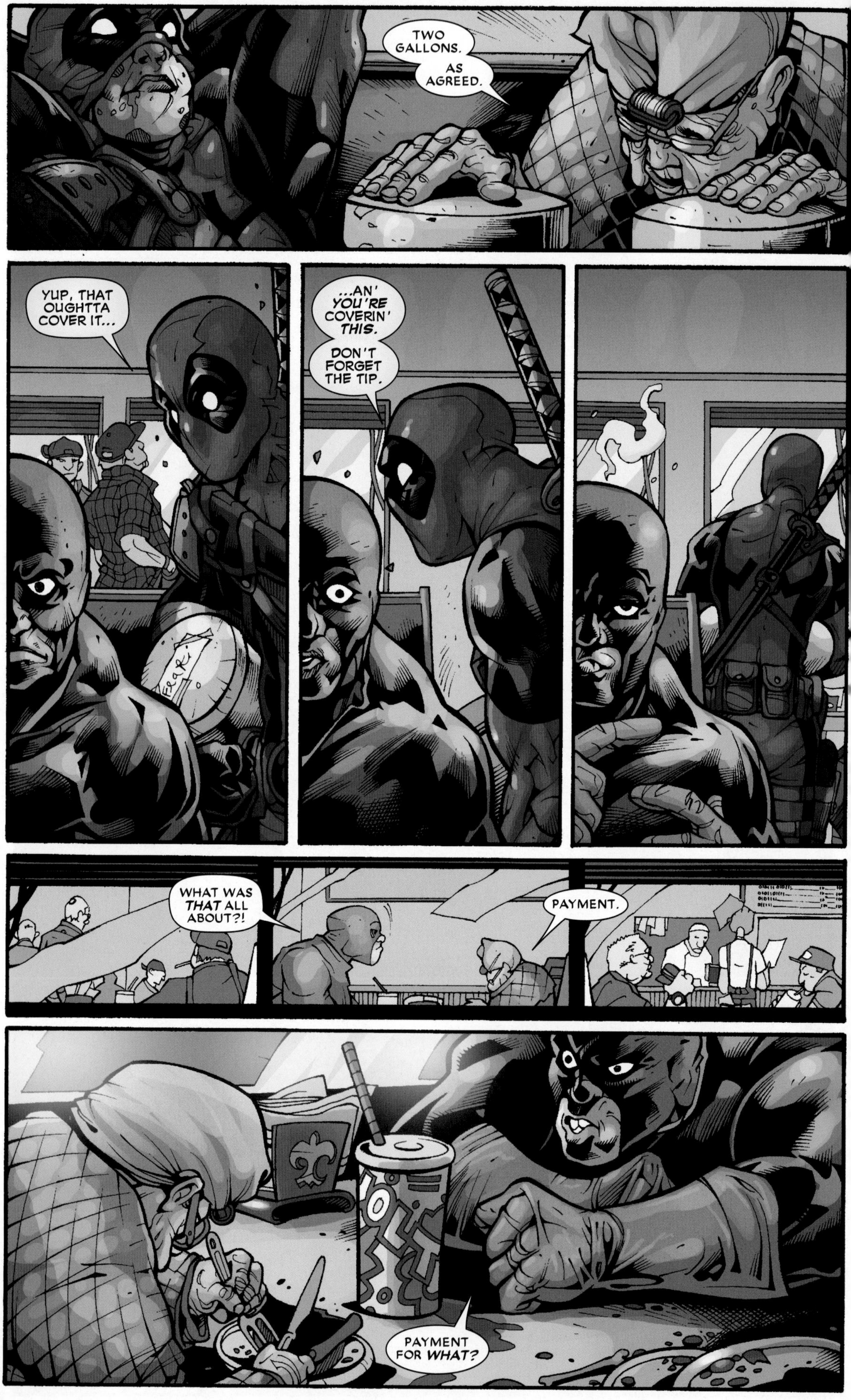
TWO GALLONS.
AS AGREED.
YUP, THAT OUGHTTA COVER IT...
...AN' YOU'RE COVERIN' THIS.
DON'T FORGET THE TIP.
WHAT WAS THAT ALL ABOUT?!
PAYMENT.
PAYMENT FOR WHAT?

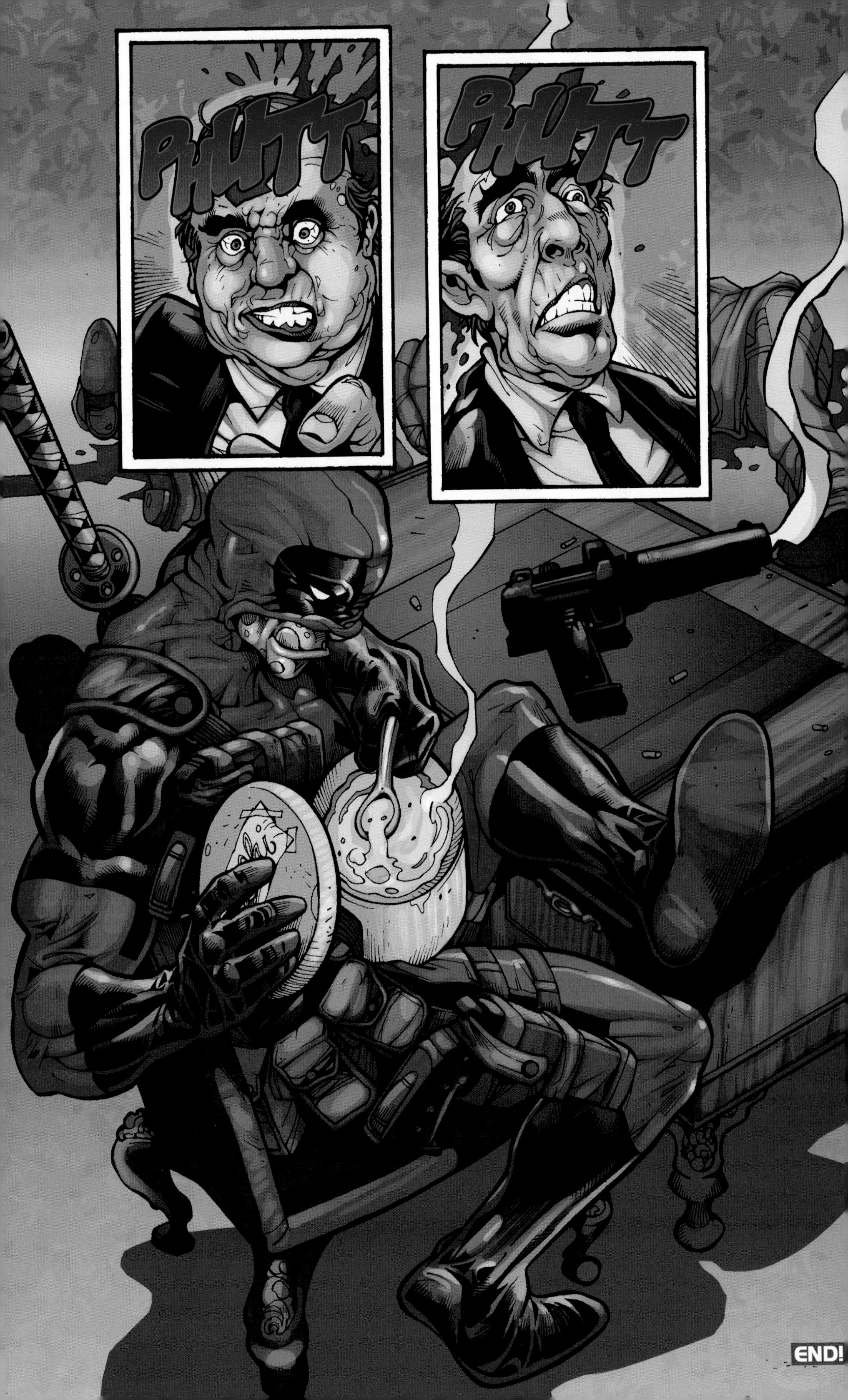
PHUTT
PHUTT
END!

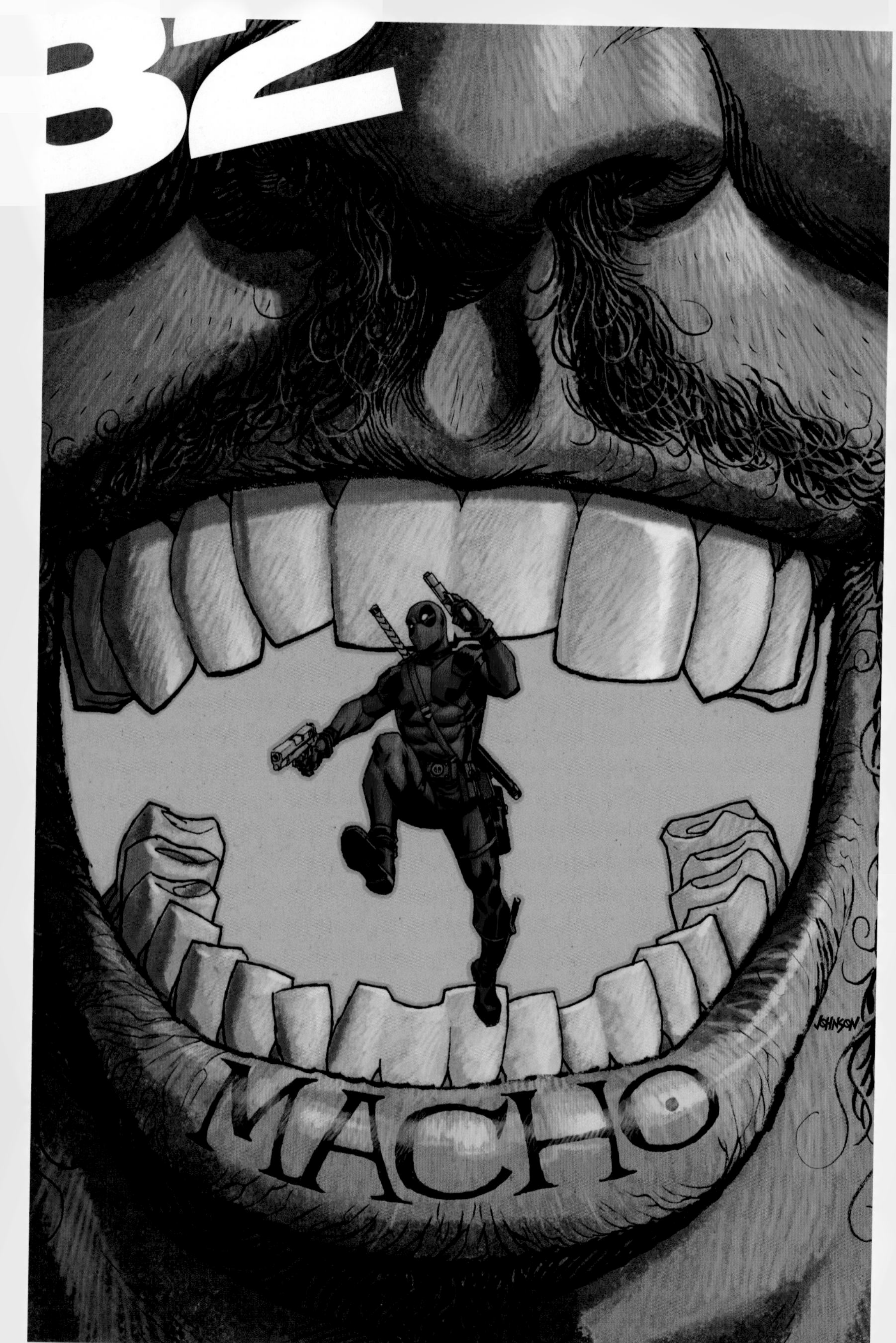
32
MACHO
JOHNSON

Some jobs are just too tough for your average fast-talkin' high-tech gun-for-hire. Sometimes...to get the job done right...you need someone crazier than a sack'a ferrets. You need Wade Wilson. The Crimson Comedian. The Regeneratin' Degenerate. The Merc with a Mouth...

DEADPOOL

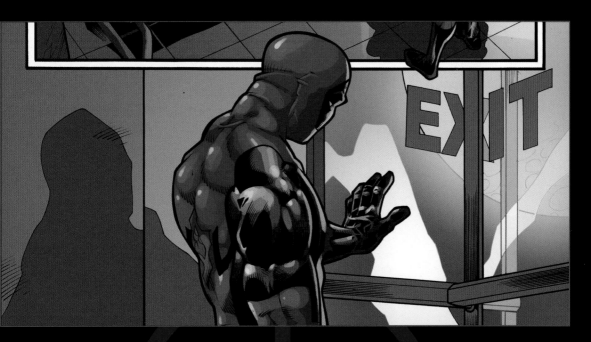

Tired of being feared and hated as a mercenary, recently Wade has been touring the country trying to figure out what it takes to be a hero. Needless to say, things haven't been going well. In San Francisco Deadpool tried to join the X-Men but was only offered "probational membership" and after a publicity stunt gone wrong, no membership at all. In New York his plans to learn from Spider-Man were thwarted by a mercenary-hunting primate known only as Hit-Monkey. In Las Vegas his attempt to become the protector of the city ended abruptly when his employers made the mistake of offering a job with "responsibilities." Later it seemed Wade finally found a place on the Secret Avengers with Steve Rogers, Black Widow, and Moon Knight, only to discover that his fellow heroes were only clones. Most recently he saved a clan of peace-loving vampires from their bloodthirsty counterparts but in the end failed to get the girl. And when you think about it, what's the point of being a hero if you don't get the girl?

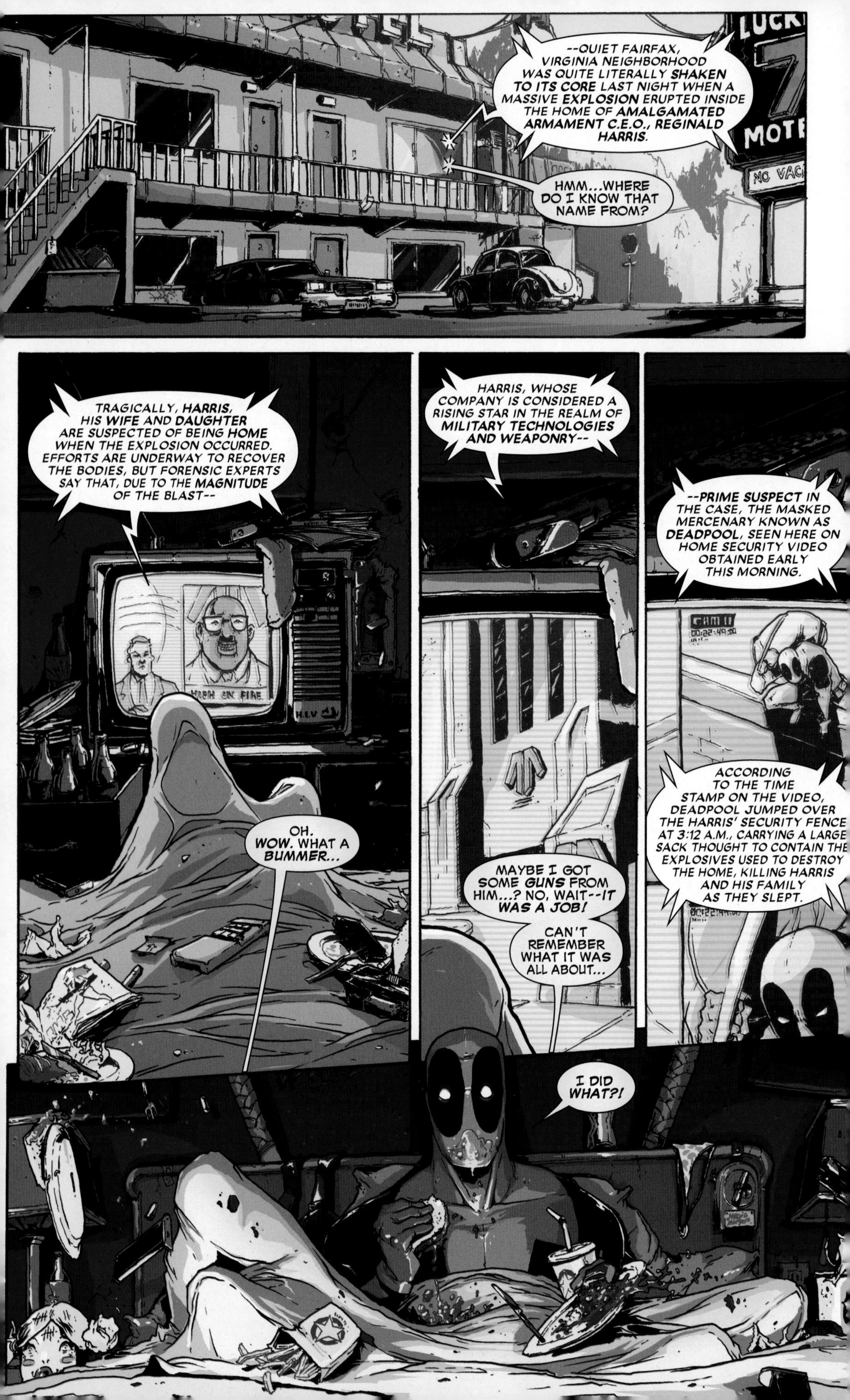

--QUIET FAIRFAX, VIRGINIA NEIGHBORHOOD WAS QUITE LITERALLY SHAKEN TO ITS CORE LAST NIGHT WHEN A MASSIVE EXPLOSION ERUPTED INSIDE THE HOME OF AMALGAMATED ARMAMENT C.E.O., REGINALD HARRIS.
HMM...WHERE DO I KNOW THAT NAME FROM?
TRAGICALLY, HARRIS, HIS WIFE AND DAUGHTER ARE SUSPECTED OF BEING HOME WHEN THE EXPLOSION OCCURRED. EFFORTS ARE UNDERWAY TO RECOVER THE BODIES, BUT FORENSIC EXPERTS SAY THAT, DUE TO THE MAGNITUDE OF THE BLAST--
OH. WOW. WHAT A BUMMER...
HARRIS, WHOSE COMPANY IS CONSIDERED A RISING STAR IN THE REALM OF MILITARY TECHNOLOGIES AND WEAPONRY--
MAYBE I GOT SOME GUNS FROM HIM...? NO, WAIT--IT WAS A JOB!
CAN'T REMEMBER WHAT IT WAS ALL ABOUT...
--PRIME SUSPECT IN THE CASE, THE MASKED MERCENARY KNOWN AS DEADPOOL, SEEN HERE ON HOME SECURITY VIDEO OBTAINED EARLY THIS MORNING.
ACCORDING TO THE TIME STAMP ON THE VIDEO, DEADPOOL JUMPED OVER THE HARRIS' SECURITY FENCE AT 3:12 A.M., CARRYING A LARGE SACK THOUGHT TO CONTAIN THE EXPLOSIVES USED TO DESTROY THE HOME, KILLING HARRIS AND HIS FAMILY AS THEY SLEPT.
I DID WHAT?!

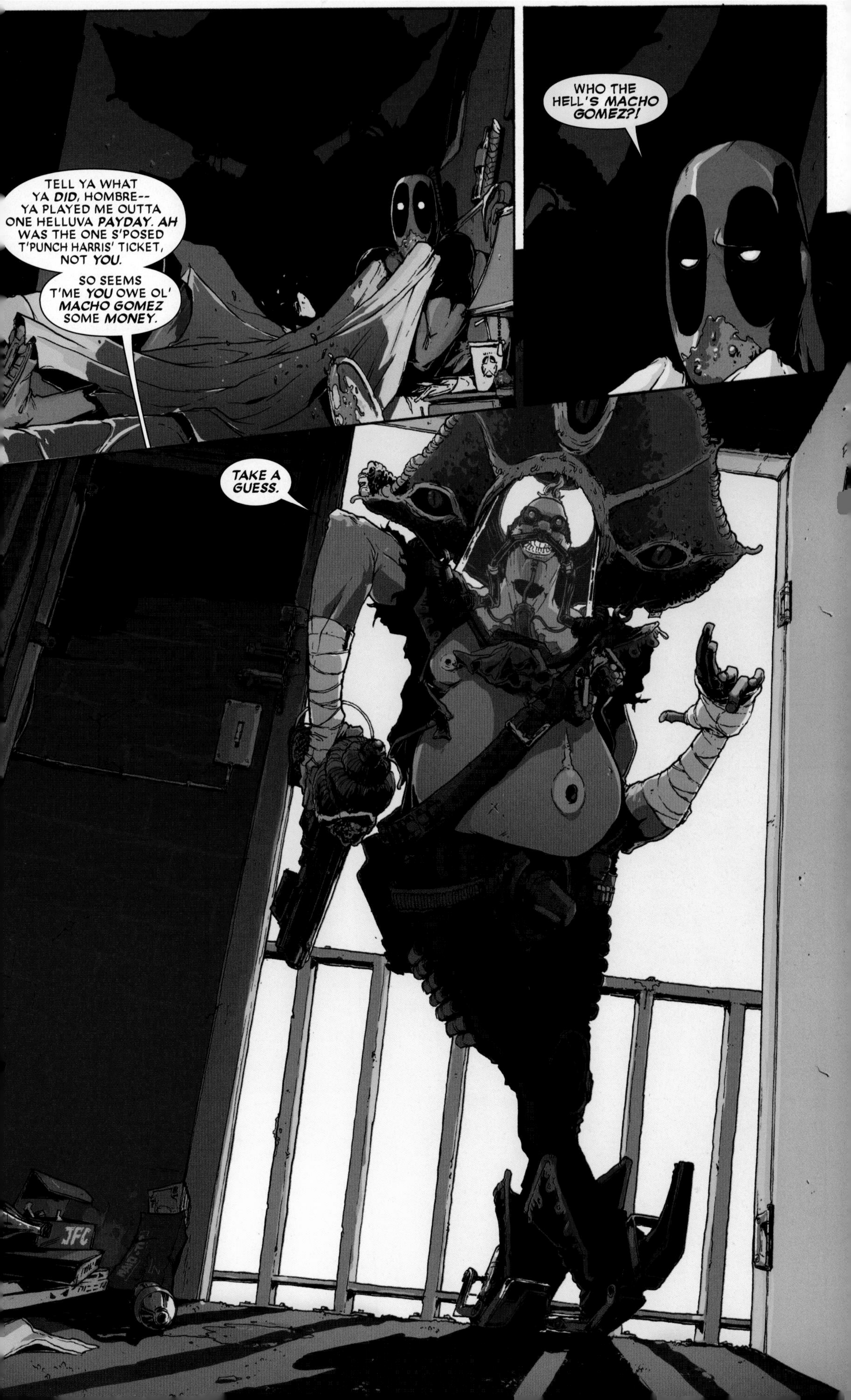
TELL YA WHAT YA *DID*, HOMBRE-- YA PLAYED ME OUTTA ONE HELLUVA *PAYDAY*. *AH* WAS THE ONE S'POSED T'PUNCH HARRIS' TICKET, NOT *YOU*.
SO SEEMS T'ME *YOU* OWE OL' *MACHO GOMEZ* SOME *MONEY*.
WHO THE HELL'S *MACHO GOMEZ?!*
TAKE A GUESS.

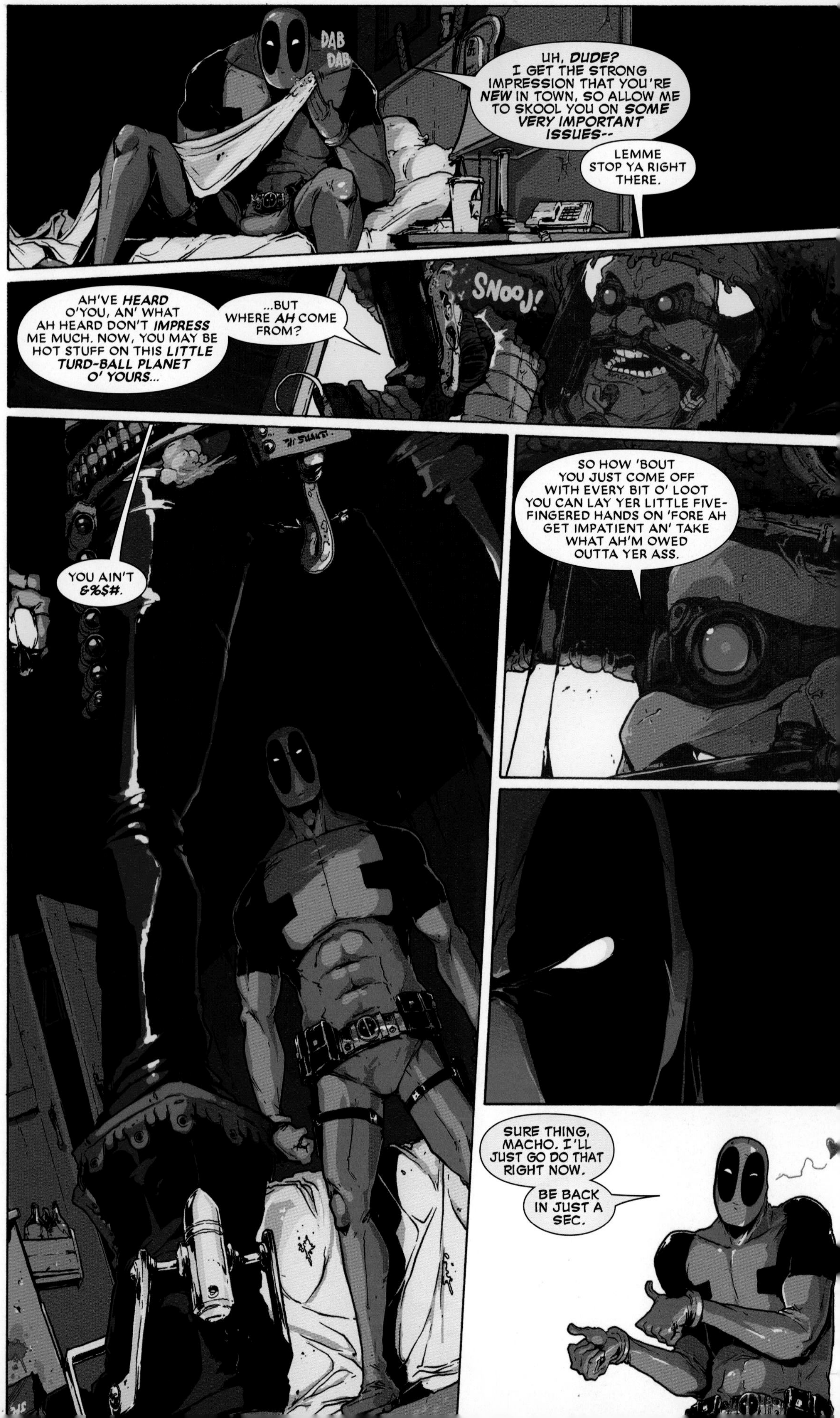
DAB DAB
UH, DUDE? I GET THE STRONG IMPRESSION THAT YOU'RE NEW IN TOWN, SO ALLOW ME TO SKOOL YOU ON SOME VERY IMPORTANT ISSUES--
LEMME STOP YA RIGHT THERE.
SNOOJ!
AH'VE HEARD O'YOU, AN' WHAT AH HEARD DON'T IMPRESS ME MUCH. NOW, YOU MAY BE HOT STUFF ON THIS LITTLE TURD-BALL PLANET O' YOURS...
...BUT WHERE AH COME FROM?
YOU AIN'T &%$#.
SO HOW 'BOUT YOU JUST COME OFF WITH EVERY BIT O' LOOT YOU CAN LAY YER LITTLE FIVE-FINGERED HANDS ON 'FORE AH GET IMPATIENT AN' TAKE WHAT AH'M OWED OUTTA YER ASS.
SURE THING, MACHO. I'LL JUST GO DO THAT RIGHT NOW.
BE BACK IN JUST A SEC.

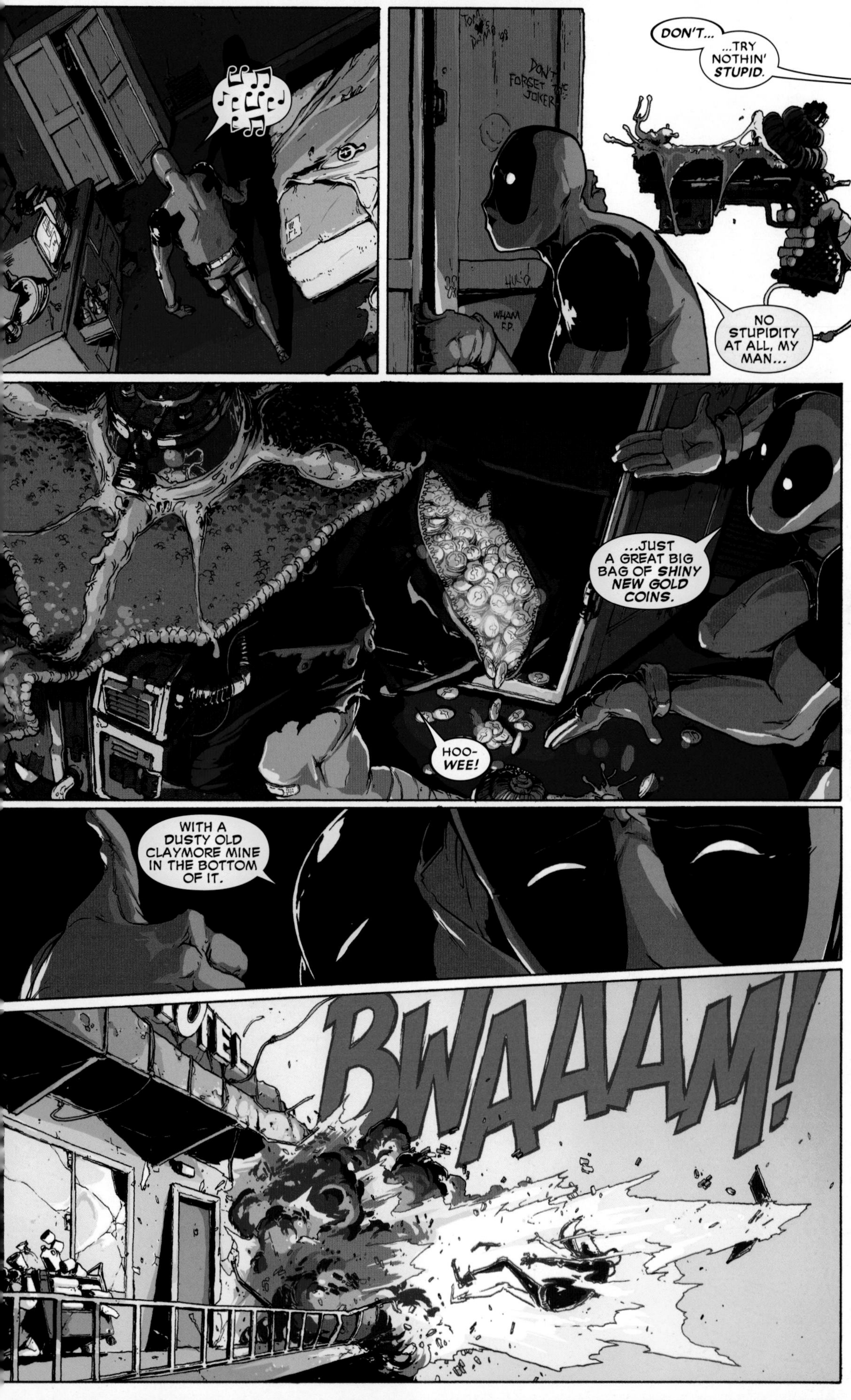
DON'T FORGET THE JOKER
DON'T... ...TRY NOTHIN' STUPID.
NO STUPIDITY AT ALL, MY MAN...
...JUST A GREAT BIG BAG OF SHINY NEW GOLD COINS.
HOO-WEE!
WITH A DUSTY OLD CLAYMORE MINE IN THE BOTTOM OF IT.
BWAAAM!

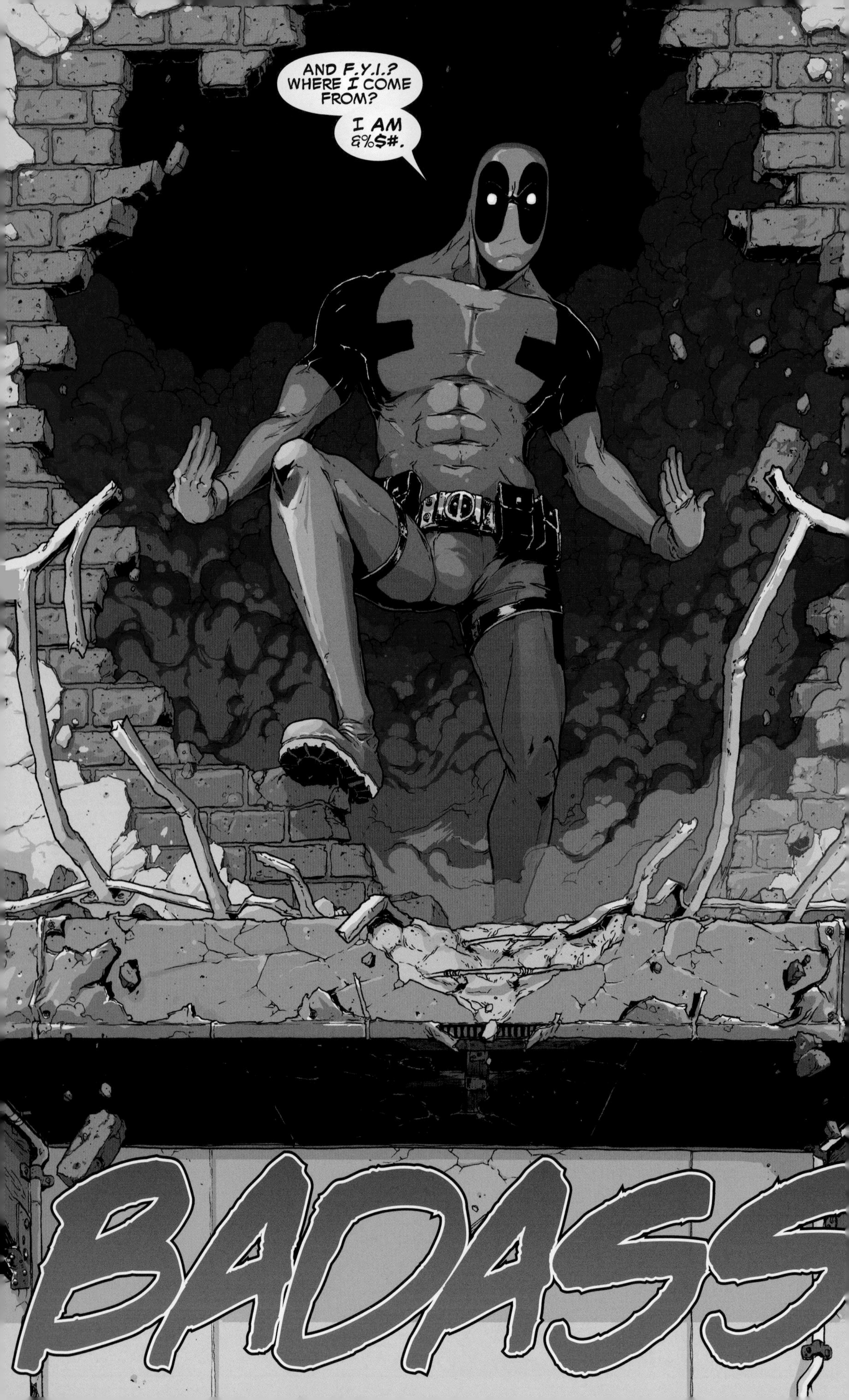
AND F.Y.I.? WHERE I COME FROM?
I AM &%$#.
BADASS

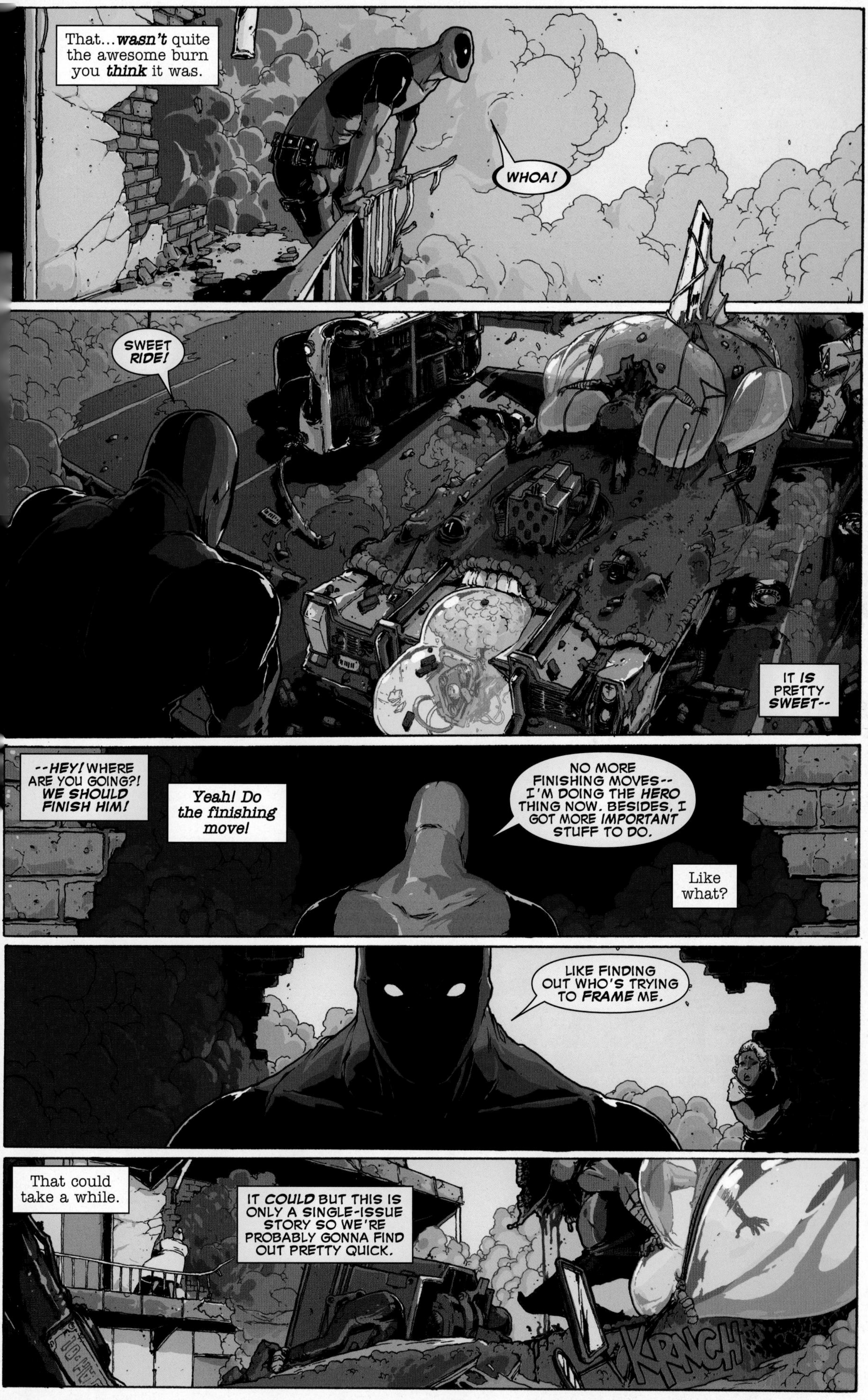
That...wasn't quite the awesome burn you think it was.
WHOA!
SWEET RIDE!
IT IS PRETTY SWEET--
--HEY! WHERE ARE YOU GOING?! WE SHOULD FINISH HIM!
Yeah! Do the finishing move!
NO MORE FINISHING MOVES--I'M DOING THE HERO THING NOW. BESIDES, I GOT MORE IMPORTANT STUFF TO DO.
Like what?
LIKE FINDING OUT WHO'S TRYING TO FRAME ME.
That could take a while.
IT COULD BUT THIS IS ONLY A SINGLE-ISSUE STORY SO WE'RE PROBABLY GONNA FIND OUT PRETTY QUICK.
KRNCH

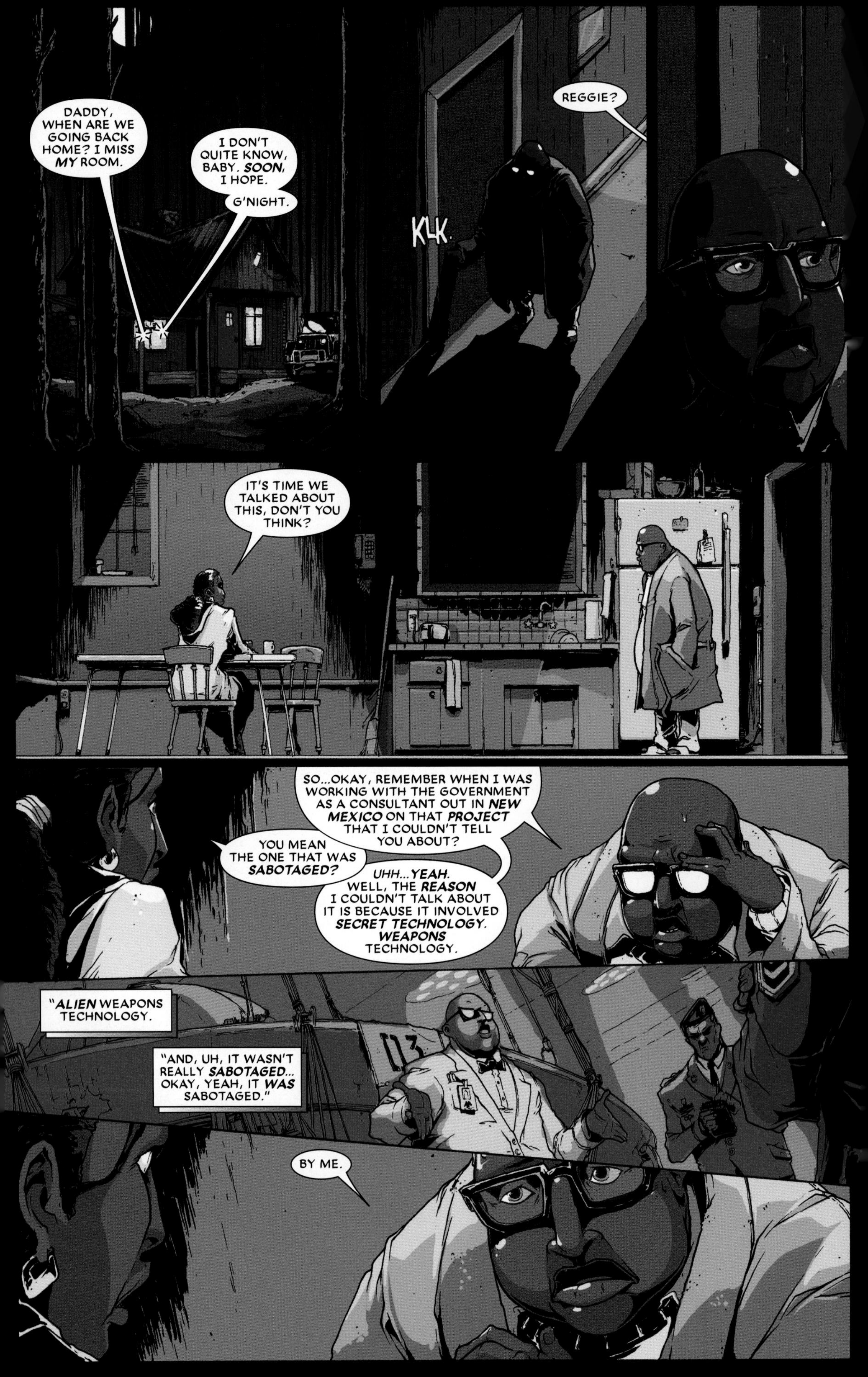
DADDY, WHEN ARE WE GOING BACK HOME? I MISS MY ROOM.
I DON'T QUITE KNOW, BABY. SOON, I HOPE.
G'NIGHT.
KLK.
REGGIE?
IT'S TIME WE TALKED ABOUT THIS, DON'T YOU THINK?
SO...OKAY, REMEMBER WHEN I WAS WORKING WITH THE GOVERNMENT AS A CONSULTANT OUT IN NEW MEXICO ON THAT PROJECT THAT I COULDN'T TELL YOU ABOUT?
YOU MEAN THE ONE THAT WAS SABOTAGED?
UHH...YEAH. WELL, THE REASON I COULDN'T TALK ABOUT IT IS BECAUSE IT INVOLVED SECRET TECHNOLOGY. WEAPONS TECHNOLOGY.
"ALIEN WEAPONS TECHNOLOGY.
"AND, UH, IT WASN'T REALLY SABOTAGED... OKAY, YEAH, IT WAS SABOTAGED."
BY ME.

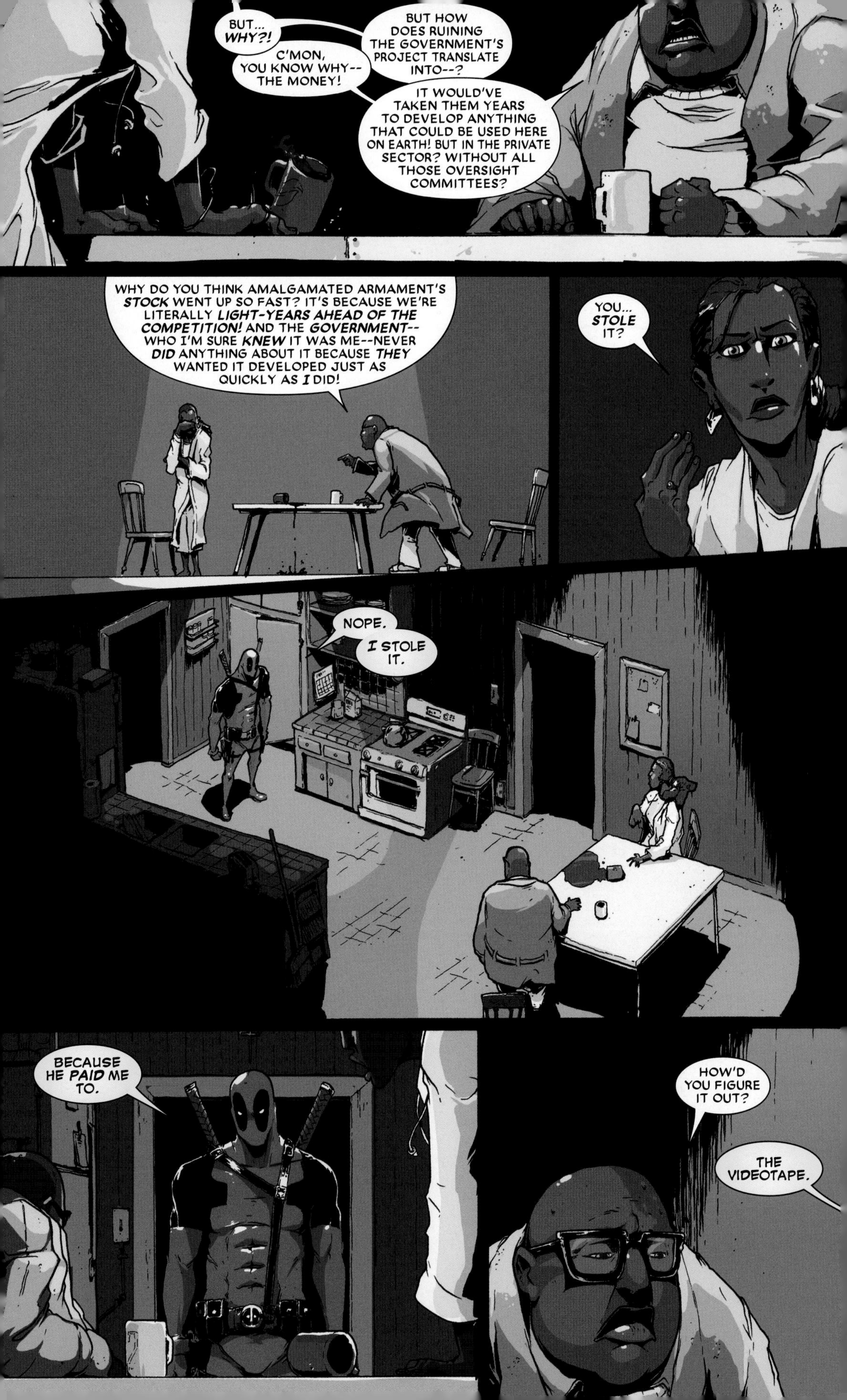
BUT... WHY?!
C'MON, YOU KNOW WHY-- THE MONEY!
BUT HOW DOES RUINING THE GOVERNMENT'S PROJECT TRANSLATE INTO--?
IT WOULD'VE TAKEN THEM YEARS TO DEVELOP ANYTHING THAT COULD BE USED HERE ON EARTH! BUT IN THE PRIVATE SECTOR? WITHOUT ALL THOSE OVERSIGHT COMMITTEES?
WHY DO YOU THINK AMALGAMATED ARMAMENT'S STOCK WENT UP SO FAST? IT'S BECAUSE WE'RE LITERALLY LIGHT-YEARS AHEAD OF THE COMPETITION! AND THE GOVERNMENT-- WHO I'M SURE KNEW IT WAS ME--NEVER DID ANYTHING ABOUT IT BECAUSE THEY WANTED IT DEVELOPED JUST AS QUICKLY AS I DID!
YOU... STOLE IT?
NOPE.
I STOLE IT.
BECAUSE HE PAID ME TO.
HOW'D YOU FIGURE IT OUT?
THE VIDEOTAPE.

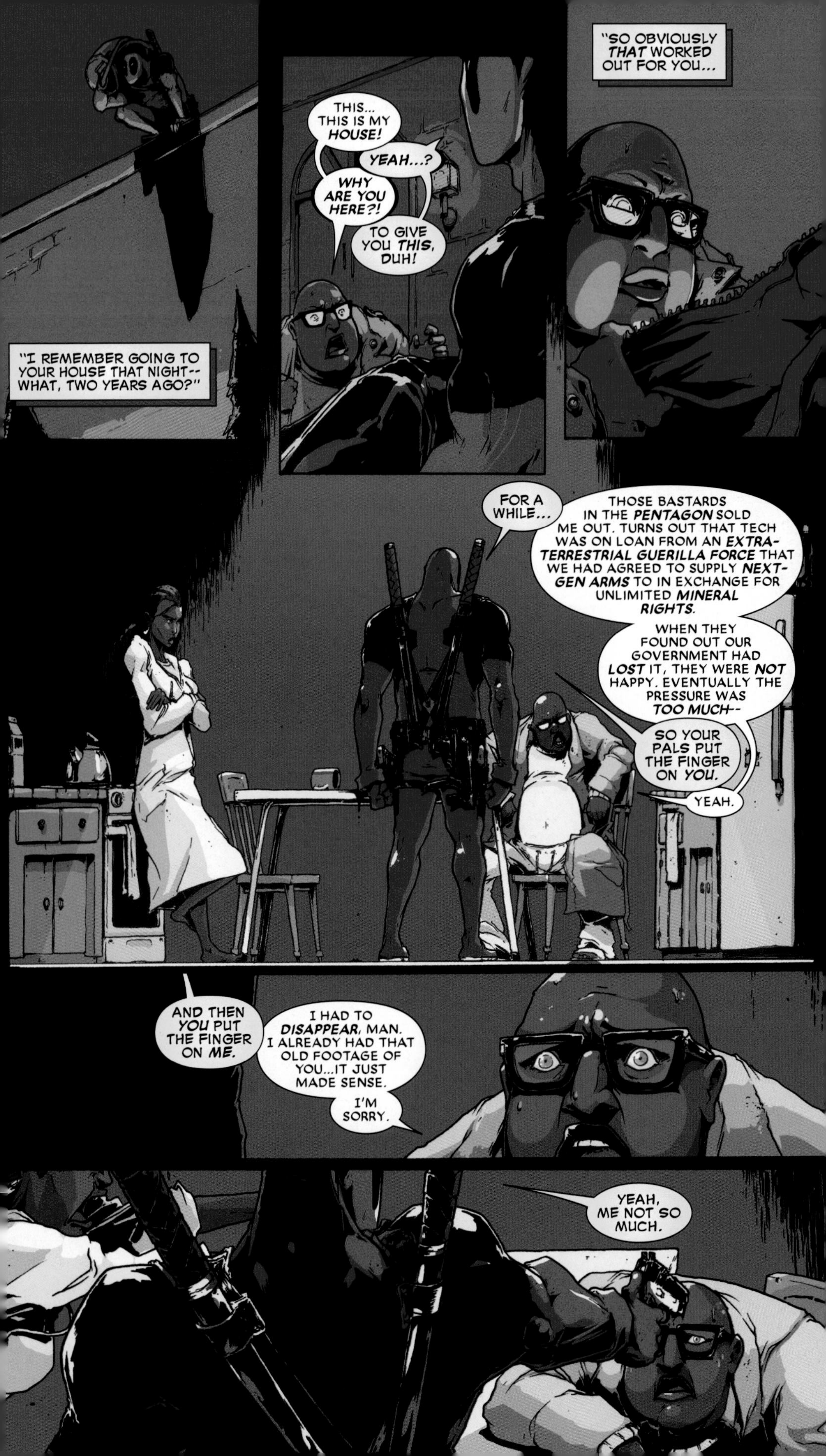
"I REMEMBER GOING TO YOUR HOUSE THAT NIGHT-- WHAT, TWO YEARS AGO?"
THIS... THIS IS MY HOUSE!
YEAH...?
WHY ARE YOU HERE?!
TO GIVE YOU THIS, DUH!
"SO OBVIOUSLY THAT WORKED OUT FOR YOU...
FOR A WHILE...
THOSE BASTARDS IN THE PENTAGON SOLD ME OUT. TURNS OUT THAT TECH WAS ON LOAN FROM AN EXTRA-TERRESTRIAL GUERILLA FORCE THAT WE HAD AGREED TO SUPPLY NEXT-GEN ARMS TO IN EXCHANGE FOR UNLIMITED MINERAL RIGHTS.
WHEN THEY FOUND OUT OUR GOVERNMENT HAD LOST IT, THEY WERE NOT HAPPY. EVENTUALLY THE PRESSURE WAS TOO MUCH--
SO YOUR PALS PUT THE FINGER ON YOU.
YEAH.
AND THEN YOU PUT THE FINGER ON ME.
I HAD TO DISAPPEAR, MAN. I ALREADY HAD THAT OLD FOOTAGE OF YOU...IT JUST MADE SENSE.
I'M SORRY.
YEAH, ME NOT SO MUCH.

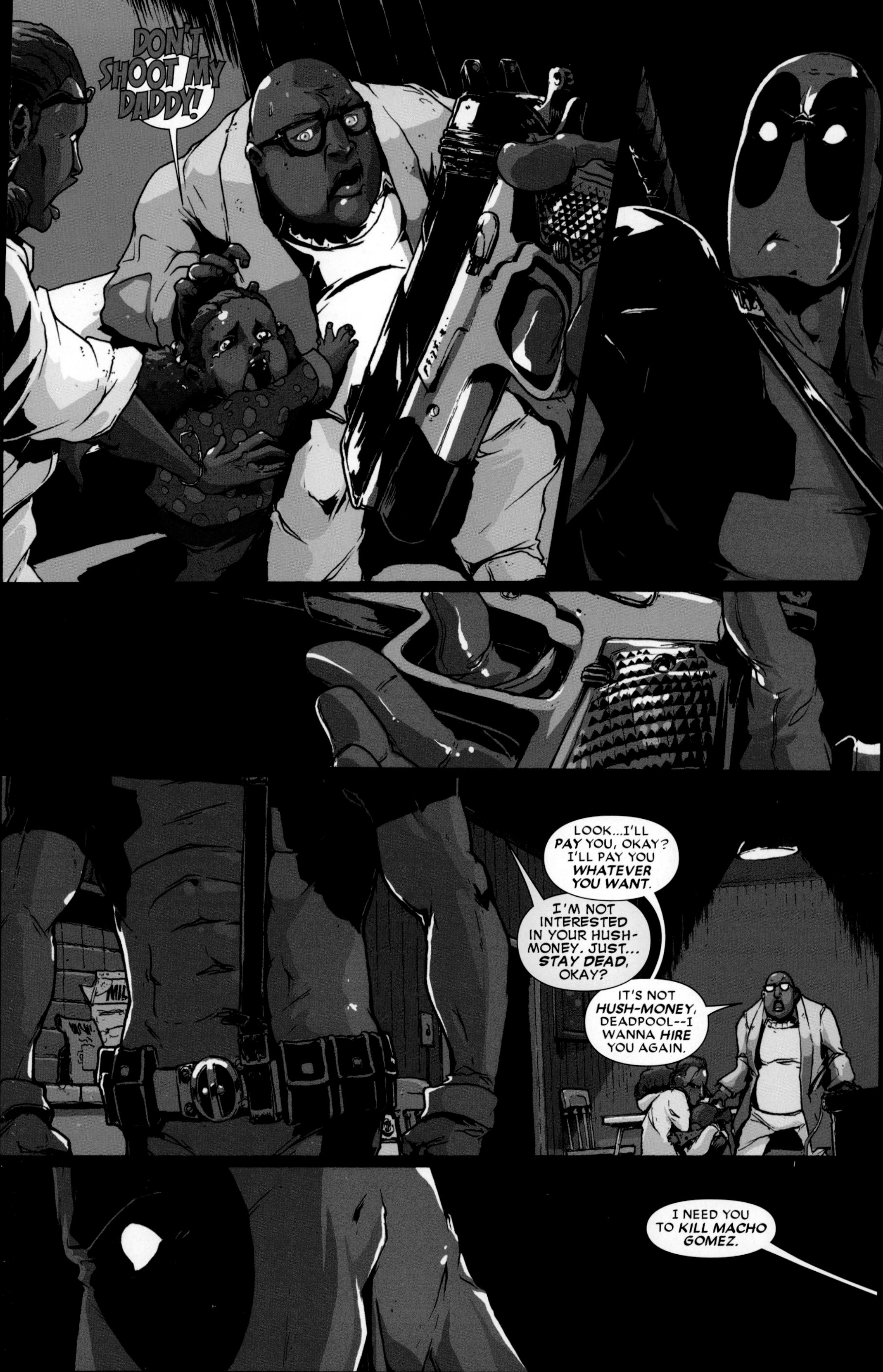
DON'T SHOOT MY DADDY!
LOOK...I'LL PAY YOU, OKAY? I'LL PAY YOU WHATEVER YOU WANT.
I'M NOT INTERESTED IN YOUR HUSH-MONEY. JUST... STAY DEAD, OKAY?
IT'S NOT HUSH-MONEY, DEADPOOL--I WANNA HIRE YOU AGAIN.
I NEED YOU TO KILL MACHO GOMEZ.

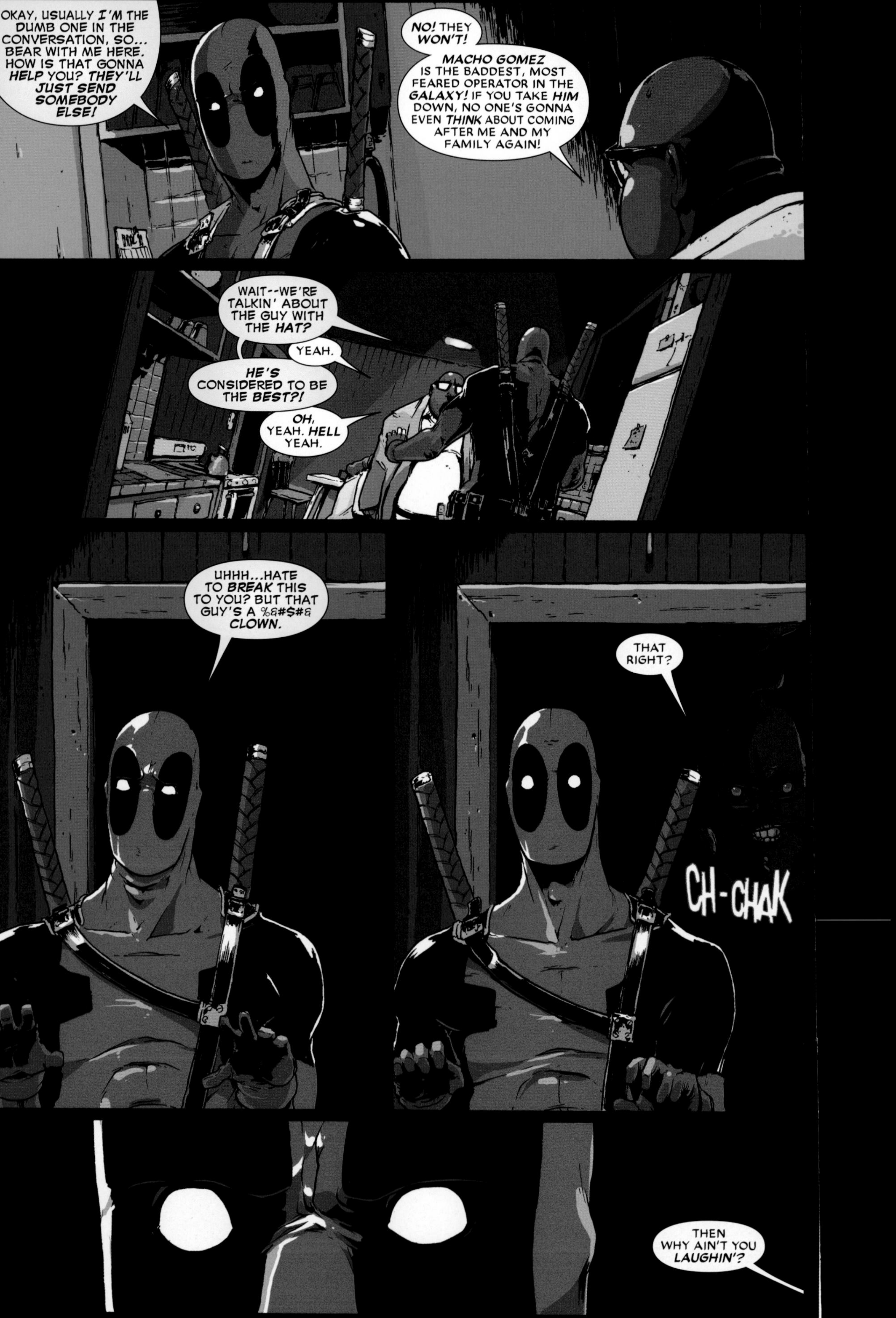
OKAY, USUALLY *I'M* THE DUMB ONE IN THE CONVERSATION, SO... BEAR WITH ME HERE. HOW IS THAT GONNA *HELP* YOU? *THEY'LL JUST SEND SOMEBODY ELSE!*
NO! THEY *WON'T!*
MACHO GOMEZ IS THE BADDEST, MOST FEARED OPERATOR IN THE *GALAXY!* IF YOU TAKE *HIM* DOWN, NO ONE'S GONNA EVEN *THINK* ABOUT COMING AFTER ME AND MY FAMILY AGAIN!
WAIT--WE'RE TALKIN' ABOUT THE GUY WITH THE *HAT?*
YEAH.
HE'S CONSIDERED TO BE THE *BEST?!*
OH, YEAH. *HELL* YEAH.
UHHH...HATE TO *BREAK* THIS TO YOU? BUT THAT GUY'S A %&#$#& *CLOWN.*
THAT RIGHT?
CH-CHAK
THEN WHY AIN'T YOU *LAUGHIN'?*

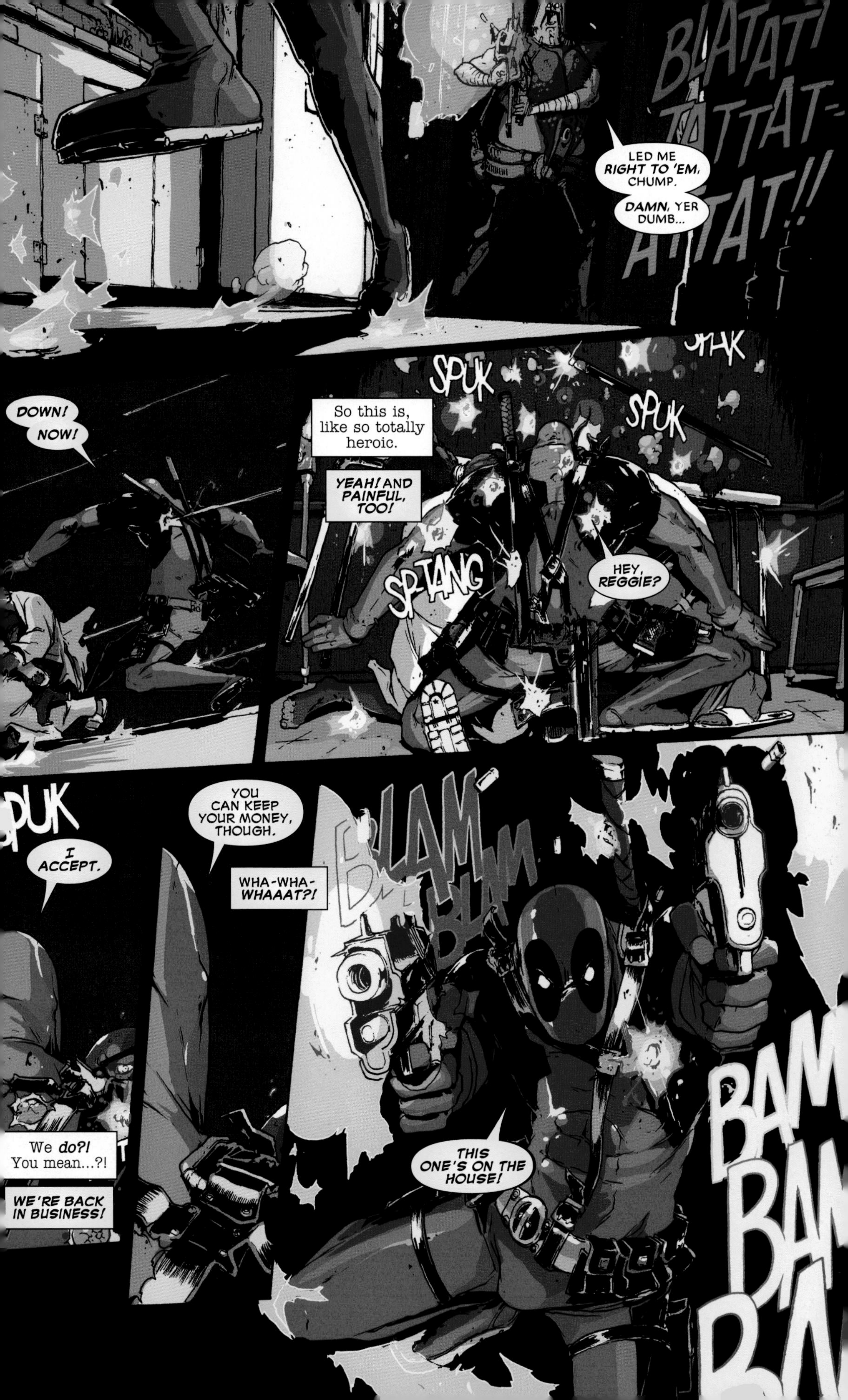
BLATAT! TATTAT-ATTTAT!!
LED ME RIGHT TO 'EM, CHUMP.
DAMN, YER DUMB...
SPUK
SPAK
SPUK
DOWN! NOW!
So this is, like so totally heroic.
YEAH! AND PAINFUL, TOO!
SPTANG
HEY, REGGIE?
SPUK
I ACCEPT.
YOU CAN KEEP YOUR MONEY, THOUGH.
WHA-WHA-WHAAAT?!
BLAM BLAM BLAM
We do?! You mean...?!
WE'RE BACK IN BUSINESS!
THIS ONE'S ON THE HOUSE!
BAM BAM

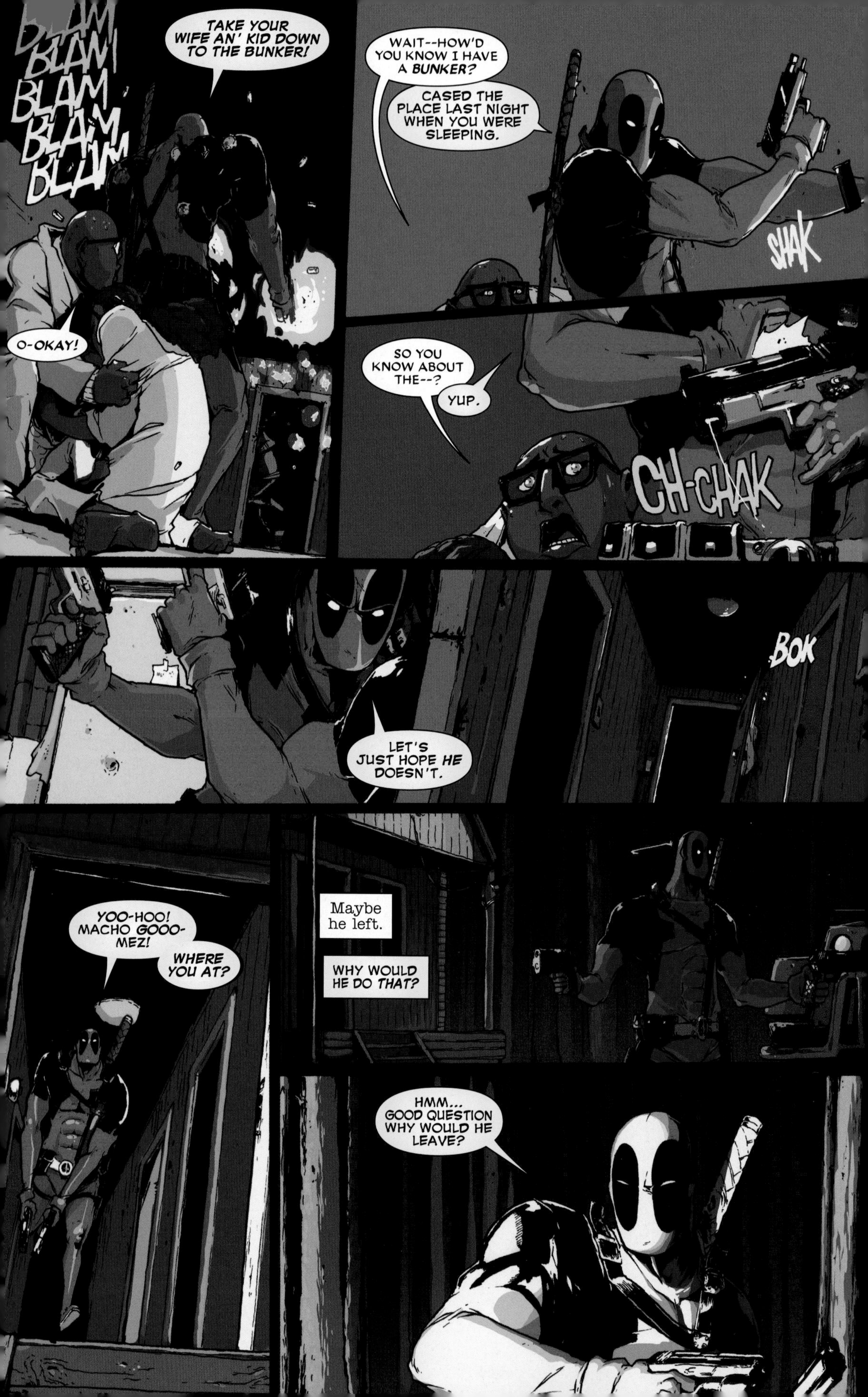
BLAM BLAM BLAM BLAM BLAM
TAKE YOUR WIFE AN' KID DOWN TO THE BUNKER!
O-OKAY!
WAIT--HOW'D YOU KNOW I HAVE A BUNKER?
CASED THE PLACE LAST NIGHT WHEN YOU WERE SLEEPING.
SHAK
SO YOU KNOW ABOUT THE--?
YUP.
CH-CHAK
BOK
LET'S JUST HOPE HE DOESN'T.
YOO-HOO! MACHO GOOO-MEZ!
WHERE YOU AT?
Maybe he left.
WHY WOULD HE DO THAT?
HMM... GOOD QUESTION WHY WOULD HE LEAVE?

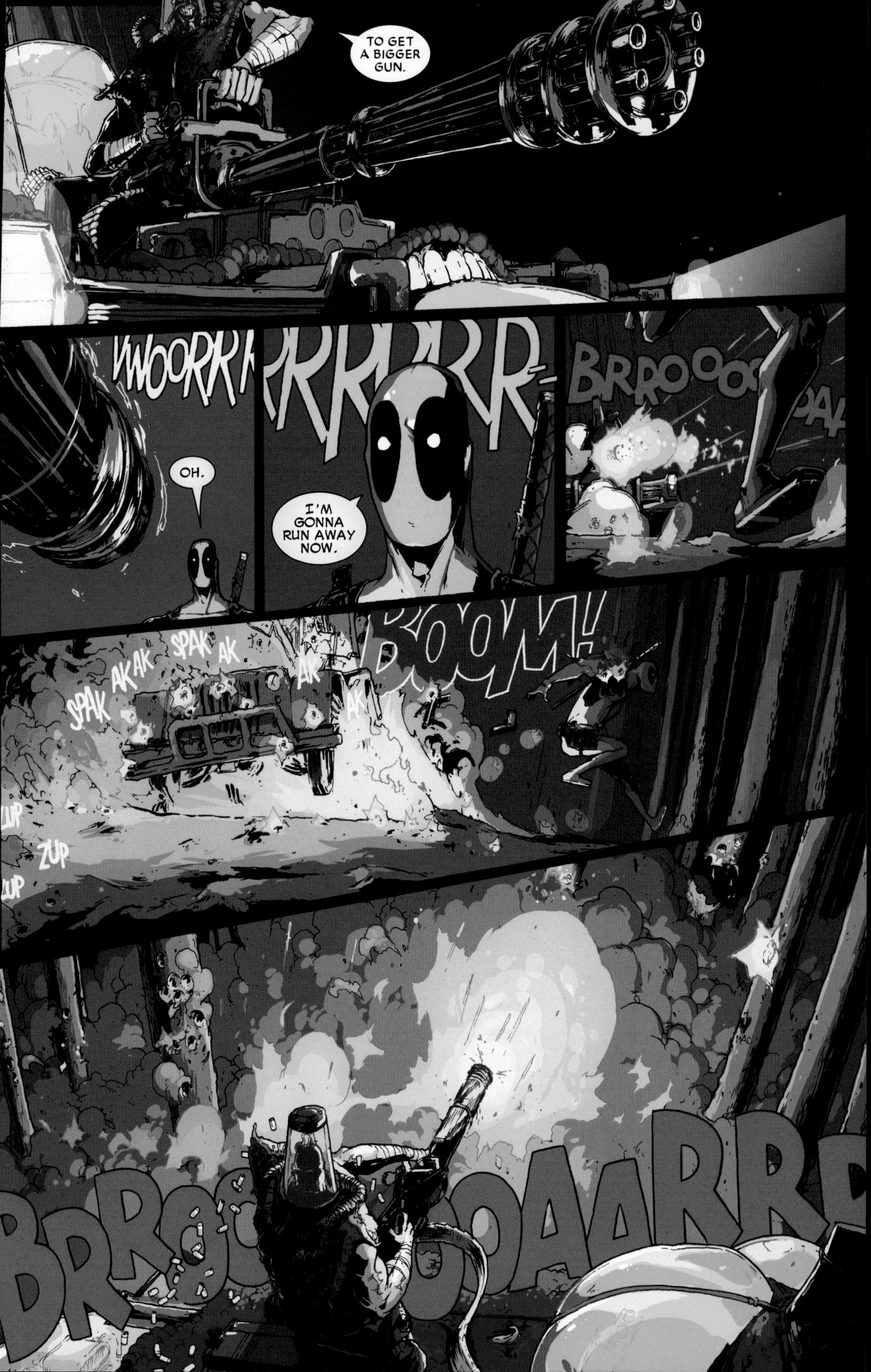
TO GET A BIGGER GUN.
VWOORRRRRRRRR-
OH.
I'M GONNA RUN AWAY NOW.
BRROOOO
SPAK
AK AK
SPAK
AK
AK
AK
BOOM!
ZUP
ZUP
ZUP
BRROOOOAARRR

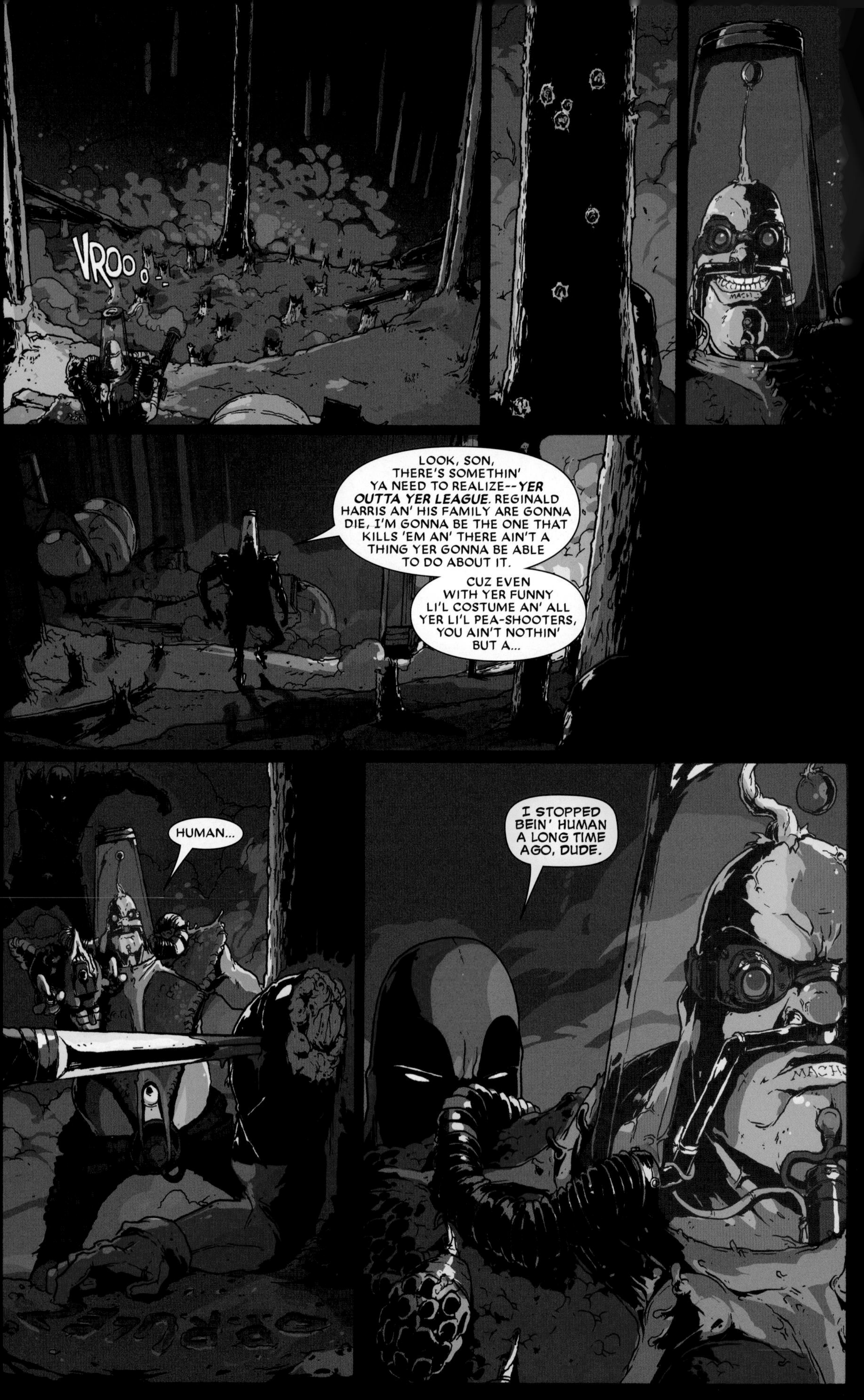
VROOo o - -
LOOK, SON, THERE'S SOMETHIN' YA NEED TO REALIZE--*YER OUTTA YER LEAGUE.* REGINALD HARRIS AN' HIS FAMILY ARE GONNA DIE, I'M GONNA BE THE ONE THAT KILLS 'EM AN' THERE AIN'T A THING YER GONNA BE ABLE TO DO ABOUT IT.
CUZ EVEN WITH YER FUNNY LI'L COSTUME AN' ALL YER LI'L PEA-SHOOTERS, YOU AIN'T NOTHIN' BUT A...
HUMAN...
I STOPPED BEIN' HUMAN A LONG TIME AGO, DUDE.

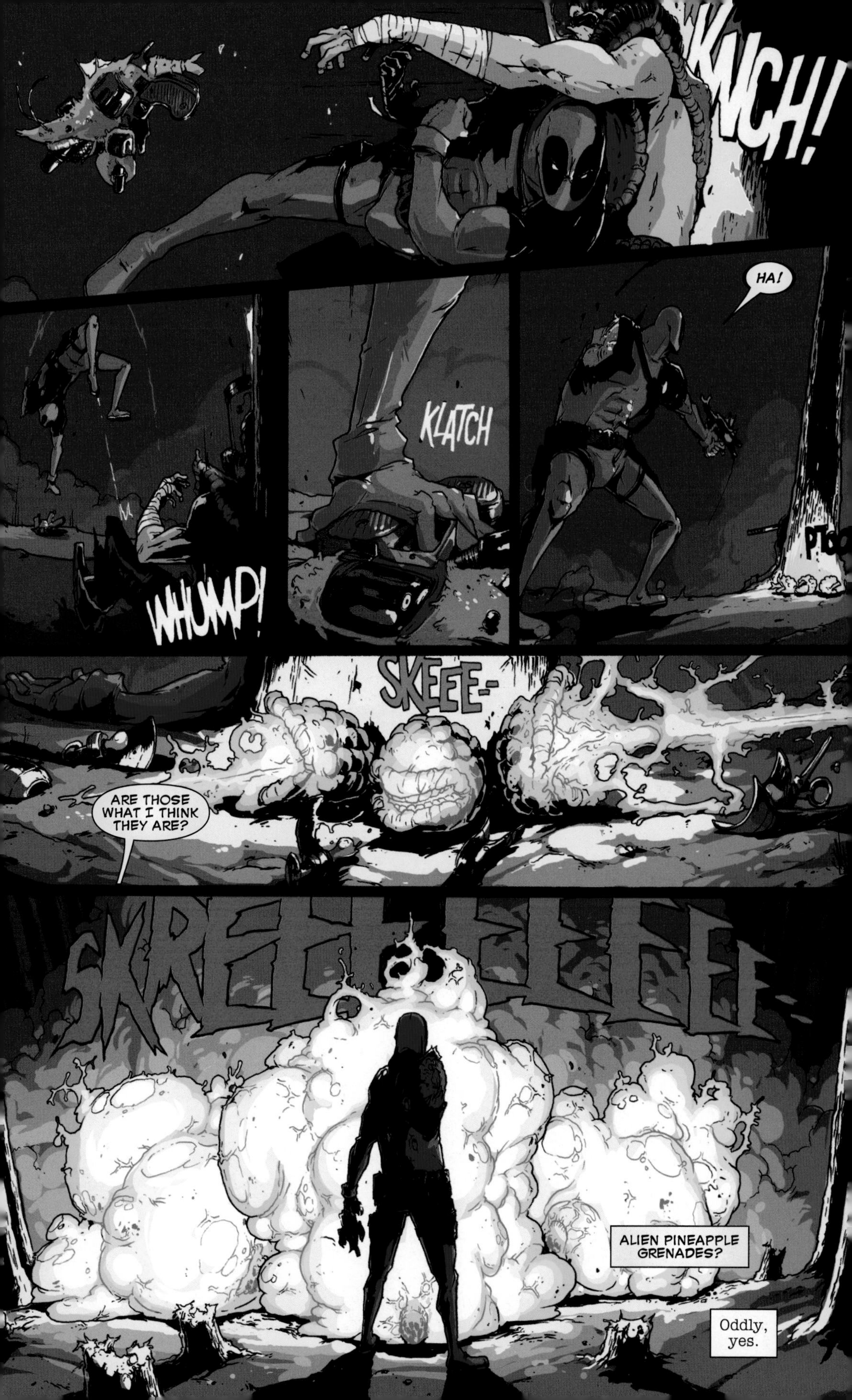
KNCH!
WHUMP!
KLATCH
HA!
PTOO
SKEEE-
ARE THOSE WHAT I THINK THEY ARE?
ALIEN PINEAPPLE GRENADES?
Oddly, yes.

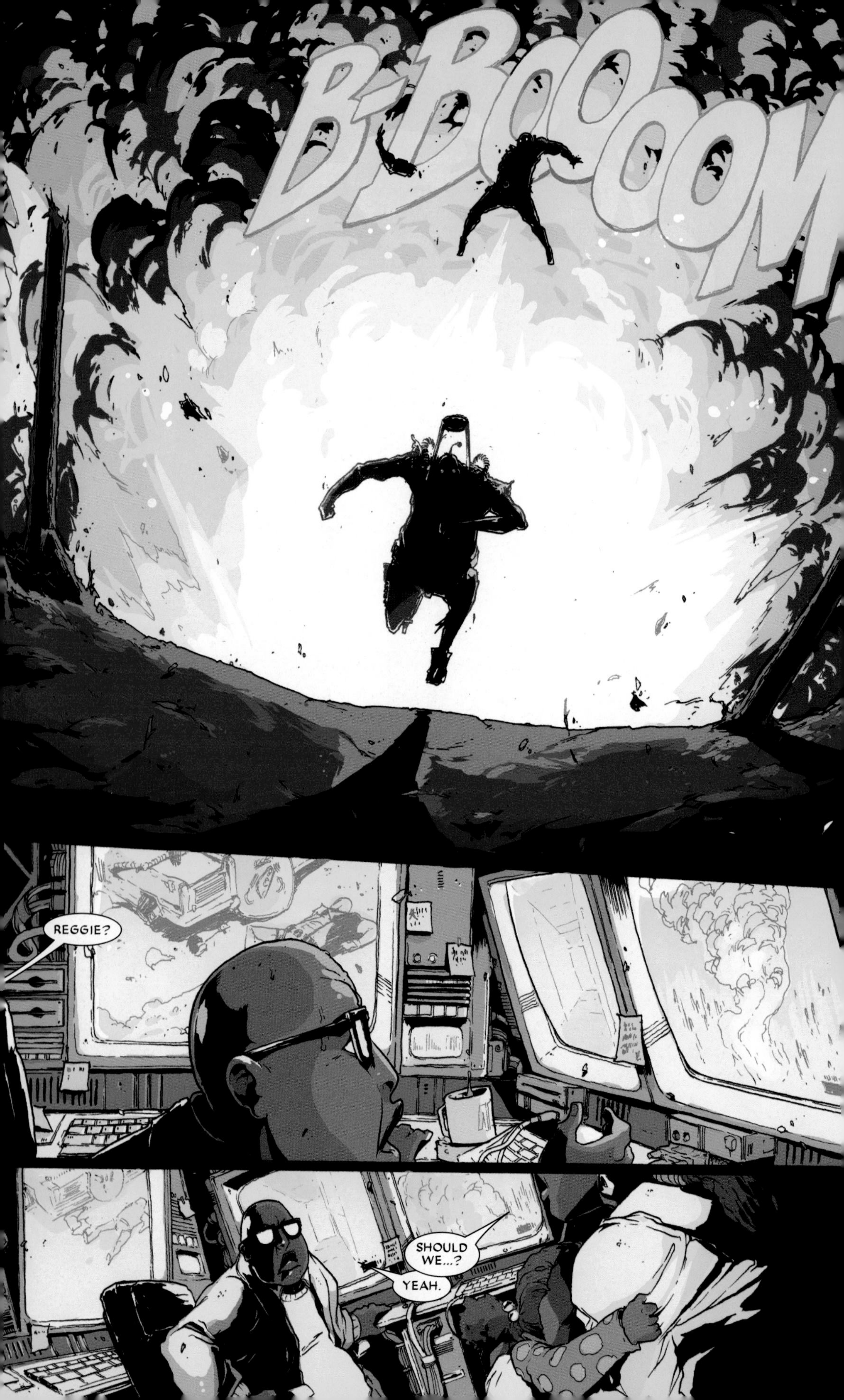
B-BOOOOM
REGGIE?
SHOULD WE...?
YEAH.

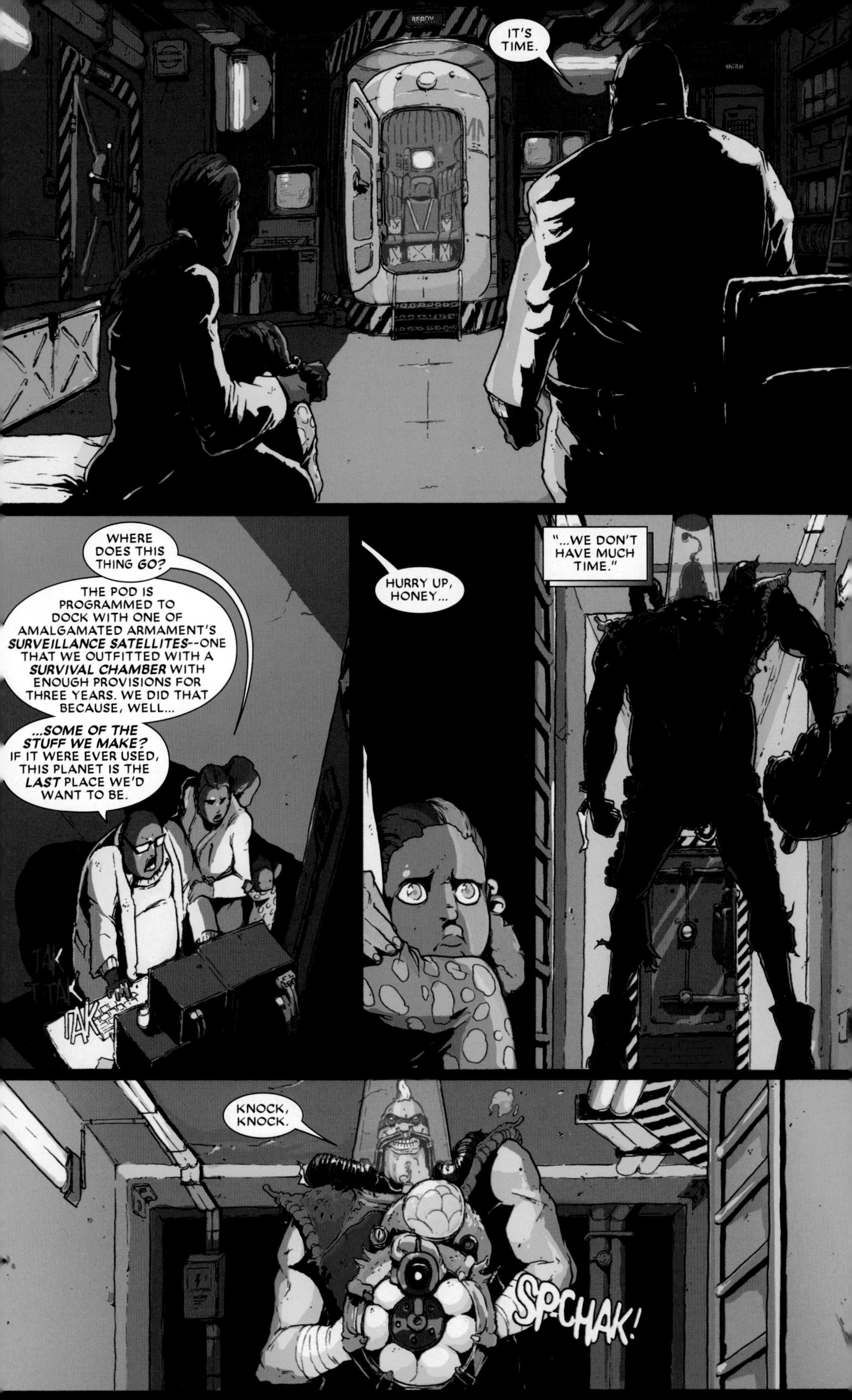
IT'S TIME.
WHERE DOES THIS THING GO?
THE POD IS PROGRAMMED TO DOCK WITH ONE OF AMALGAMATED ARMAMENT'S SURVEILLANCE SATELLITES--ONE THAT WE OUTFITTED WITH A SURVIVAL CHAMBER WITH ENOUGH PROVISIONS FOR THREE YEARS. WE DID THAT BECAUSE, WELL...
...SOME OF THE STUFF WE MAKE? IF IT WERE EVER USED, THIS PLANET IS THE LAST PLACE WE'D WANT TO BE.
TAK T-TAK TAK
HURRY UP, HONEY...
"...WE DON'T HAVE MUCH TIME."
KNOCK, KNOCK.
SP-CHAK!

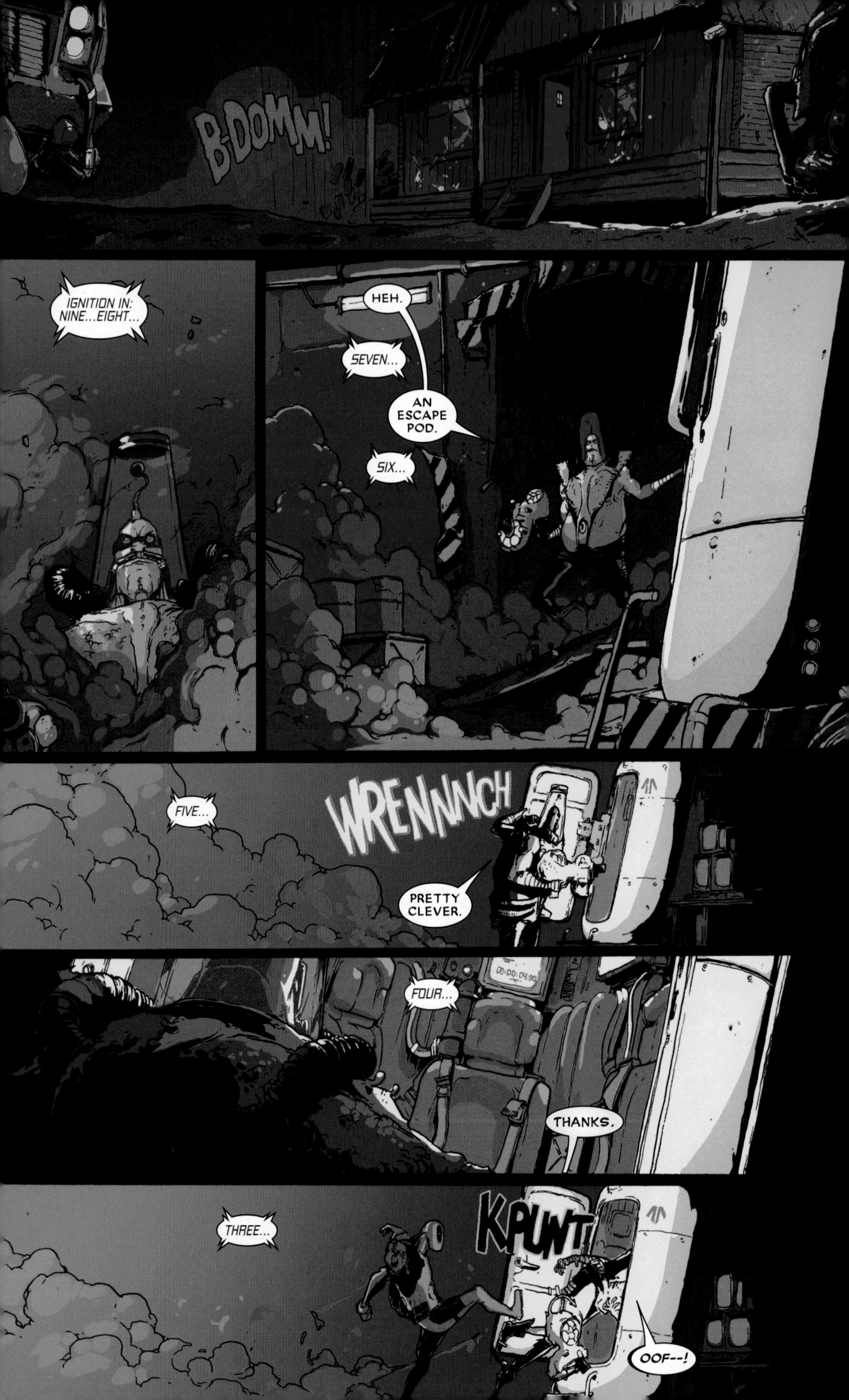
B-DOMM!
IGNITION IN:
NINE...EIGHT...
HEH.
SEVEN...
AN ESCAPE POD.
SIX...
FIVE...
WRENNNCH
PRETTY CLEVER.
FOUR...
00:00:04:00
THANKS.
THREE...
KPUNT!
OOF--!

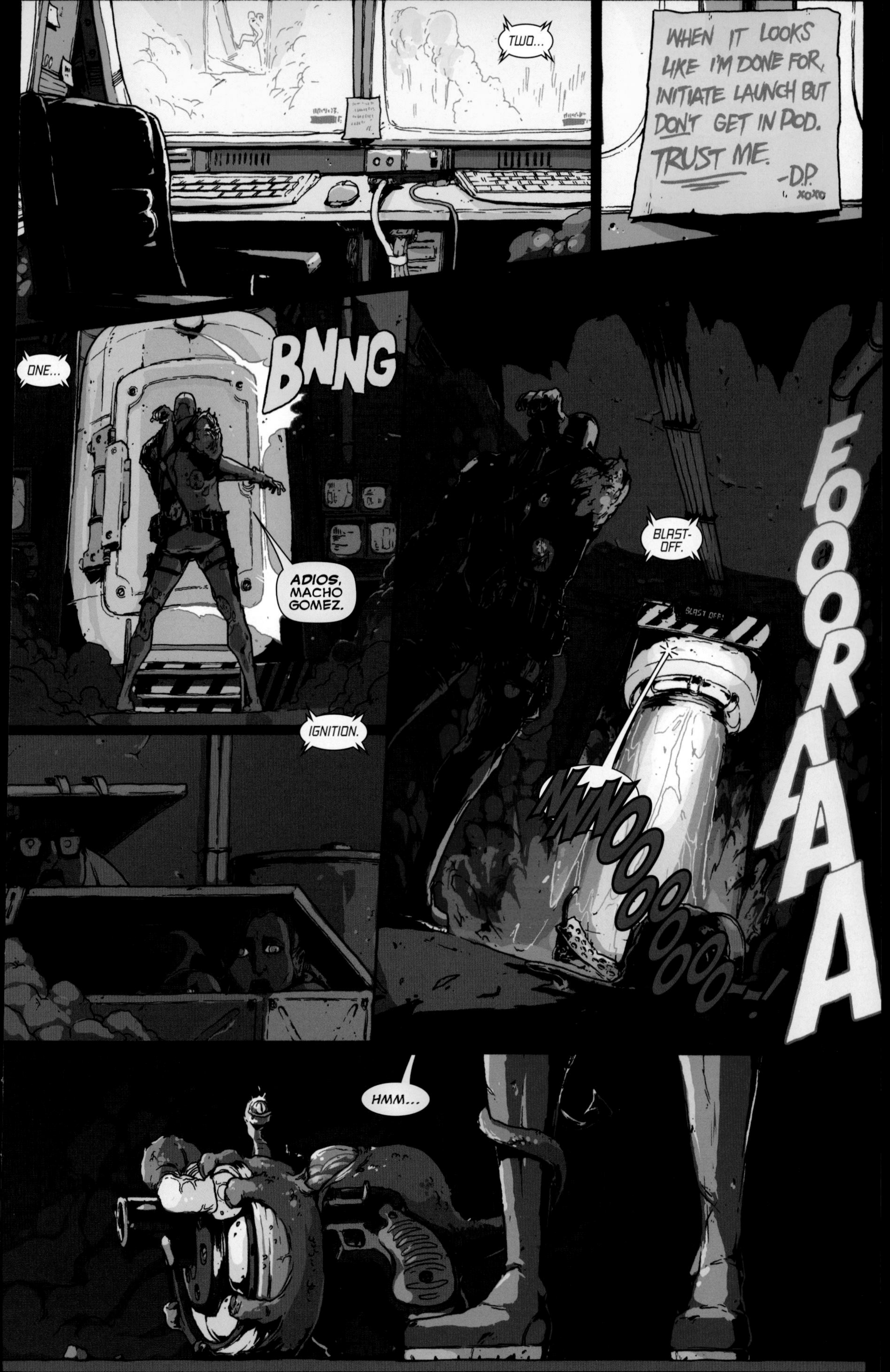
TWO...
WHEN IT LOOKS LIKE I'M DONE FOR, INITIATE LAUNCH BUT DON'T GET IN POD. TRUST ME. -D.P. XOXO
ONE...
BNNG
ADIOS, MACHO GOMEZ.
IGNITION.
BLAST-OFF.
BLAST OFF!
FOOORAAA
NNNOOOOOOOOO--!
HMM...

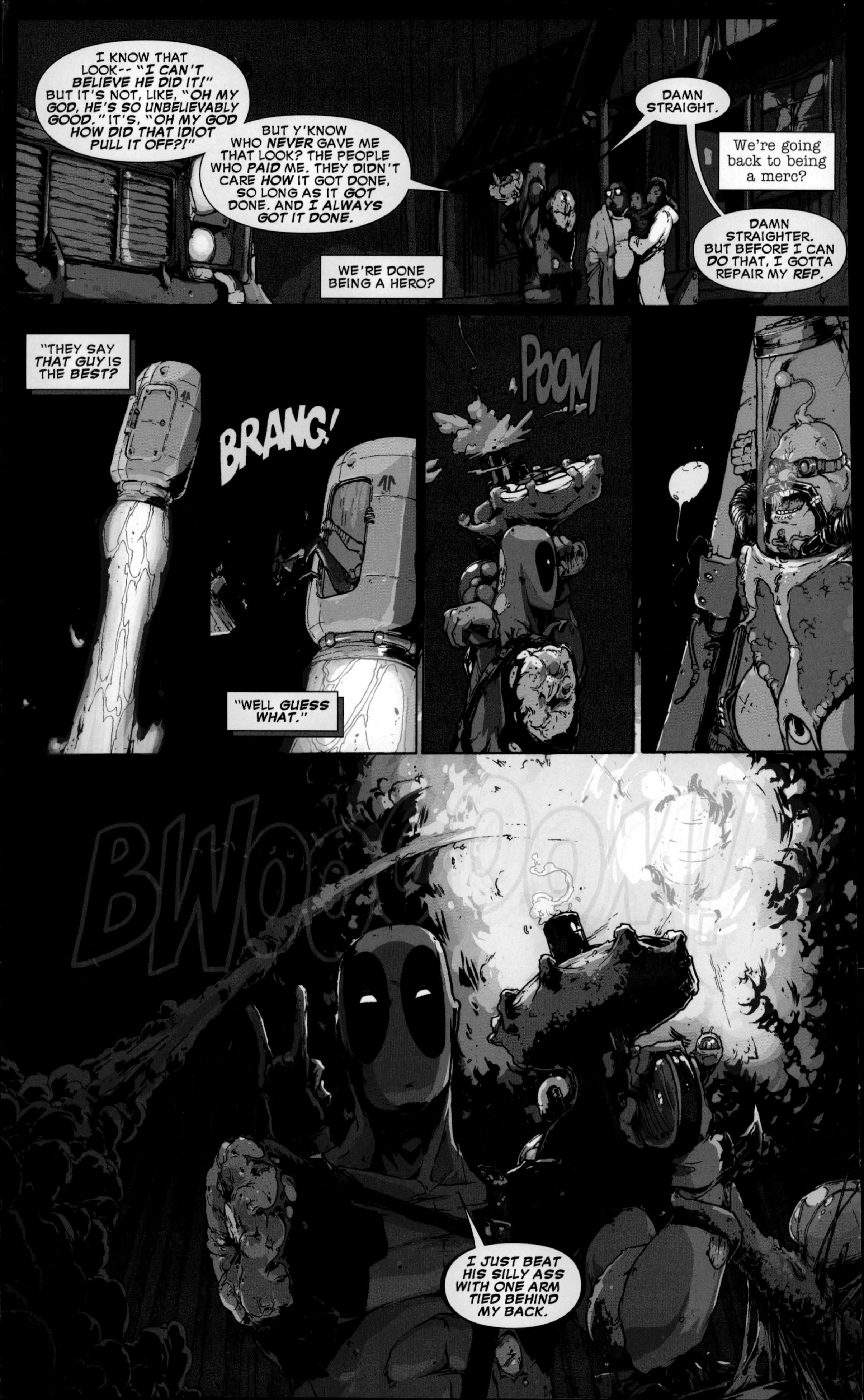
I KNOW THAT LOOK-- "I CAN'T BELIEVE HE DID IT!" BUT IT'S NOT, LIKE, "OH MY GOD, HE'S SO UNBELIEVABLY GOOD." IT'S, "OH MY GOD HOW DID THAT IDIOT PULL IT OFF?!"
BUT Y'KNOW WHO NEVER GAVE ME THAT LOOK? THE PEOPLE WHO PAID ME. THEY DIDN'T CARE HOW IT GOT DONE, SO LONG AS IT GOT DONE. AND I ALWAYS GOT IT DONE.
WE'RE DONE BEING A HERO?
DAMN STRAIGHT.
We're going back to being a merc?
DAMN STRAIGHTER. BUT BEFORE I CAN DO THAT, I GOTTA REPAIR MY REP.
"THEY SAY THAT GUY IS THE BEST?
BRANG!
"WELL GUESS WHAT."
POOM
BWOOOOOM!
I JUST BEAT HIS SILLY ASS WITH ONE ARM TIED BEHIND MY BACK.

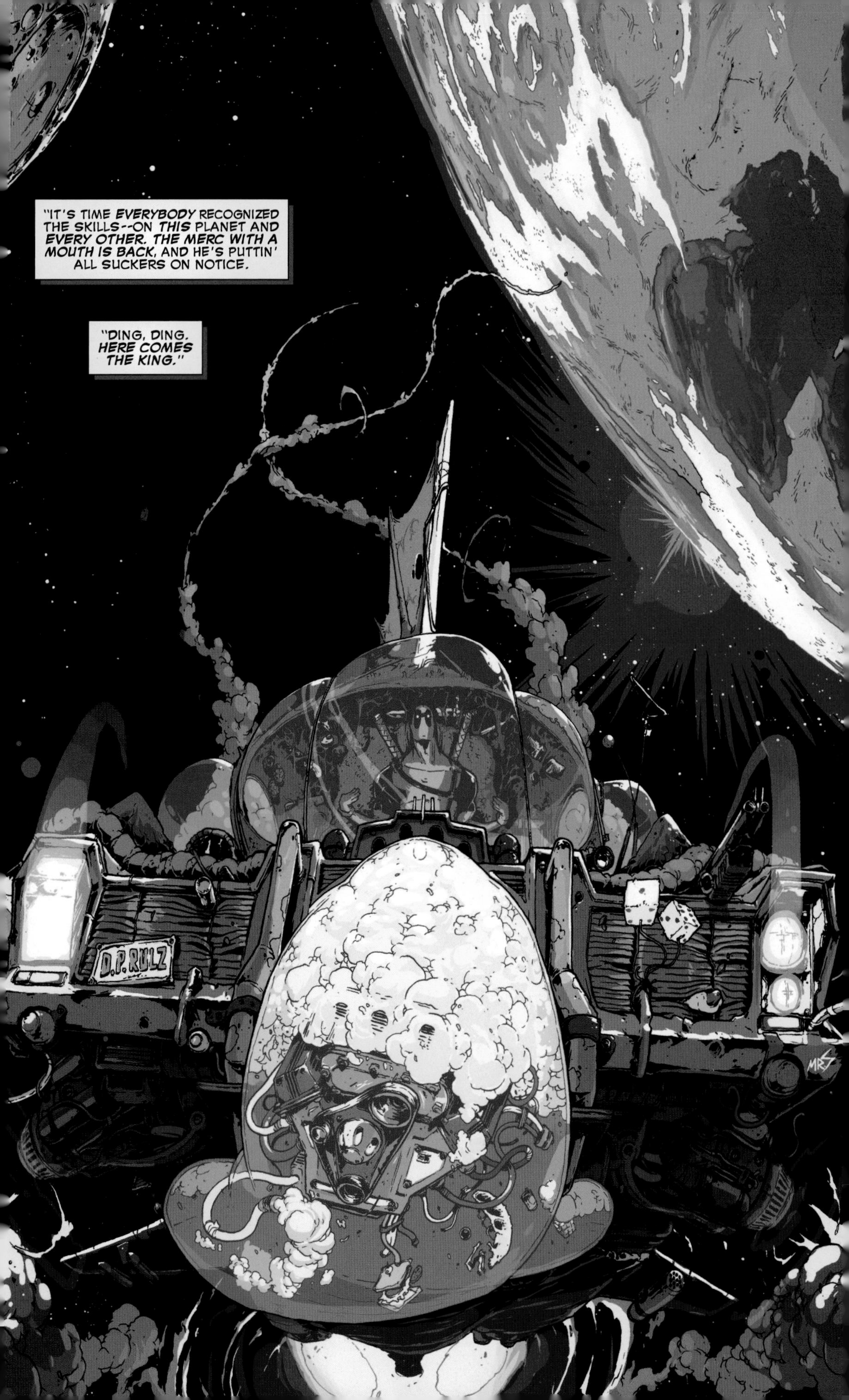
"IT'S TIME *EVERYBODY* RECOGNIZED THE SKILLS--ON *THIS* PLANET AND *EVERY OTHER. THE MERC WITH A MOUTH IS BACK,* AND HE'S PUTTIN' ALL SUCKERS ON NOTICE.
"DING, DING. *HERE COMES THE KING.*"
D.P. RULZ
MRS

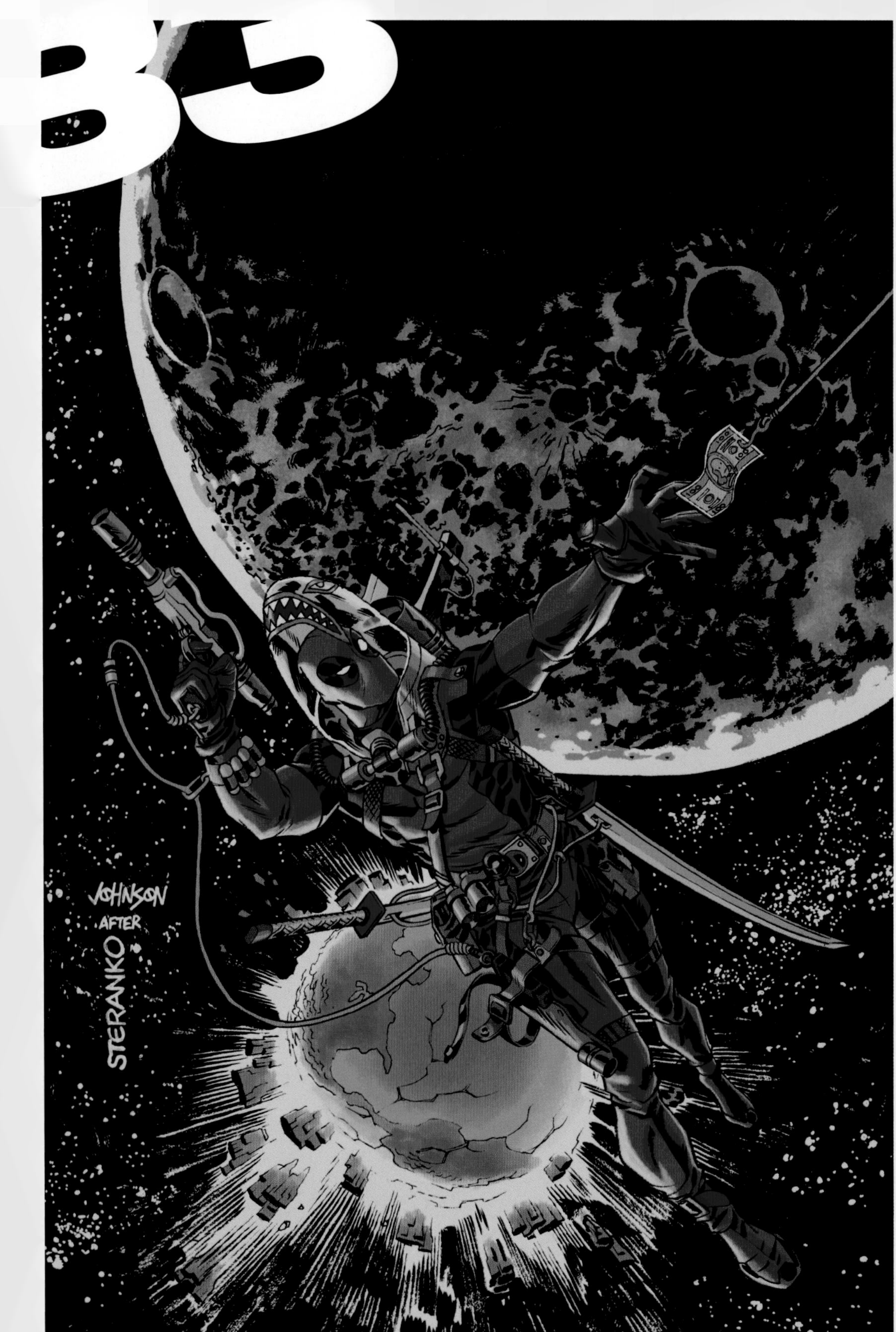
33
JOHNSON AFTER STERANKO

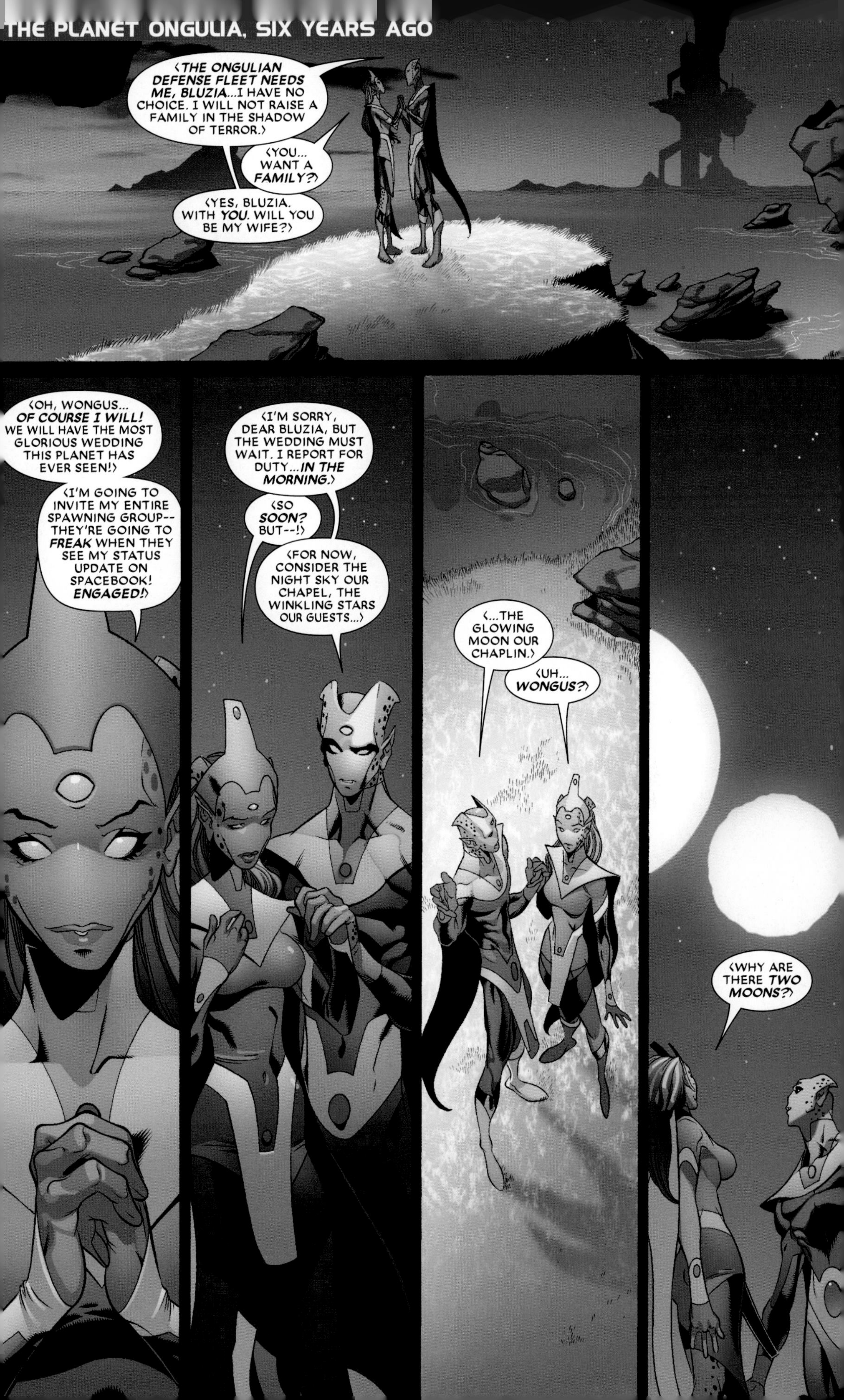
THE PLANET ONGULIA, SIX YEARS AGO
‹THE ONGULIAN DEFENSE FLEET NEEDS ME, BLUZIA...I HAVE NO CHOICE. I WILL NOT RAISE A FAMILY IN THE SHADOW OF TERROR.›
‹YOU... WANT A FAMILY?›
‹YES, BLUZIA. WITH YOU. WILL YOU BE MY WIFE?›
‹OH, WONGUS... OF COURSE I WILL! WE WILL HAVE THE MOST GLORIOUS WEDDING THIS PLANET HAS EVER SEEN!›
‹I'M GOING TO INVITE MY ENTIRE SPAWNING GROUP-- THEY'RE GOING TO FREAK WHEN THEY SEE MY STATUS UPDATE ON SPACEBOOK! ENGAGED!›
‹I'M SORRY, DEAR BLUZIA, BUT THE WEDDING MUST WAIT. I REPORT FOR DUTY...IN THE MORNING.›
‹SO SOON? BUT--!›
‹FOR NOW, CONSIDER THE NIGHT SKY OUR CHAPEL, THE WINKLING STARS OUR GUESTS...›
‹...THE GLOWING MOON OUR CHAPLIN.›
‹UH... WONGUS?›
‹WHY ARE THERE TWO MOONS?›

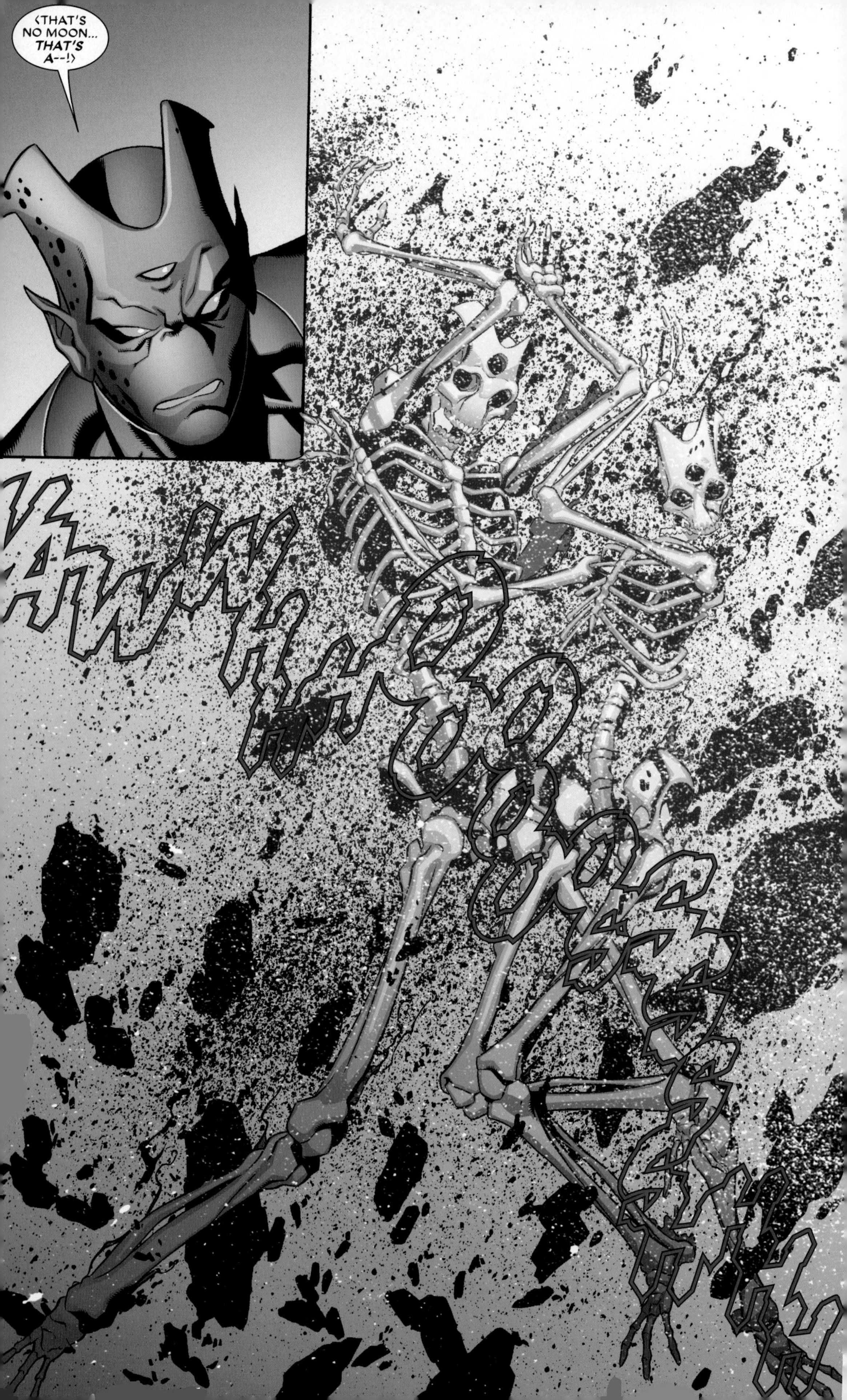
‹THAT'S NO MOON... THAT'S A--!›

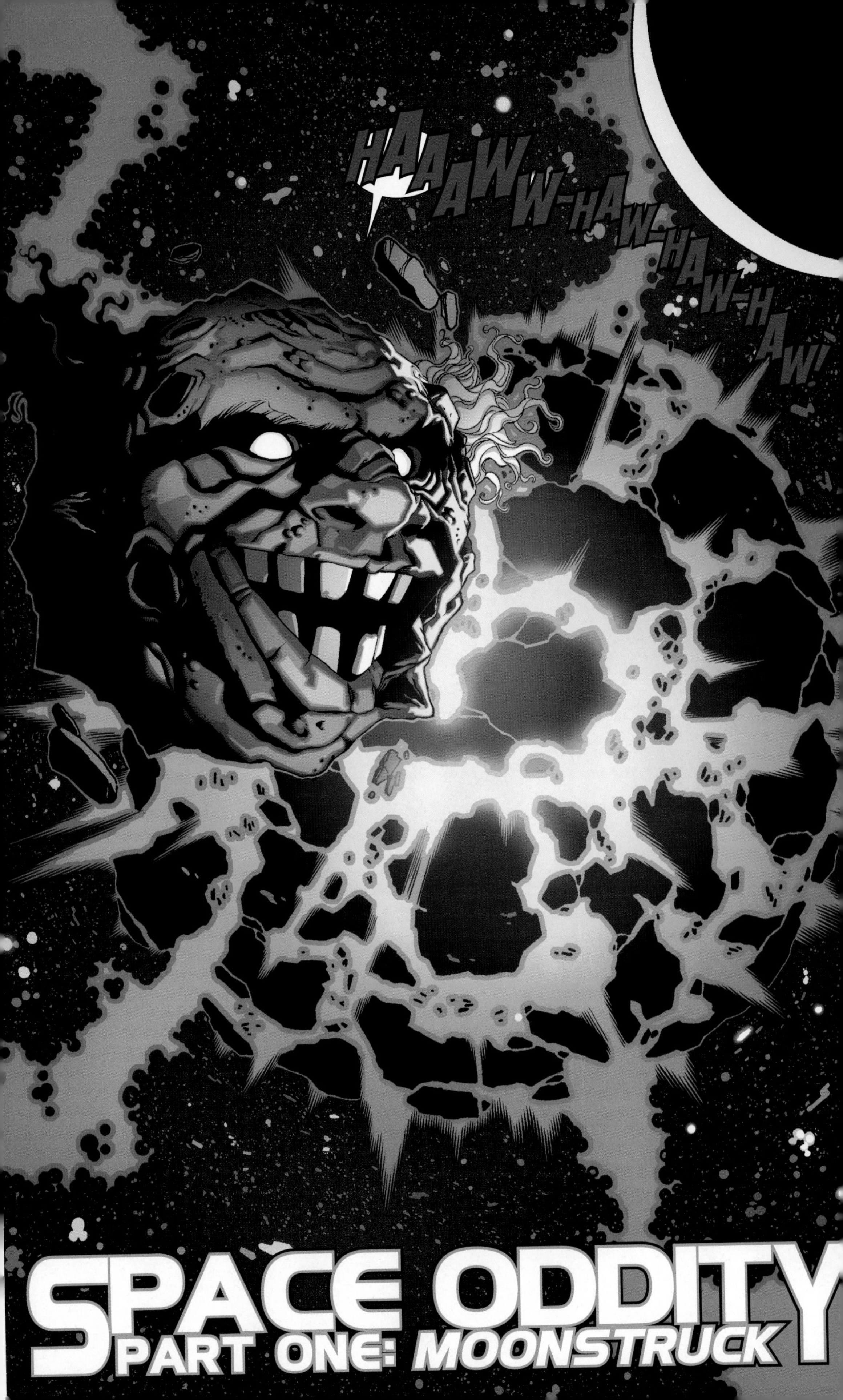
HAAAWW-HAW-HAW-HAW-HAW!
SPACE ODDITY
PART ONE: MOONSTRUCK

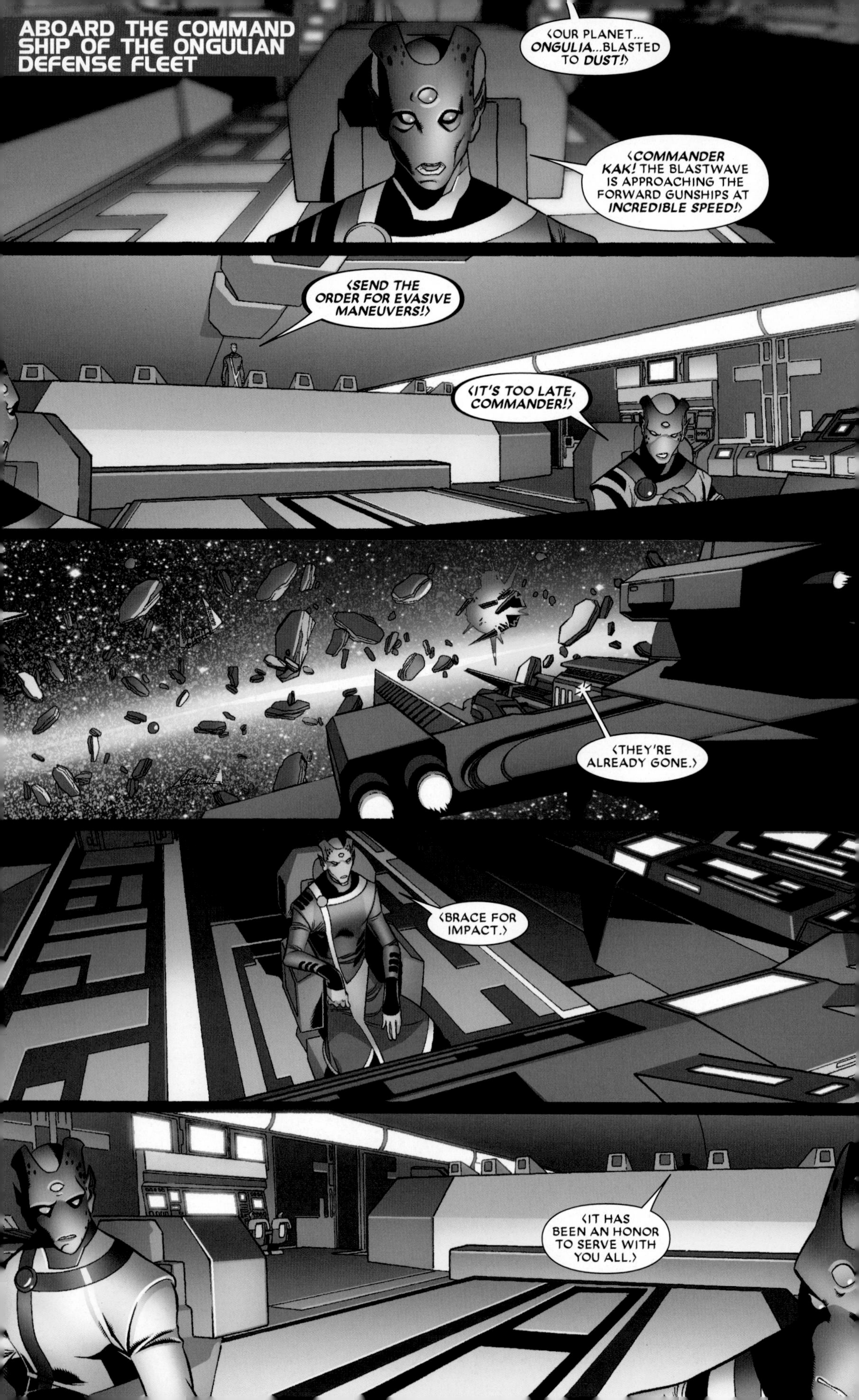
ABOARD THE COMMAND SHIP OF THE ONGULIAN DEFENSE FLEET
‹OUR PLANET... ONGULIA...BLASTED TO DUST!›
‹COMMANDER KAK! THE BLASTWAVE IS APPROACHING THE FORWARD GUNSHIPS AT INCREDIBLE SPEED!›
‹SEND THE ORDER FOR EVASIVE MANEUVERS!›
‹IT'S TOO LATE, COMMANDER!›
‹THEY'RE ALREADY GONE.›
‹BRACE FOR IMPACT.›
‹IT HAS BEEN AN HONOR TO SERVE WITH YOU ALL.›

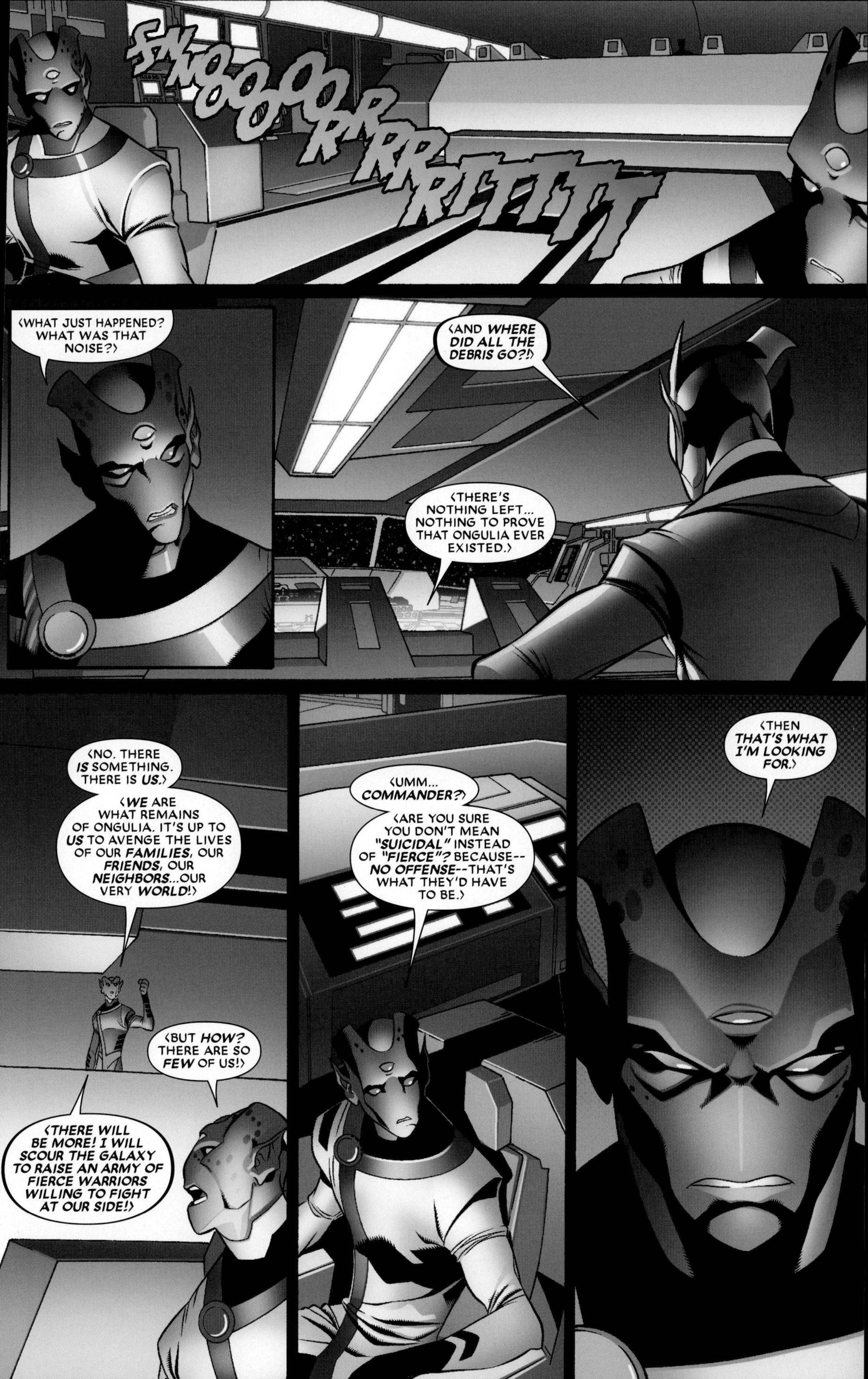
SNOOOOORRRRRRITTTTT
‹WHAT JUST HAPPENED? WHAT WAS THAT NOISE?›
‹AND WHERE DID ALL THE DEBRIS GO?!›
‹THERE'S NOTHING LEFT... NOTHING TO PROVE THAT ONGULIA EVER EXISTED.›
‹NO. THERE IS SOMETHING. THERE IS US.›
‹WE ARE WHAT REMAINS OF ONGULIA. IT'S UP TO US TO AVENGE THE LIVES OF OUR FAMILIES, OUR FRIENDS, OUR NEIGHBORS...OUR VERY WORLD!›
‹BUT HOW? THERE ARE SO FEW OF US!›
‹THERE WILL BE MORE! I WILL SCOUR THE GALAXY TO RAISE AN ARMY OF FIERCE WARRIORS WILLING TO FIGHT AT OUR SIDE!›
‹UMM... COMMANDER?›
‹ARE YOU SURE YOU DON'T MEAN "SUICIDAL" INSTEAD OF "FIERCE"? BECAUSE--NO OFFENSE--THAT'S WHAT THEY'D HAVE TO BE.›
‹THEN THAT'S WHAT I'M LOOKING FOR.›

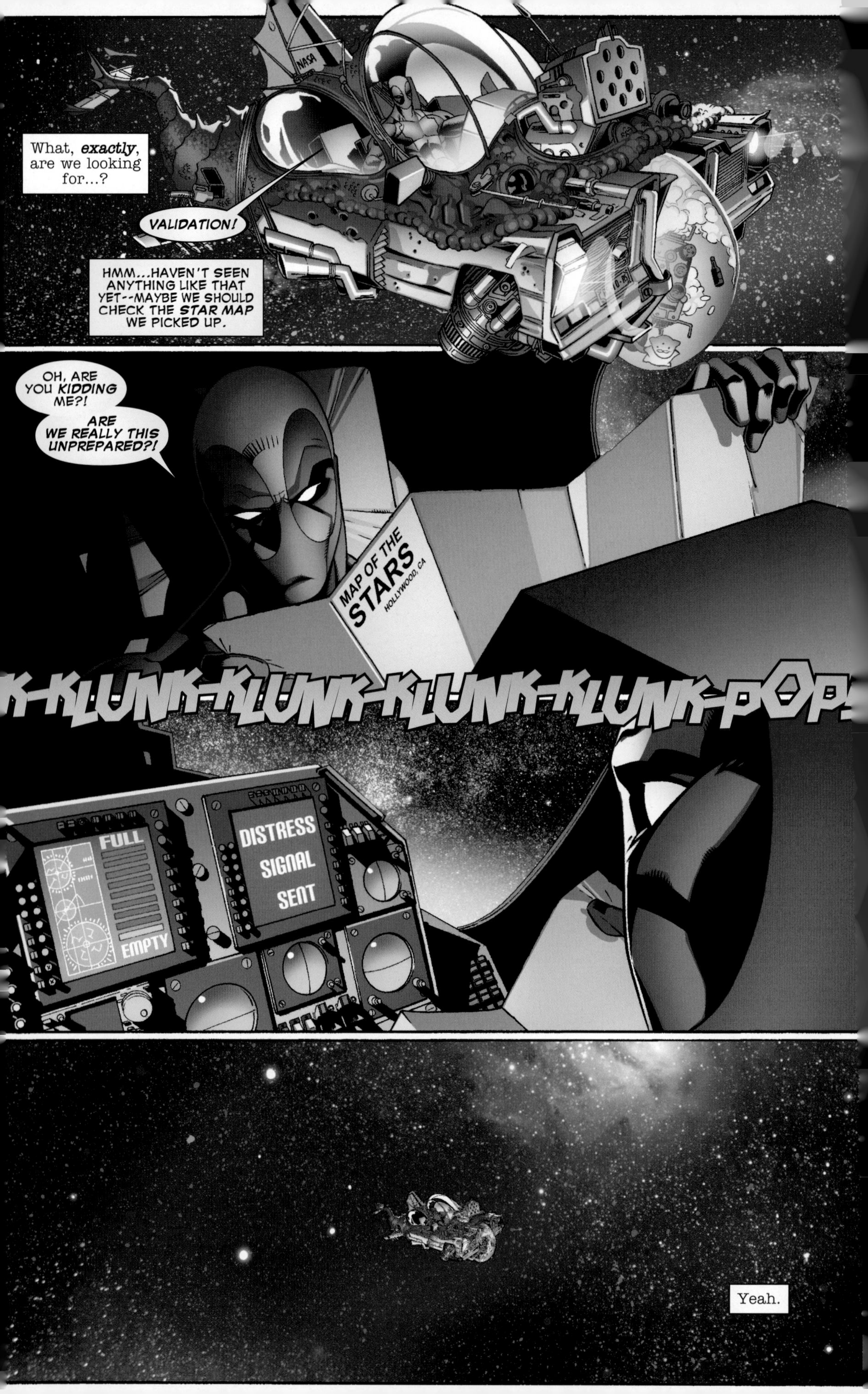
What, *exactly*, are we looking for...?
VALIDATION!
HMM...HAVEN'T SEEN ANYTHING LIKE THAT YET--MAYBE WE SHOULD CHECK THE STAR MAP WE PICKED UP.
OH, ARE YOU KIDDING ME?!
ARE WE REALLY THIS UNPREPARED?!
MAP OF THE STARS HOLLYWOOD, CA
K-KLUNK-KLUNK-KLUNK-KLUNK-pOP!
FULL
EMPTY
DISTRESS SIGNAL SENT
Yeah.

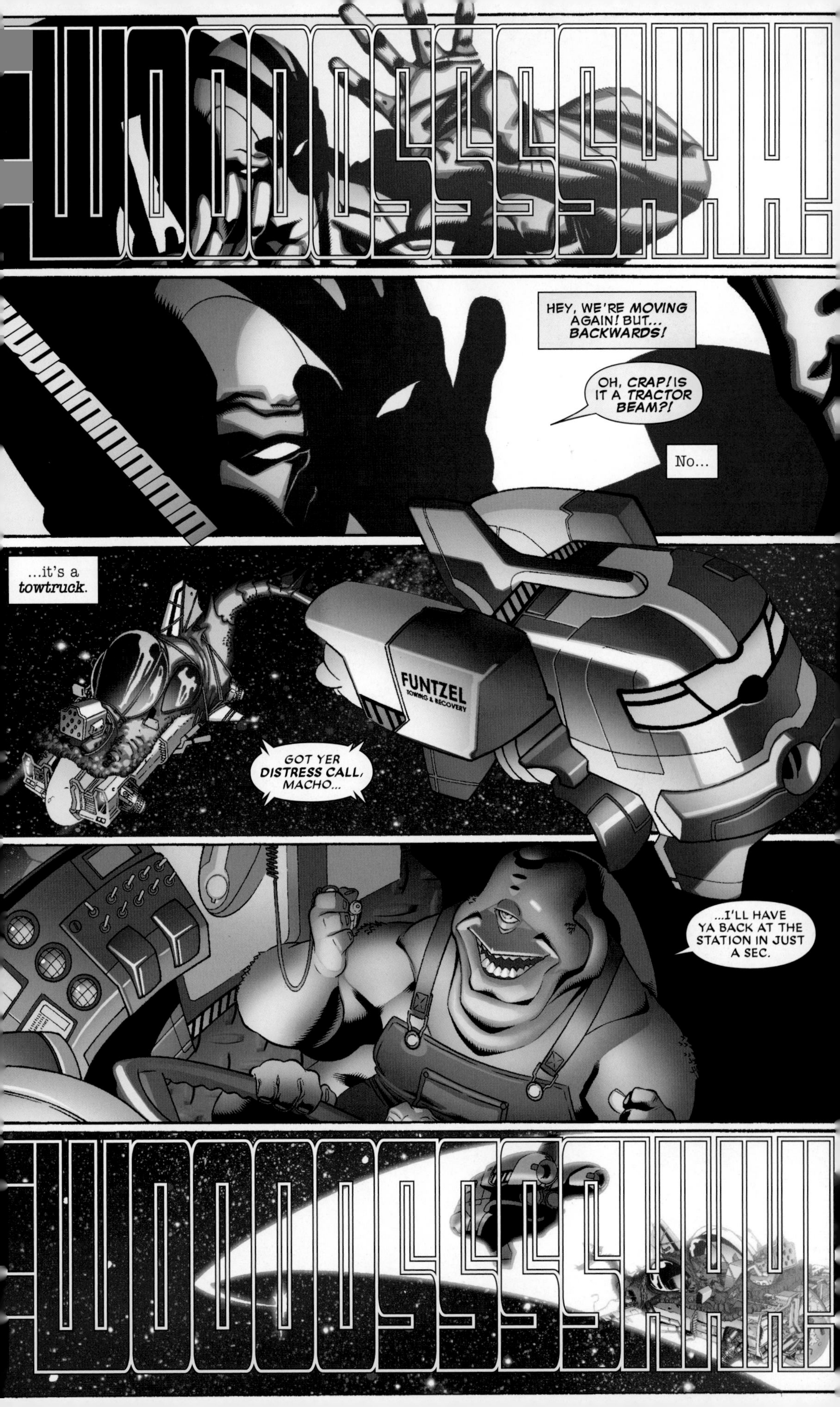
WOOOOSSSSHHH!
HEY, WE'RE MOVING AGAIN! BUT... BACKWARDS!
OH, CRAP! IS IT A TRACTOR BEAM?!
No...
...it's a towtruck.
FUNTZEL TOWING & RECOVERY
GOT YER DISTRESS CALL, MACHO...
...I'LL HAVE YA BACK AT THE STATION IN JUST A SEC.
WOOOOSSSSHHH!

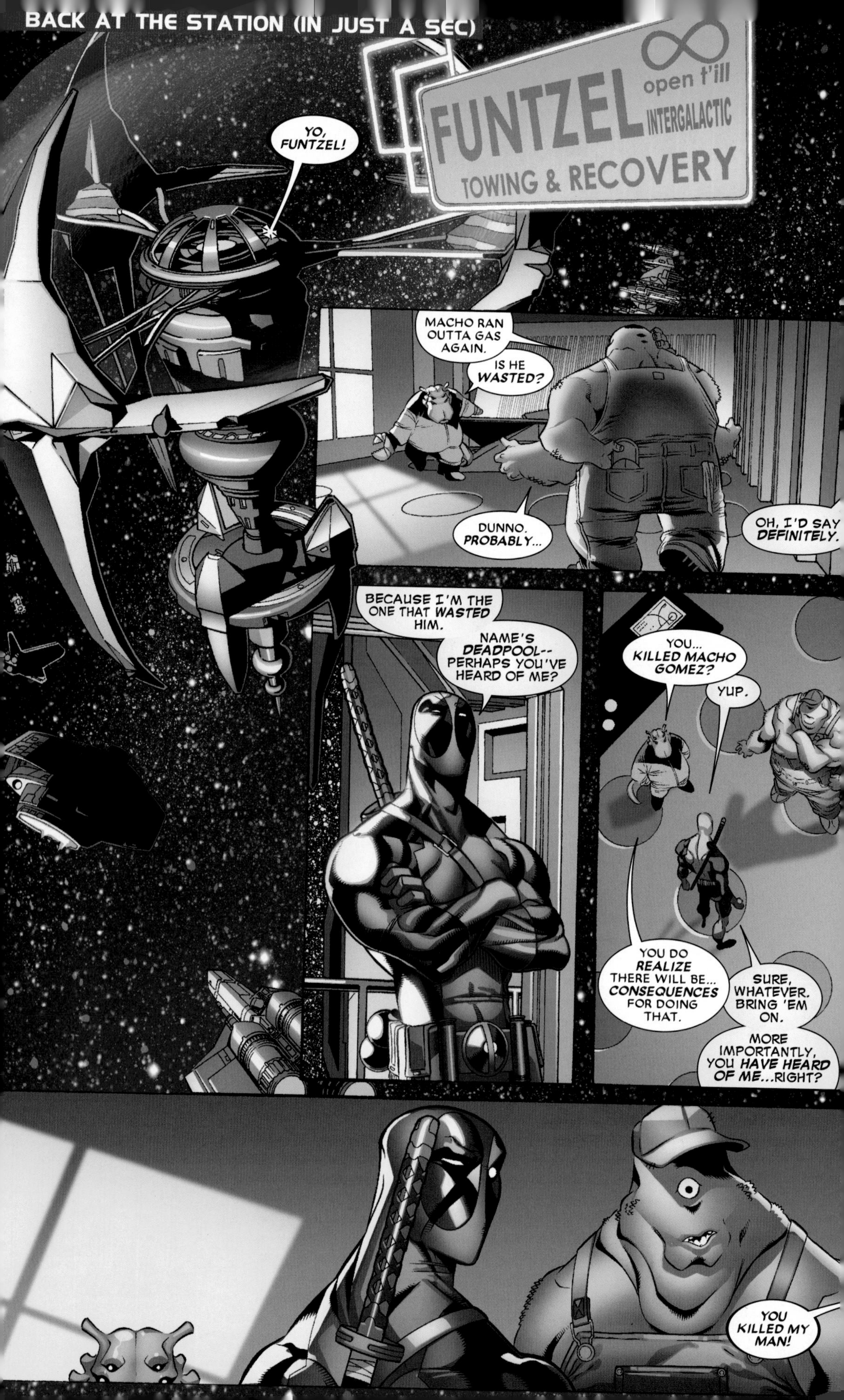
BACK AT THE STATION (IN JUST A SEC)
FUNTZEL open t'ill ∞ INTERGALACTIC TOWING & RECOVERY
YO, FUNTZEL!
MACHO RAN OUTTA GAS AGAIN.
IS HE WASTED?
DUNNO. PROBABLY...
OH, I'D SAY DEFINITELY.
BECAUSE I'M THE ONE THAT WASTED HIM.
NAME'S DEADPOOL-- PERHAPS YOU'VE HEARD OF ME?
YOU... KILLED MACHO GOMEZ?
YUP.
YOU DO REALIZE THERE WILL BE... CONSEQUENCES FOR DOING THAT.
SURE, WHATEVER. BRING 'EM ON.
MORE IMPORTANTLY, YOU HAVE HEARD OF ME...RIGHT?
YOU KILLED MY MAN!

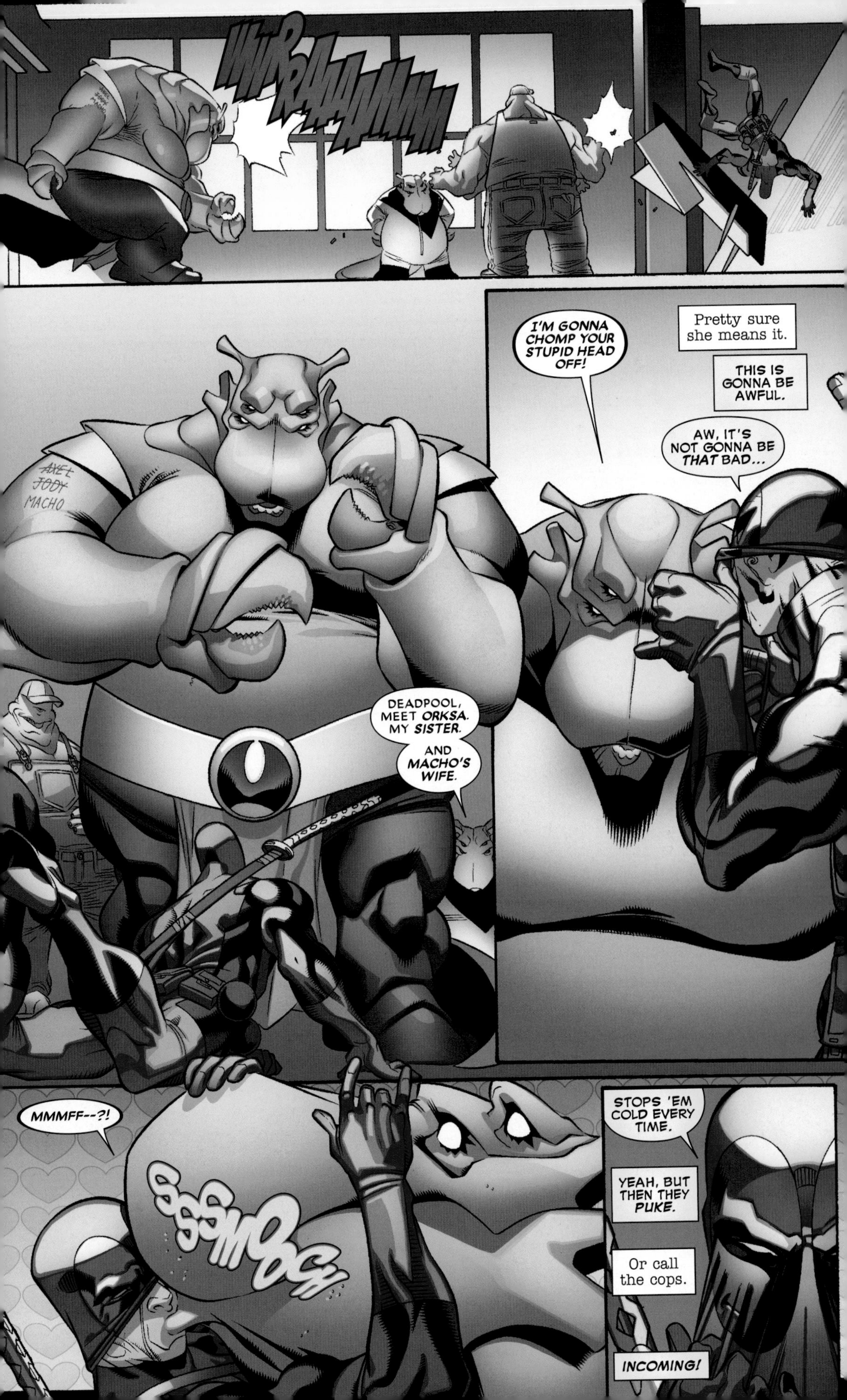
WHRAAAAMMM
AXEL
JODY
MACHO
I'M GONNA CHOMP YOUR STUPID HEAD OFF!
Pretty sure she means it.
THIS IS GONNA BE AWFUL.
AW, IT'S NOT GONNA BE *THAT* BAD...
DEADPOOL, MEET *ORKSA*. MY *SISTER*.
AND *MACHO'S* *WIFE*.
MMMFF--?!
SSSMOOCH
STOPS 'EM COLD EVERY TIME.
YEAH, BUT THEN THEY *PUKE*.
Or call the cops.
INCOMING!

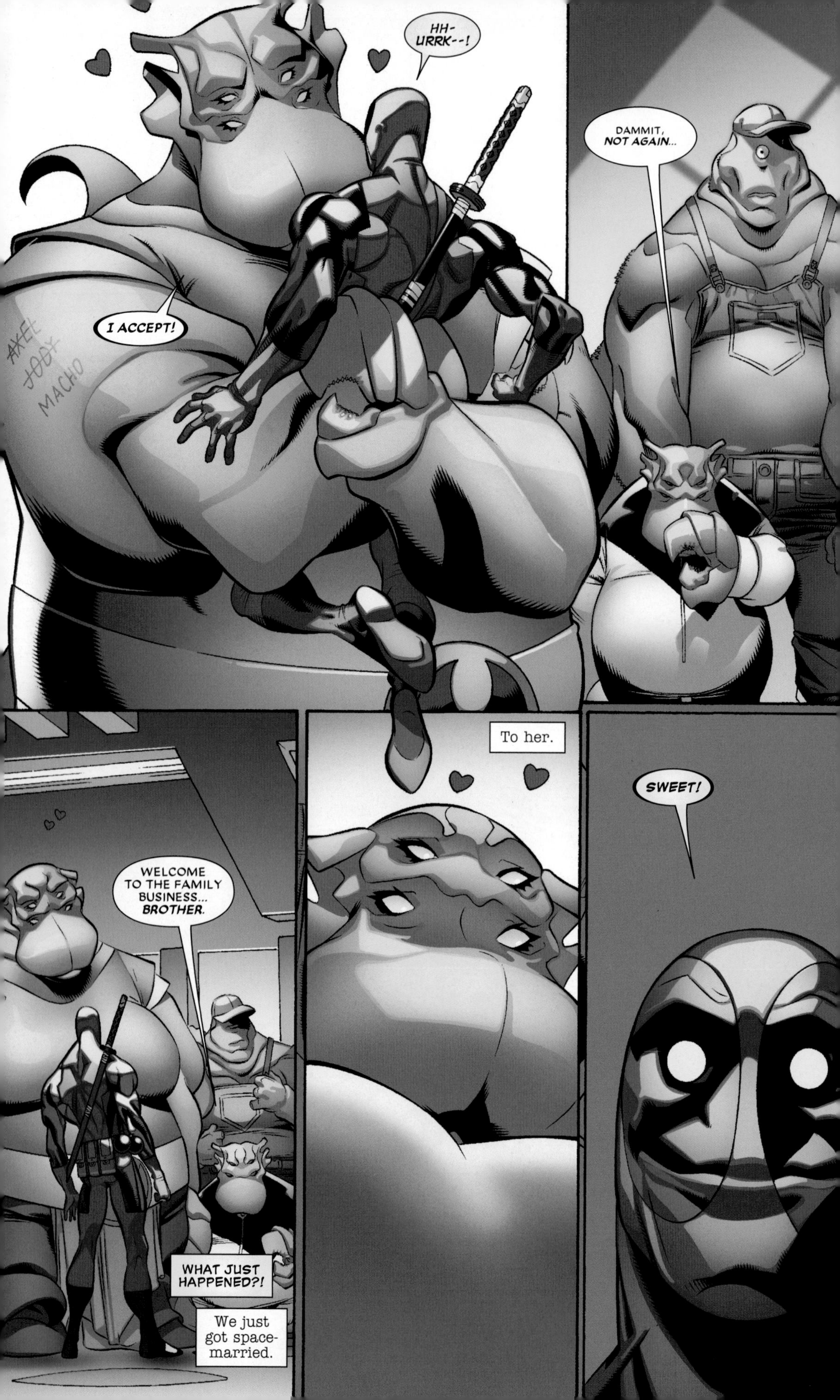
HH-URRK--!
I ACCEPT!
AXEL
JOBY
MACHO
DAMMIT, NOT AGAIN...
WELCOME TO THE FAMILY BUSINESS... BROTHER.
WHAT JUST HAPPENED?!
We just got space-married.
To her.
SWEET!

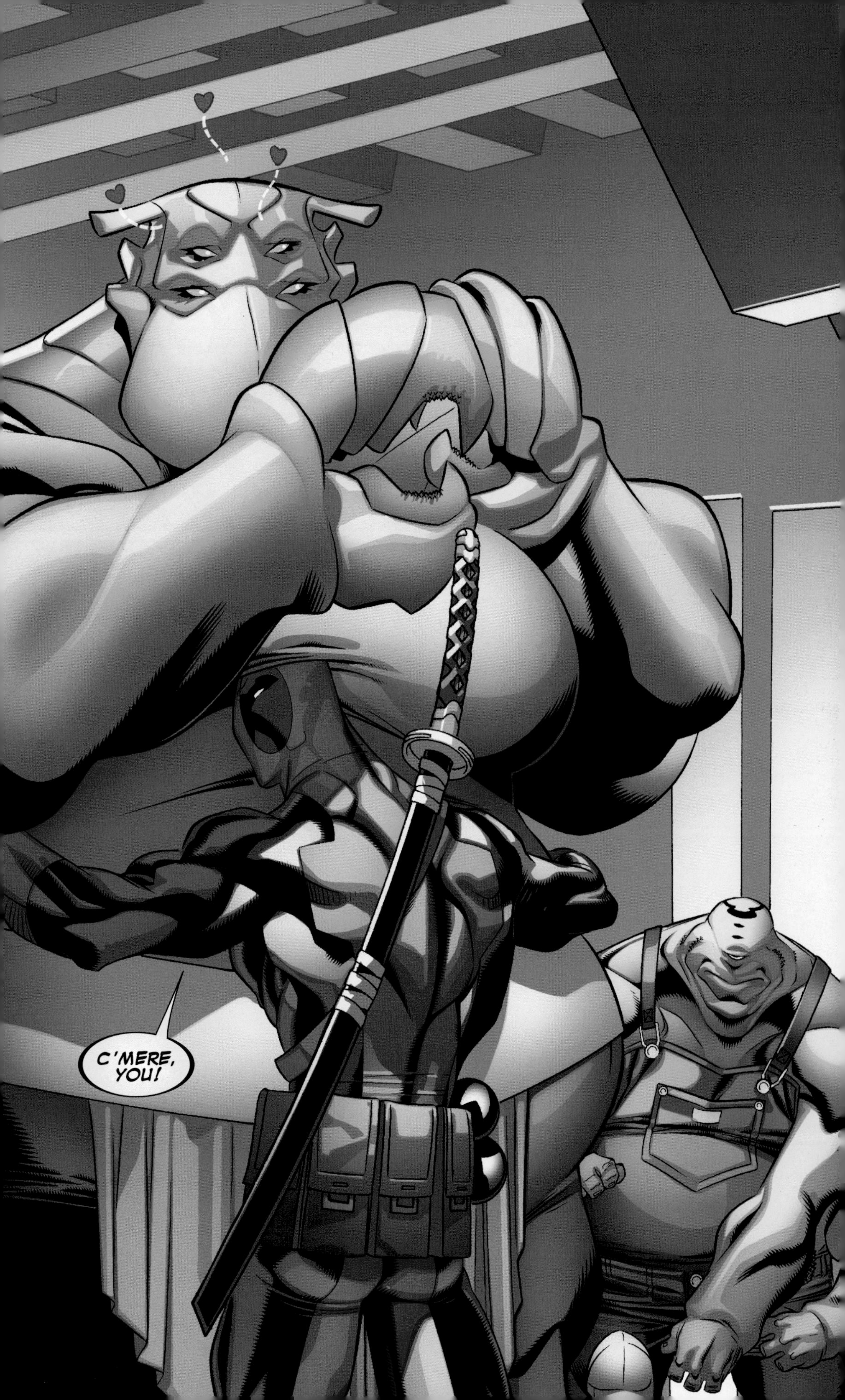
C'MERE, YOU!

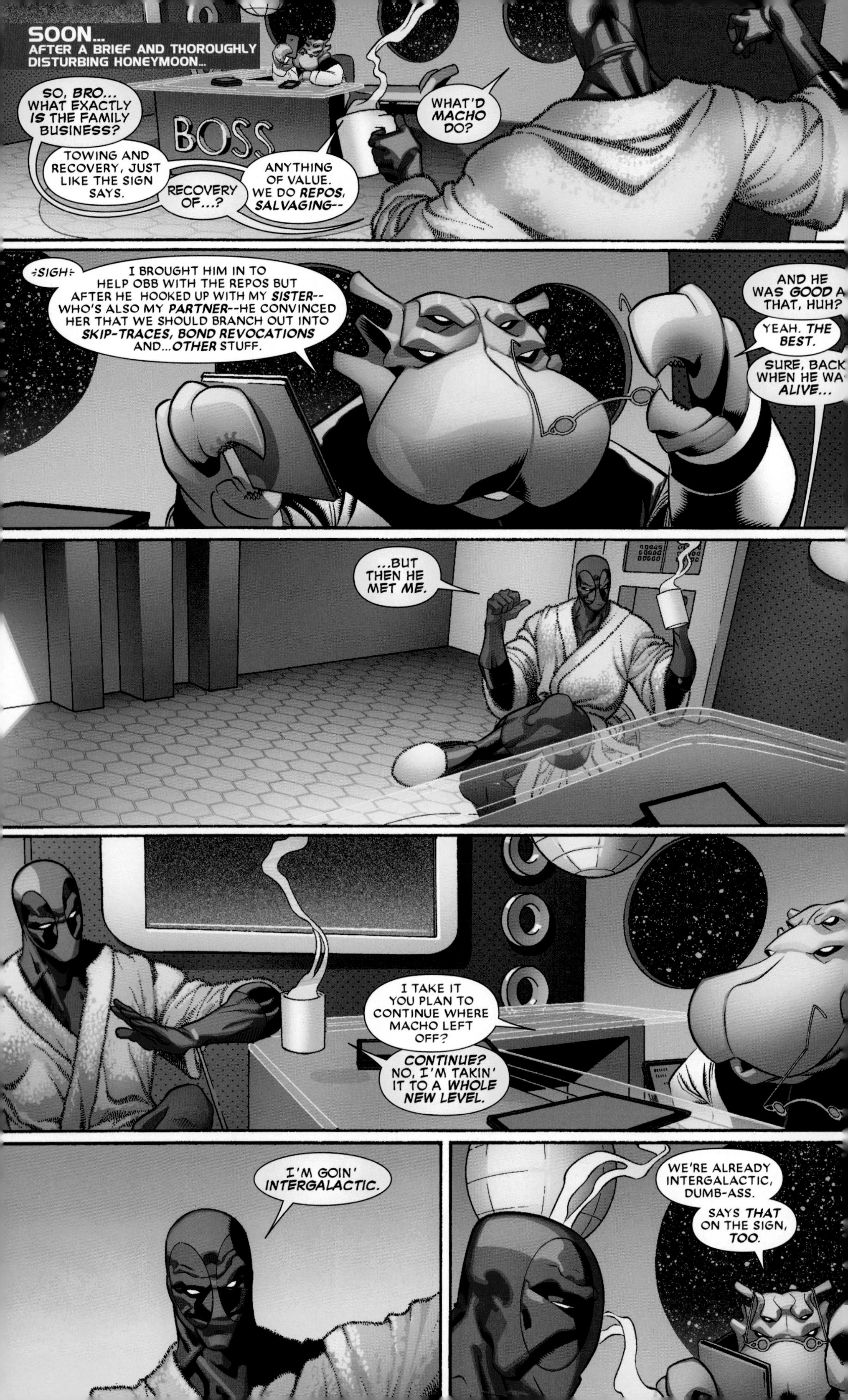
SOON... AFTER A BRIEF AND THOROUGHLY DISTURBING HONEYMOON...
BOSS
SO, BRO... WHAT EXACTLY IS THE FAMILY BUSINESS?
TOWING AND RECOVERY, JUST LIKE THE SIGN SAYS.
RECOVERY OF...?
ANYTHING OF VALUE. WE DO REPOS, SALVAGING--
WHAT'D MACHO DO?
≑SIGH≑
I BROUGHT HIM IN TO HELP OBB WITH THE REPOS BUT AFTER HE HOOKED UP WITH MY SISTER-- WHO'S ALSO MY PARTNER--HE CONVINCED HER THAT WE SHOULD BRANCH OUT INTO SKIP-TRACES, BOND REVOCATIONS AND...OTHER STUFF.
AND HE WAS GOOD A THAT, HUH?
YEAH. THE BEST.
SURE, BACK WHEN HE WA ALIVE...
...BUT THEN HE MET ME.
I TAKE IT YOU PLAN TO CONTINUE WHERE MACHO LEFT OFF?
CONTINUE? NO, I'M TAKIN' IT TO A WHOLE NEW LEVEL.
I'M GOIN' INTERGALACTIC.
WE'RE ALREADY INTERGALACTIC, DUMB-ASS.
SAYS THAT ON THE SIGN, TOO.

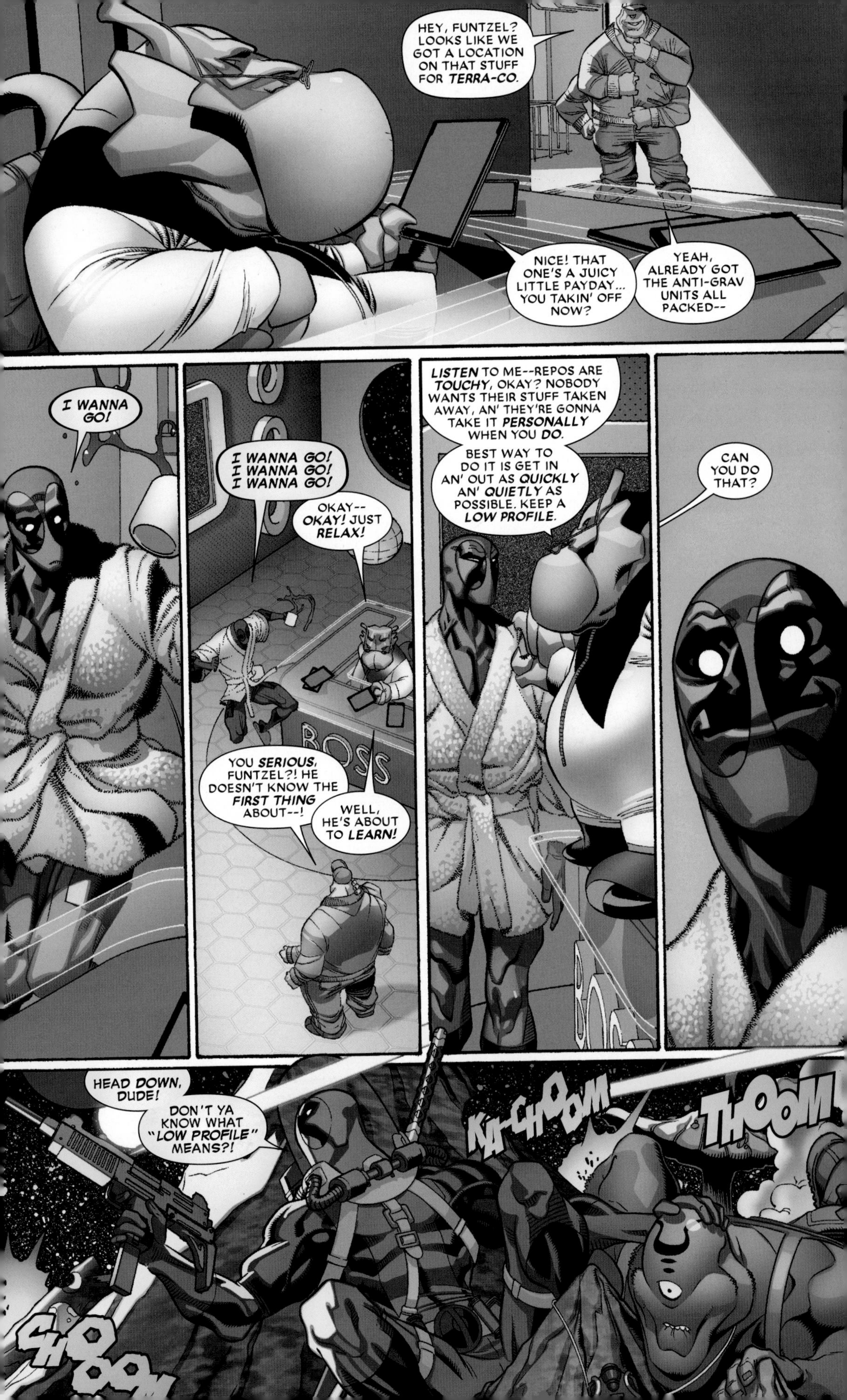
HEY, FUNTZEL? LOOKS LIKE WE GOT A LOCATION ON THAT STUFF FOR TERRA-CO.
NICE! THAT ONE'S A JUICY LITTLE PAYDAY... YOU TAKIN' OFF NOW?
YEAH, ALREADY GOT THE ANTI-GRAV UNITS ALL PACKED--
I WANNA GO!
I WANNA GO! I WANNA GO! I WANNA GO!
OKAY-- OKAY! JUST RELAX!
BOSS
YOU SERIOUS, FUNTZEL?! HE DOESN'T KNOW THE FIRST THING ABOUT--!
WELL, HE'S ABOUT TO LEARN!
LISTEN TO ME--REPOS ARE TOUCHY, OKAY? NOBODY WANTS THEIR STUFF TAKEN AWAY, AN' THEY'RE GONNA TAKE IT PERSONALLY WHEN YOU DO.
BEST WAY TO DO IT IS GET IN AN' OUT AS QUICKLY AN' QUIETLY AS POSSIBLE. KEEP A LOW PROFILE.
CAN YOU DO THAT?
HEAD DOWN, DUDE!
DON'T YA KNOW WHAT "LOW PROFILE" MEANS?!
KA-CHOOOM
THOOOM
CHOOOM

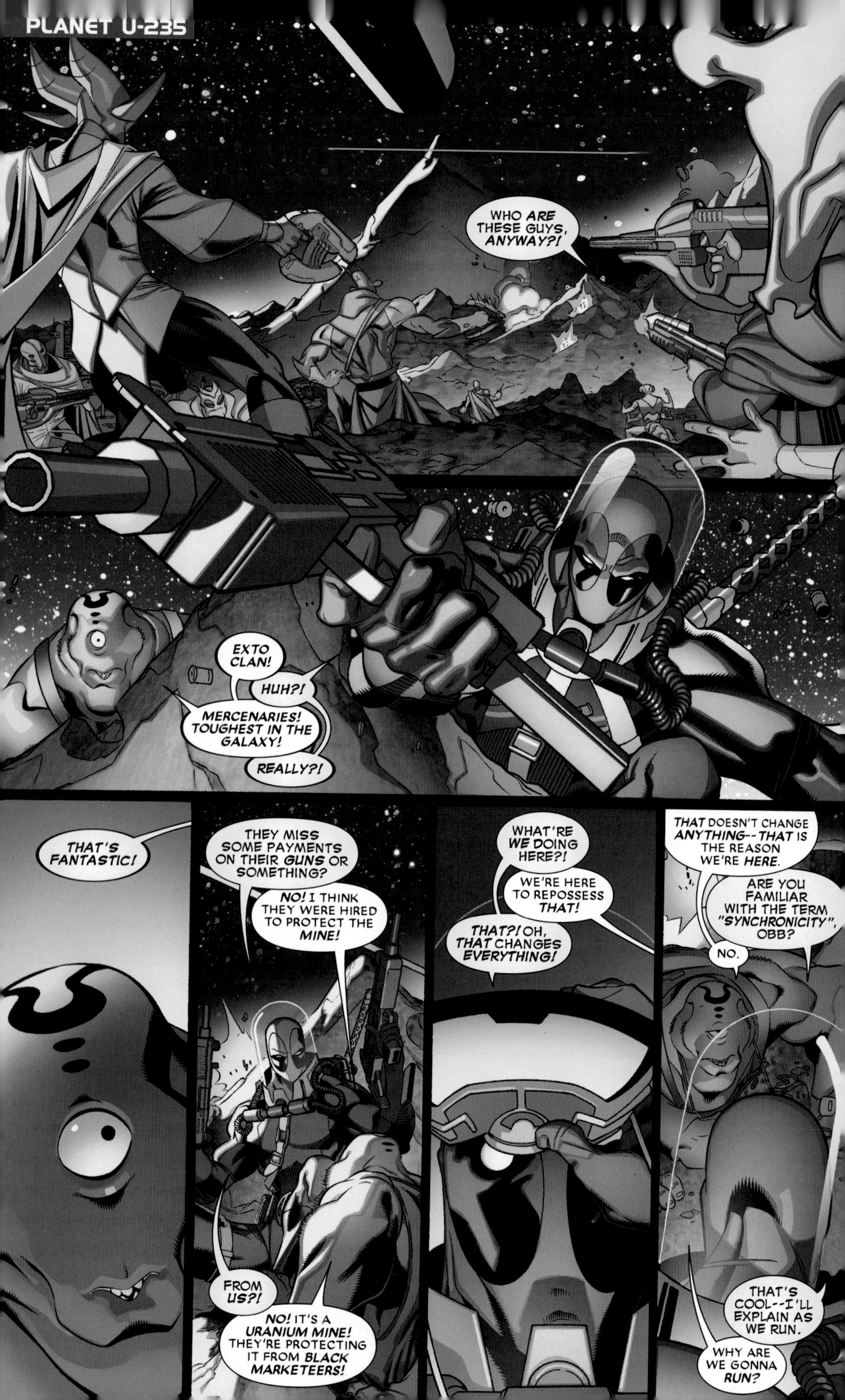
PLANET U-235
WHO ARE THESE GUYS, ANYWAY?!
EXTO CLAN!
HUH?!
MERCENARIES! TOUGHEST IN THE GALAXY!
REALLY?!
THAT'S FANTASTIC!
THEY MISS SOME PAYMENTS ON THEIR GUNS OR SOMETHING?
NO! I THINK THEY WERE HIRED TO PROTECT THE MINE!
FROM US?!
NO! IT'S A URANIUM MINE! THEY'RE PROTECTING IT FROM BLACK MARKETEERS!
WHAT'RE WE DOING HERE?!
WE'RE HERE TO REPOSSESS THAT!
THAT?! OH, THAT CHANGES EVERYTHING!
THAT DOESN'T CHANGE ANYTHING--THAT IS THE REASON WE'RE HERE.
ARE YOU FAMILIAR WITH THE TERM "SYNCHRONICITY", OBB?
NO.
THAT'S COOL--I'LL EXPLAIN AS WE RUN.
WHY ARE WE GONNA RUN?

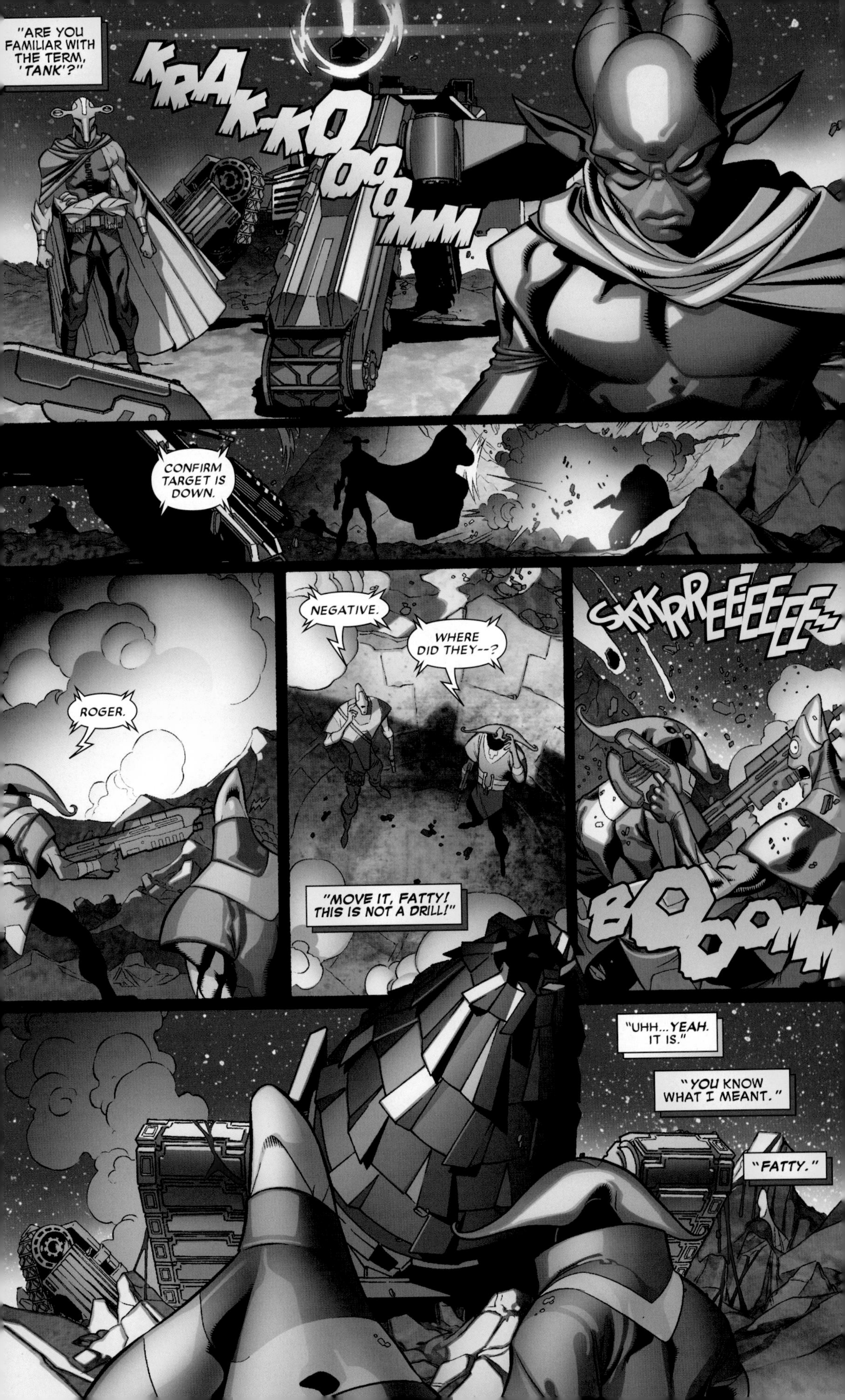
"ARE YOU FAMILIAR WITH THE TERM, 'TANK'?"
KRAK-KOOOOOMM
CONFIRM TARGET IS DOWN.
ROGER.
NEGATIVE.
WHERE DID THEY--?
"MOVE IT, FATTY! THIS IS NOT A DRILL!"
SKKRREEEEEEE
BOOOMM
"UHH...YEAH. IT IS."
"YOU KNOW WHAT I MEANT."
"FATTY."

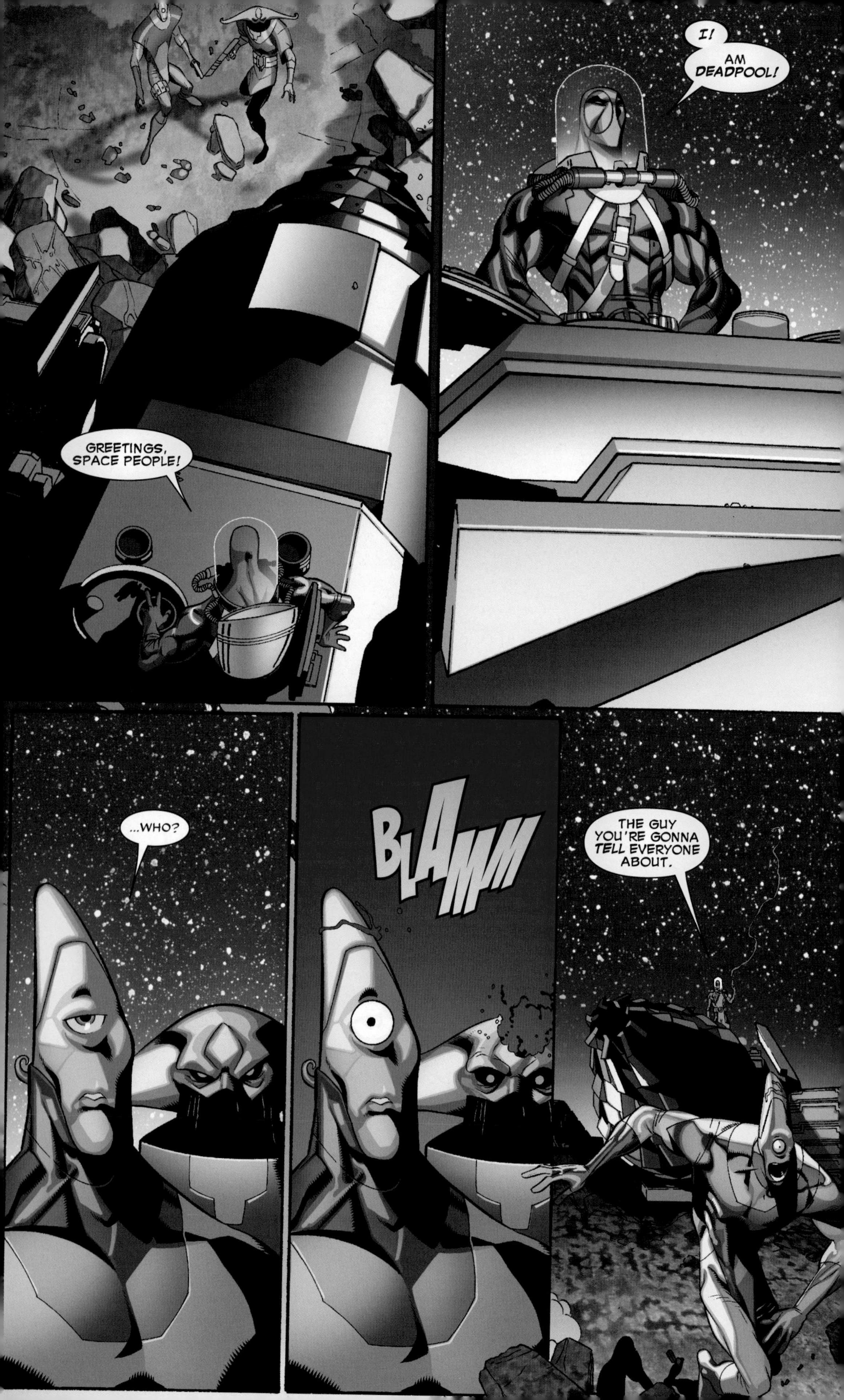
GREETINGS, SPACE PEOPLE!
I! AM DEADPOOL!
...WHO?
BLAMM
THE GUY YOU'RE GONNA TELL EVERYONE ABOUT.

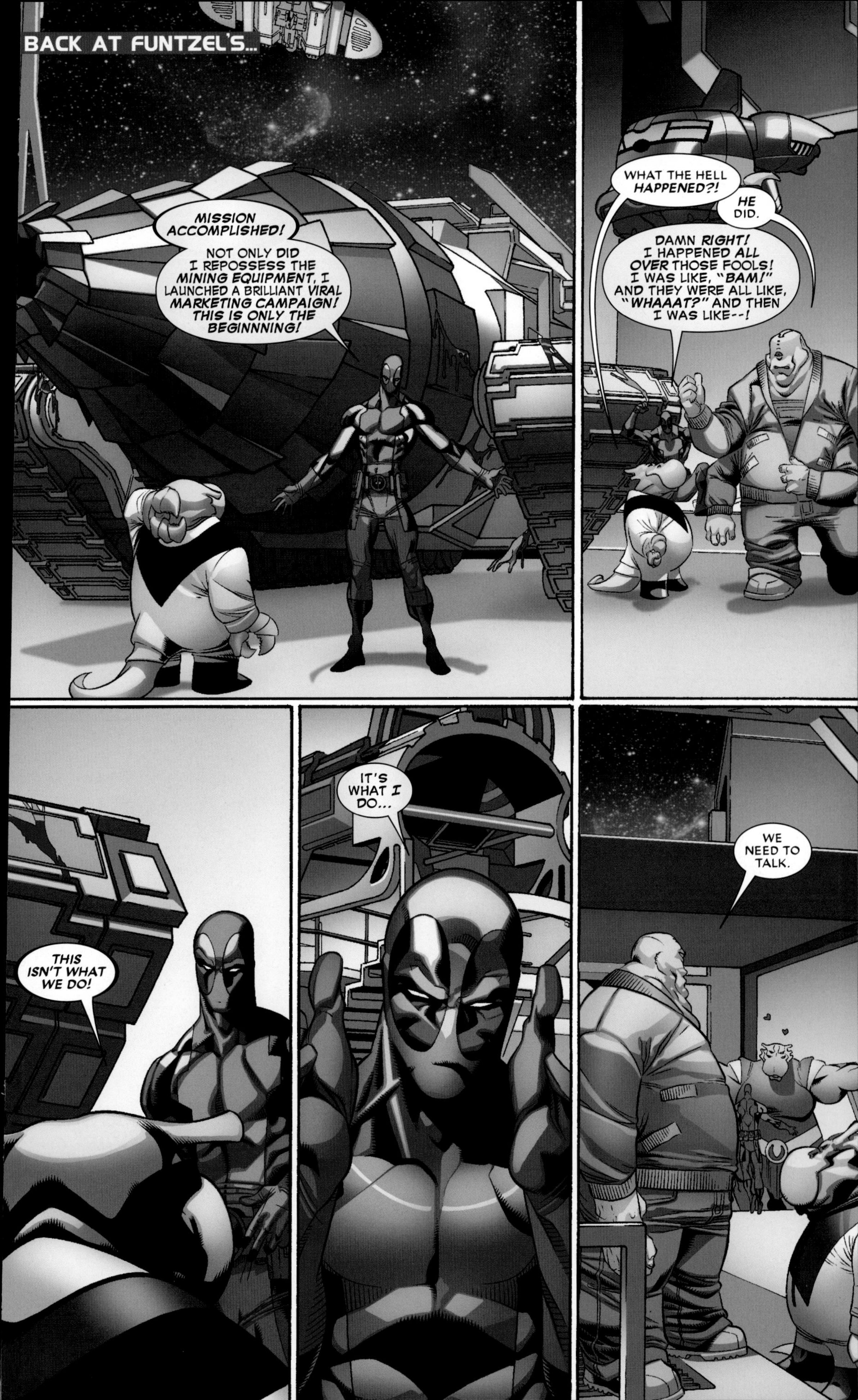
BACK AT FUNTZEL'S...
MISSION ACCOMPLISHED!
NOT ONLY DID I REPOSSESS THE MINING EQUIPMENT, I LAUNCHED A BRILLIANT VIRAL MARKETING CAMPAIGN! THIS IS ONLY THE BEGINNNING!
WHAT THE HELL HAPPENED?!
HE DID.
DAMN RIGHT! I HAPPENED ALL OVER THOSE FOOLS! I WAS LIKE, "BAM!" AND THEY WERE ALL LIKE, "WHAAAT?" AND THEN I WAS LIKE--!
THIS ISN'T WHAT WE DO!
IT'S WHAT I DO...
WE NEED TO TALK.

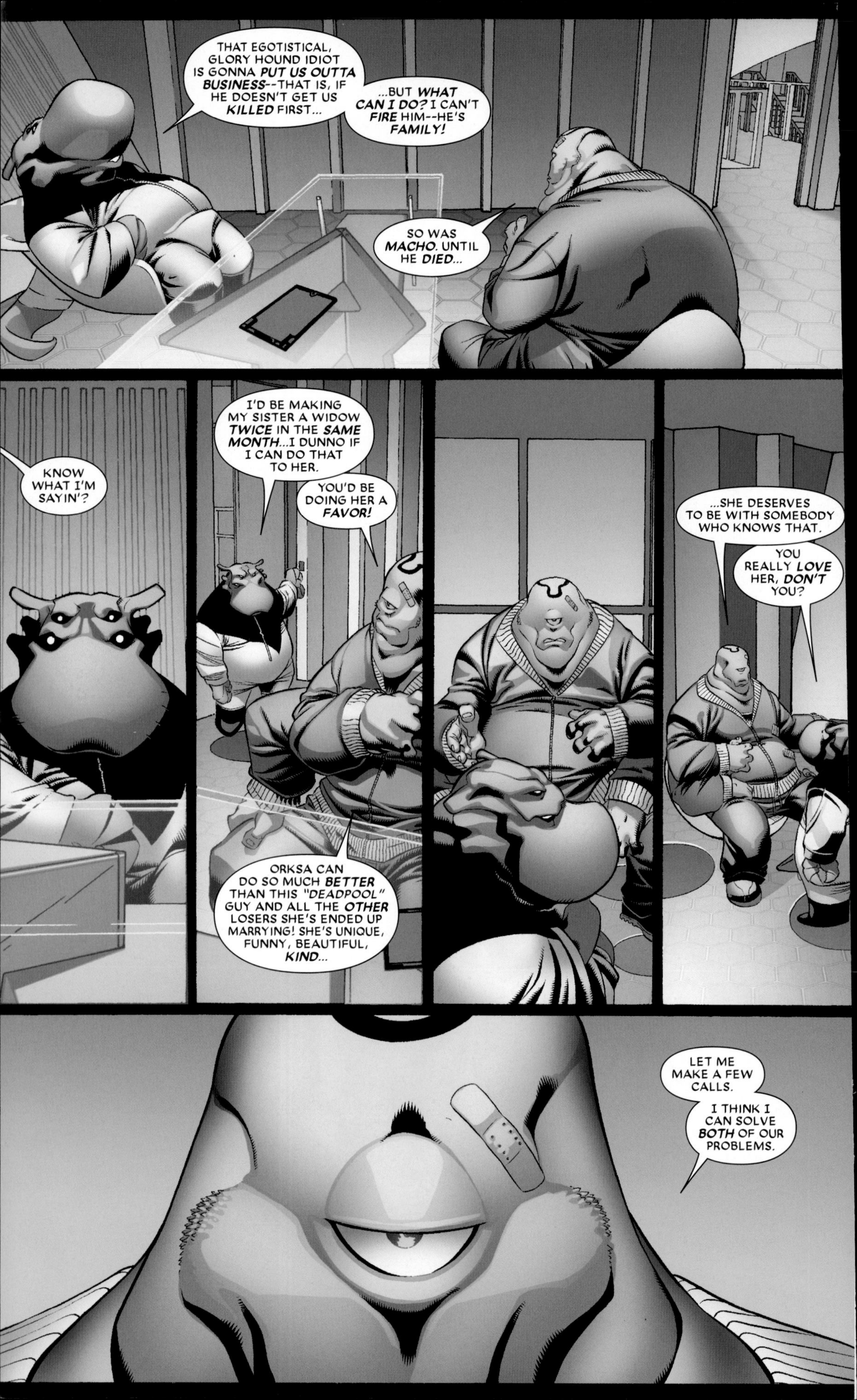
THAT EGOTISTICAL, GLORY HOUND IDIOT IS GONNA PUT US OUTTA BUSINESS--THAT IS, IF HE DOESN'T GET US KILLED FIRST...
...BUT WHAT CAN I DO? I CAN'T FIRE HIM--HE'S FAMILY!
SO WAS MACHO. UNTIL HE DIED...
KNOW WHAT I'M SAYIN'?
I'D BE MAKING MY SISTER A WIDOW TWICE IN THE SAME MONTH...I DUNNO IF I CAN DO THAT TO HER.
YOU'D BE DOING HER A FAVOR!
ORKSA CAN DO SO MUCH BETTER THAN THIS "DEADPOOL" GUY AND ALL THE OTHER LOSERS SHE'S ENDED UP MARRYING! SHE'S UNIQUE, FUNNY, BEAUTIFUL, KIND...
...SHE DESERVES TO BE WITH SOMEBODY WHO KNOWS THAT.
YOU REALLY LOVE HER, DON'T YOU?
LET ME MAKE A FEW CALLS.
I THINK I CAN SOLVE BOTH OF OUR PROBLEMS.

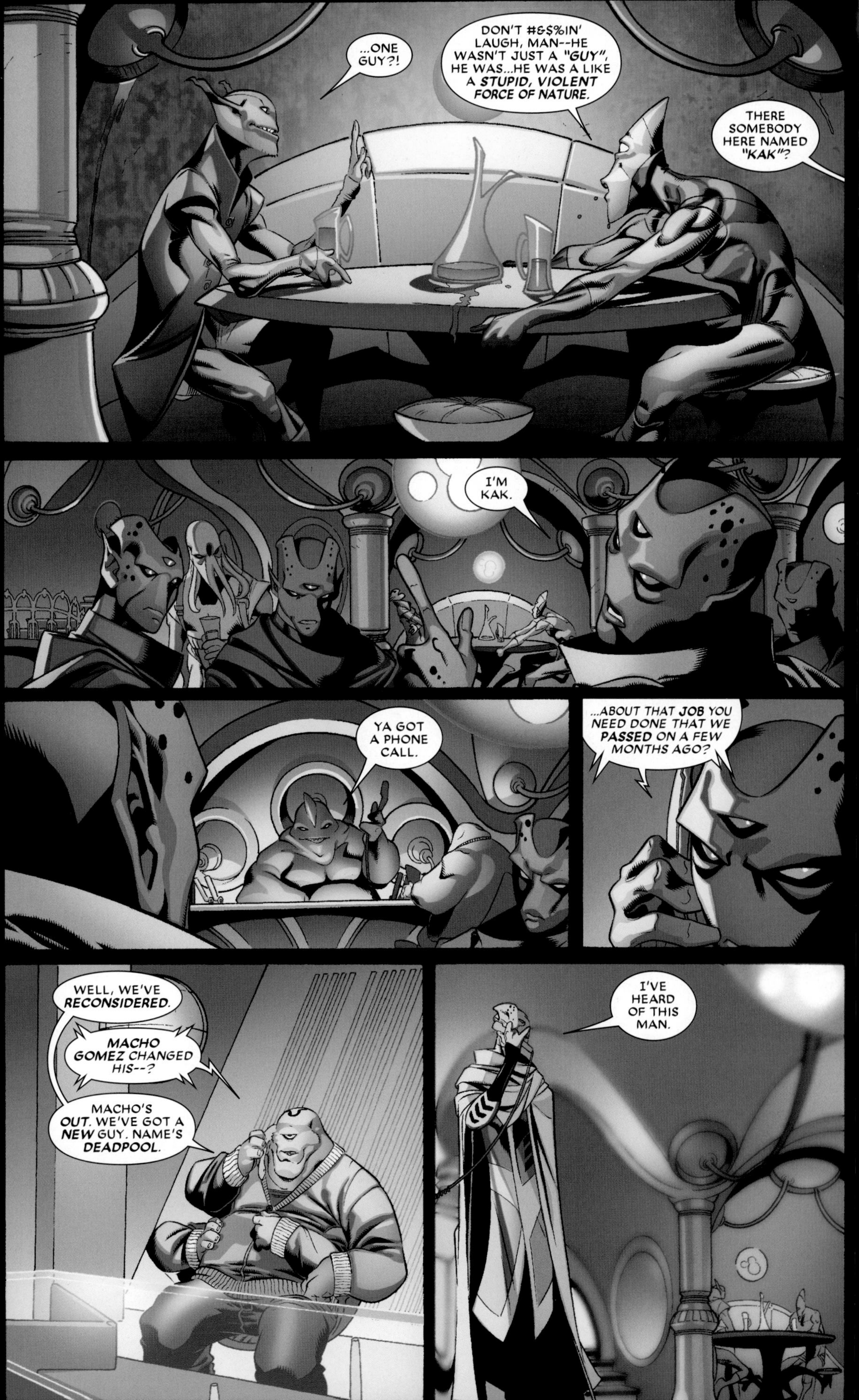

...ONE GUY?!
DON'T #&$%IN' LAUGH, MAN--HE WASN'T JUST A "GUY", HE WAS...HE WAS A LIKE A STUPID, VIOLENT FORCE OF NATURE.
THERE SOMEBODY HERE NAMED "KAK"?
I'M KAK.
YA GOT A PHONE CALL.
...ABOUT THAT JOB YOU NEED DONE THAT WE PASSED ON A FEW MONTHS AGO?
WELL, WE'VE RECONSIDERED.
MACHO GOMEZ CHANGED HIS--?
MACHO'S OUT. WE'VE GOT A NEW GUY. NAME'S DEADPOOL.
I'VE HEARD OF THIS MAN.

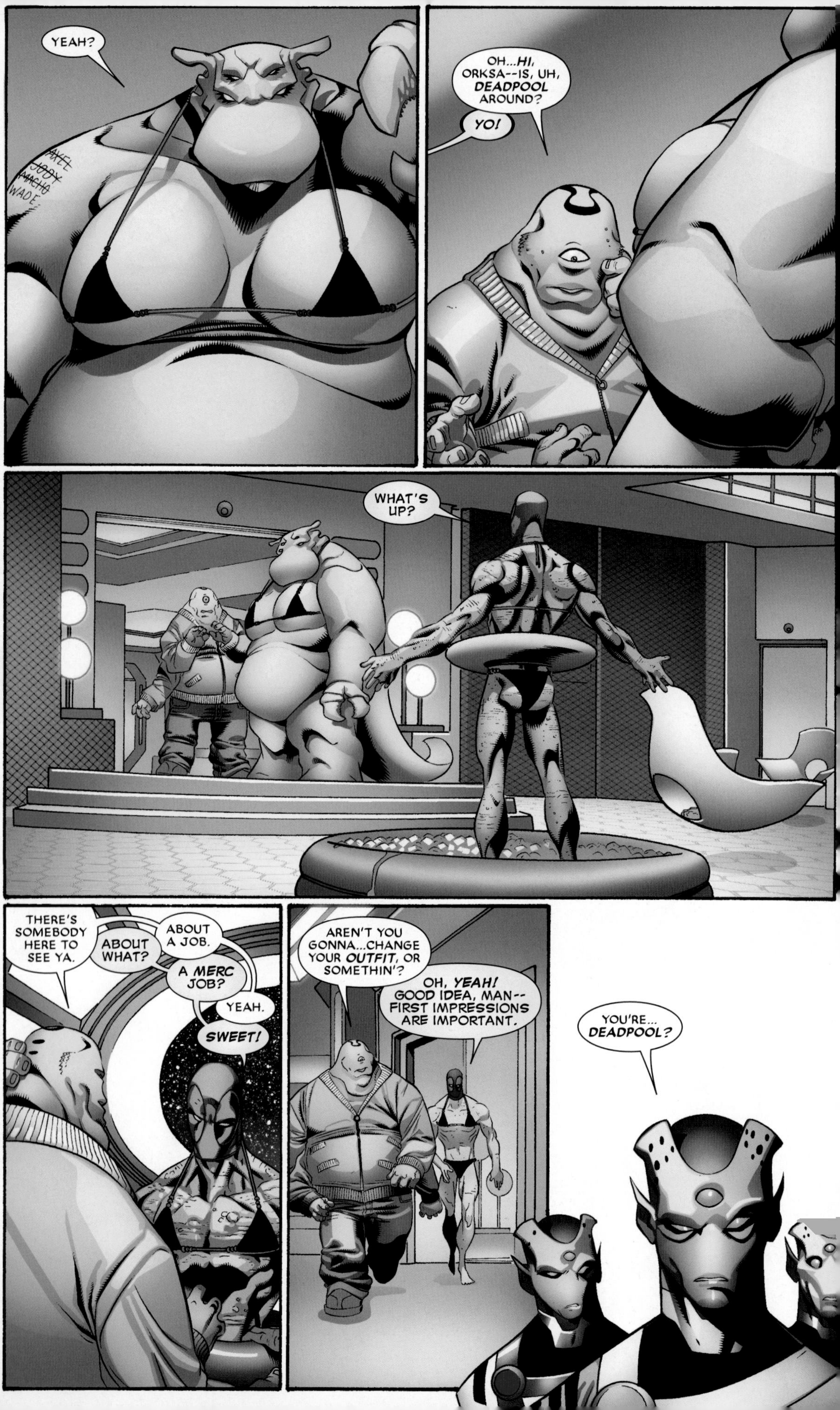
YEAH?
AXEL
JODY
MACHO
WADE
OH...HI, ORKSA--IS, UH, DEADPOOL AROUND?
YO!
WHAT'S UP?
THERE'S SOMEBODY HERE TO SEE YA.
ABOUT WHAT?
ABOUT A JOB.
A MERC JOB?
YEAH.
SWEET!
AREN'T YOU GONNA...CHANGE YOUR OUTFIT, OR SOMETHIN'?
OH, YEAH! GOOD IDEA, MAN--FIRST IMPRESSIONS ARE IMPORTANT.
YOU'RE... DEADPOOL?

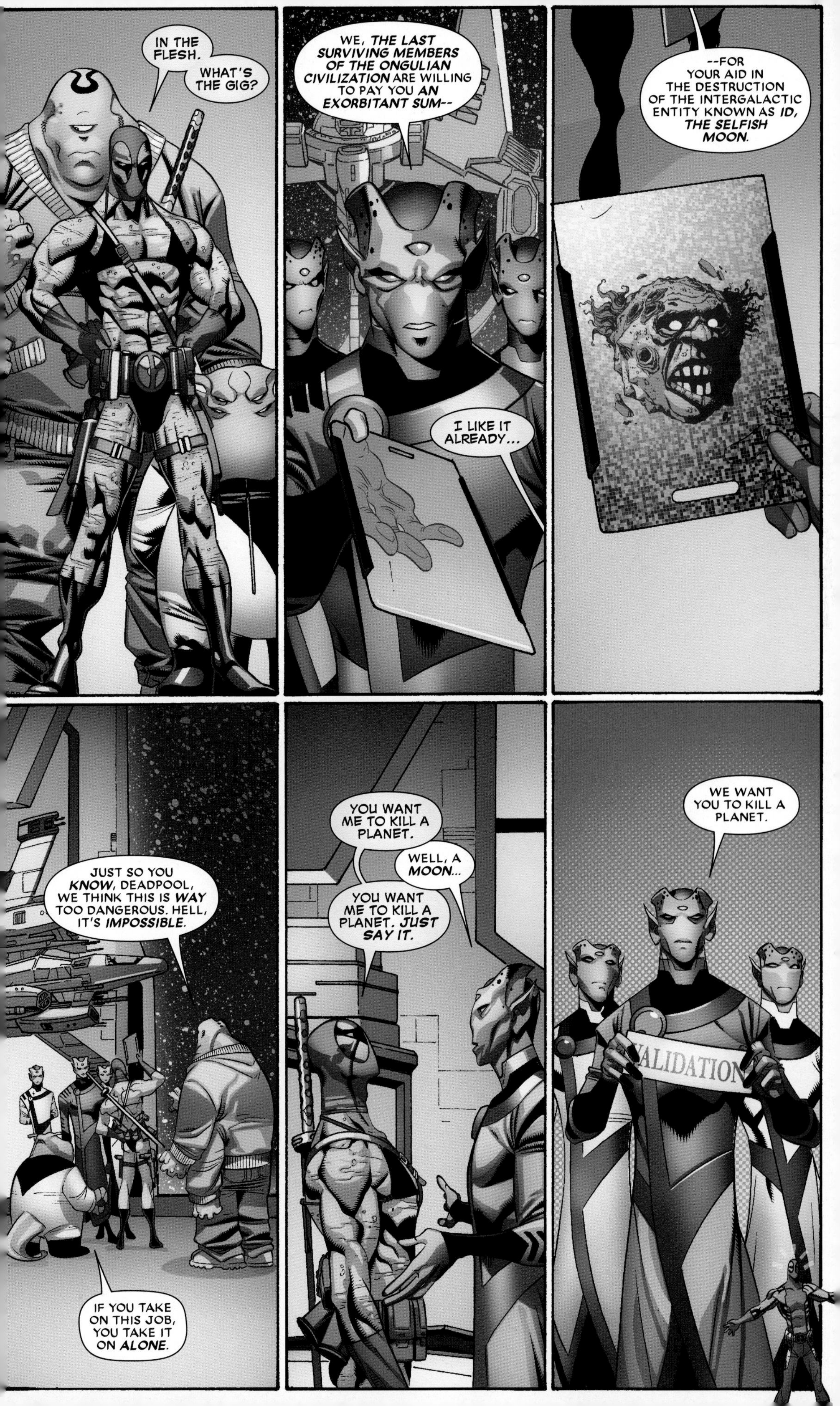
IN THE FLESH.
WHAT'S THE GIG?
WE, THE LAST SURVIVING MEMBERS OF THE ONGULIAN CIVILIZATION ARE WILLING TO PAY YOU AN EXORBITANT SUM--
I LIKE IT ALREADY...
--FOR YOUR AID IN THE DESTRUCTION OF THE INTERGALACTIC ENTITY KNOWN AS ID, THE SELFISH MOON.
JUST SO YOU KNOW, DEADPOOL, WE THINK THIS IS WAY TOO DANGEROUS. HELL, IT'S IMPOSSIBLE.
IF YOU TAKE ON THIS JOB, YOU TAKE IT ON ALONE.
YOU WANT ME TO KILL A PLANET.
WELL, A MOON...
YOU WANT ME TO KILL A PLANET. JUST SAY IT.
WE WANT YOU TO KILL A PLANET.
VALIDATION

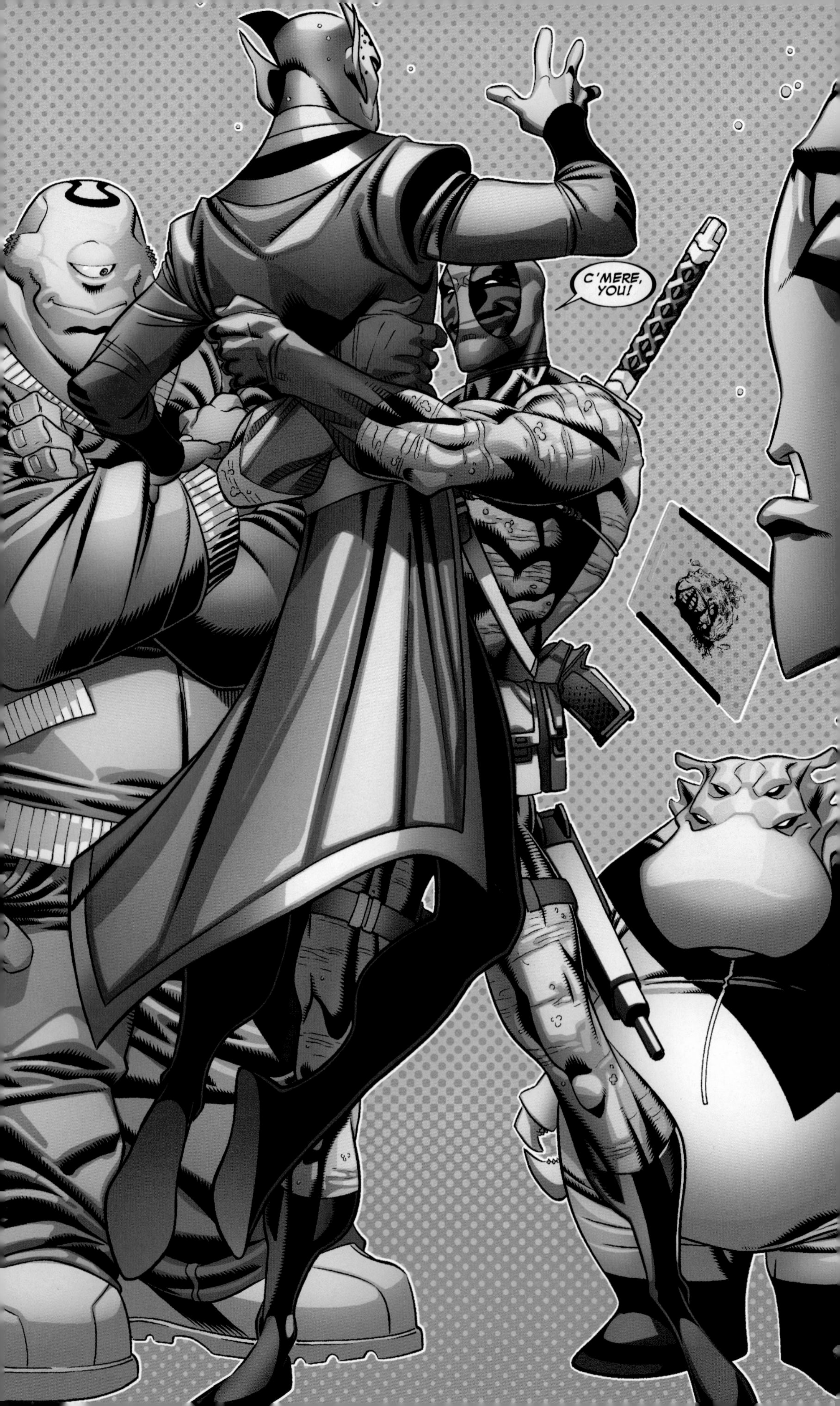
C'MERE, YOU!

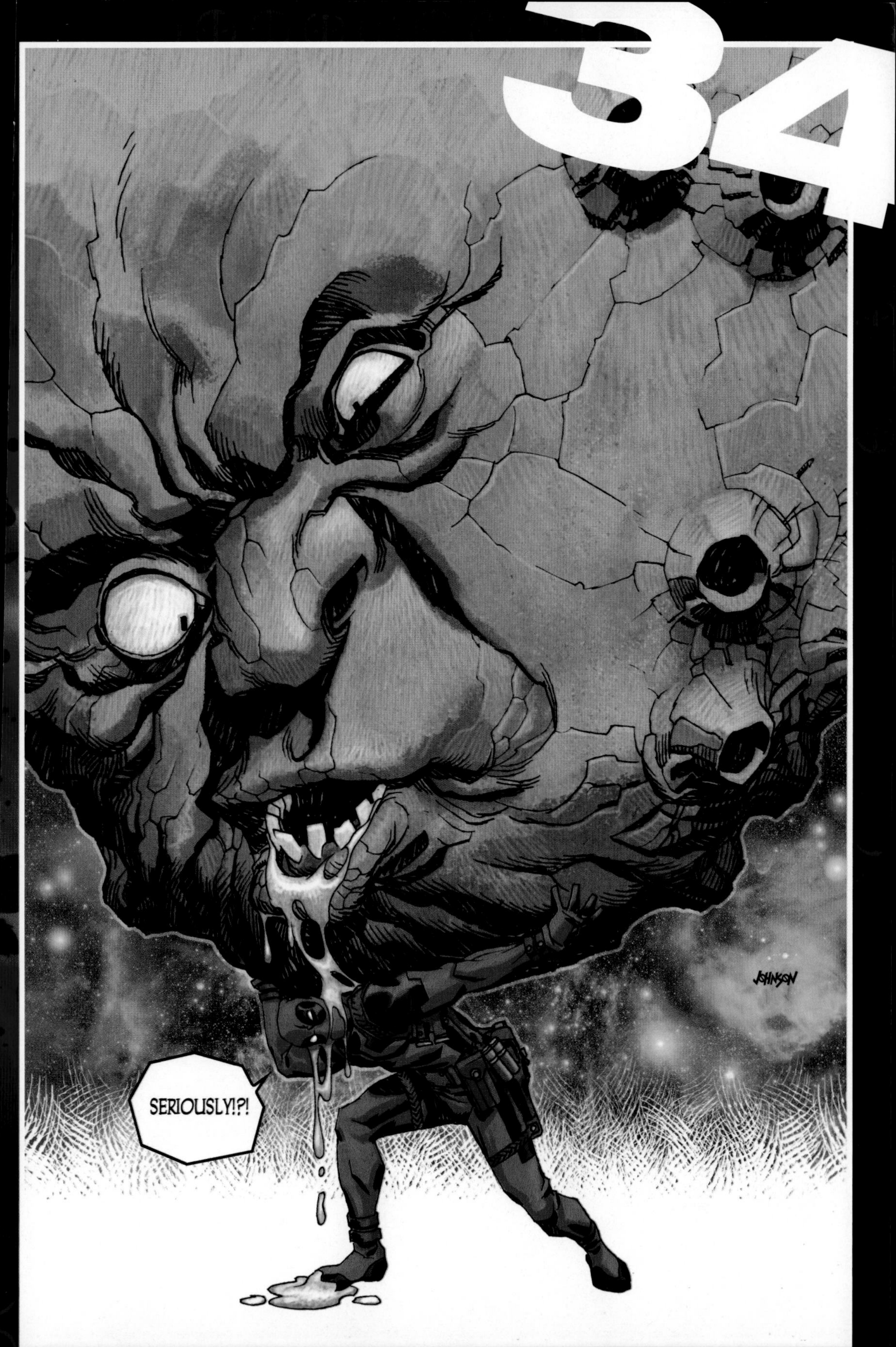
34
SERIOUSLY!?!
JOHNSON

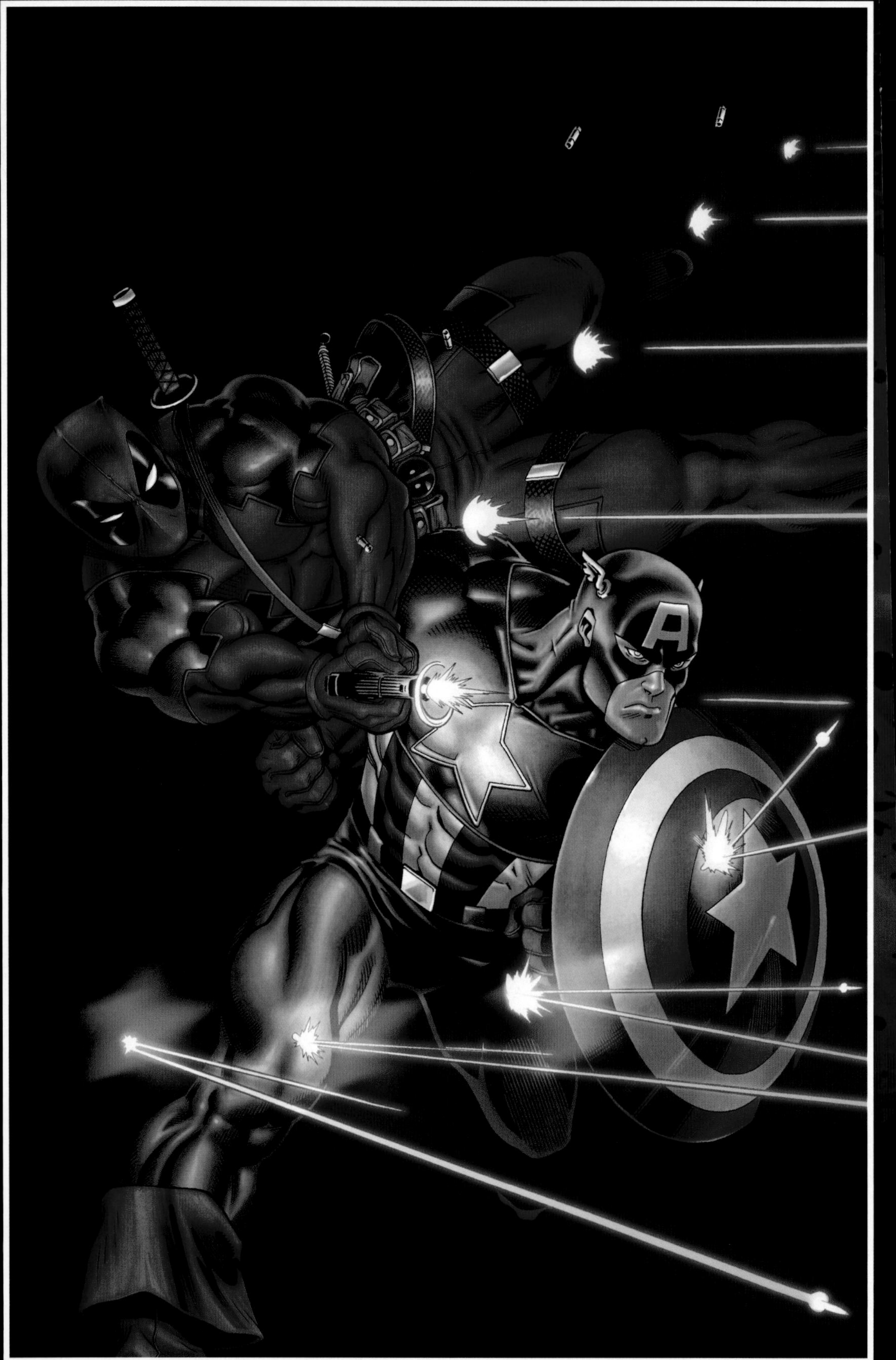

DEADPOOL #34 CAPTAIN AMERICA 70TH ANNIVERSARY VARIANT
by Ed McGuinness

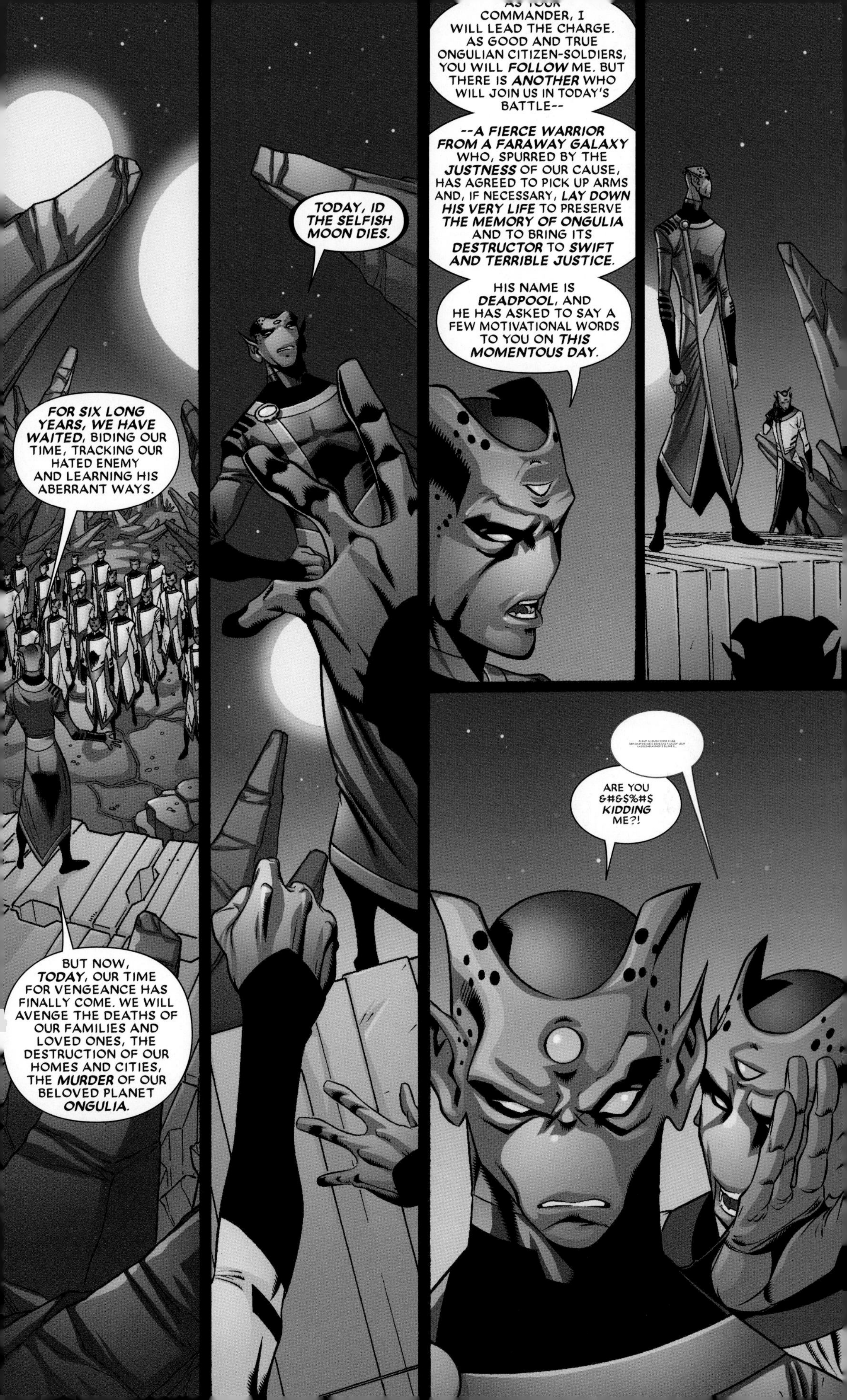
FOR SIX LONG YEARS, WE HAVE WAITED, BIDING OUR TIME, TRACKING OUR HATED ENEMY AND LEARNING HIS ABERRANT WAYS.
BUT NOW, TODAY, OUR TIME FOR VENGEANCE HAS FINALLY COME. WE WILL AVENGE THE DEATHS OF OUR FAMILIES AND LOVED ONES, THE DESTRUCTION OF OUR HOMES AND CITIES, THE MURDER OF OUR BELOVED PLANET ONGULIA.
TODAY, ID THE SELFISH MOON DIES.
AS YOUR COMMANDER, I WILL LEAD THE CHARGE. AS GOOD AND TRUE ONGULIAN CITIZEN-SOLDIERS, YOU WILL FOLLOW ME. BUT THERE IS ANOTHER WHO WILL JOIN US IN TODAY'S BATTLE--
--A FIERCE WARRIOR FROM A FARAWAY GALAXY WHO, SPURRED BY THE JUSTNESS OF OUR CAUSE, HAS AGREED TO PICK UP ARMS AND, IF NECESSARY, LAY DOWN HIS VERY LIFE TO PRESERVE THE MEMORY OF ONGULIA AND TO BRING ITS DESTRUCTOR TO SWIFT AND TERRIBLE JUSTICE.
HIS NAME IS DEADPOOL, AND HE HAS ASKED TO SAY A FEW MOTIVATIONAL WORDS TO YOU ON THIS MOMENTOUS DAY.
ARE YOU &#&$%#$ KIDDING ME?!

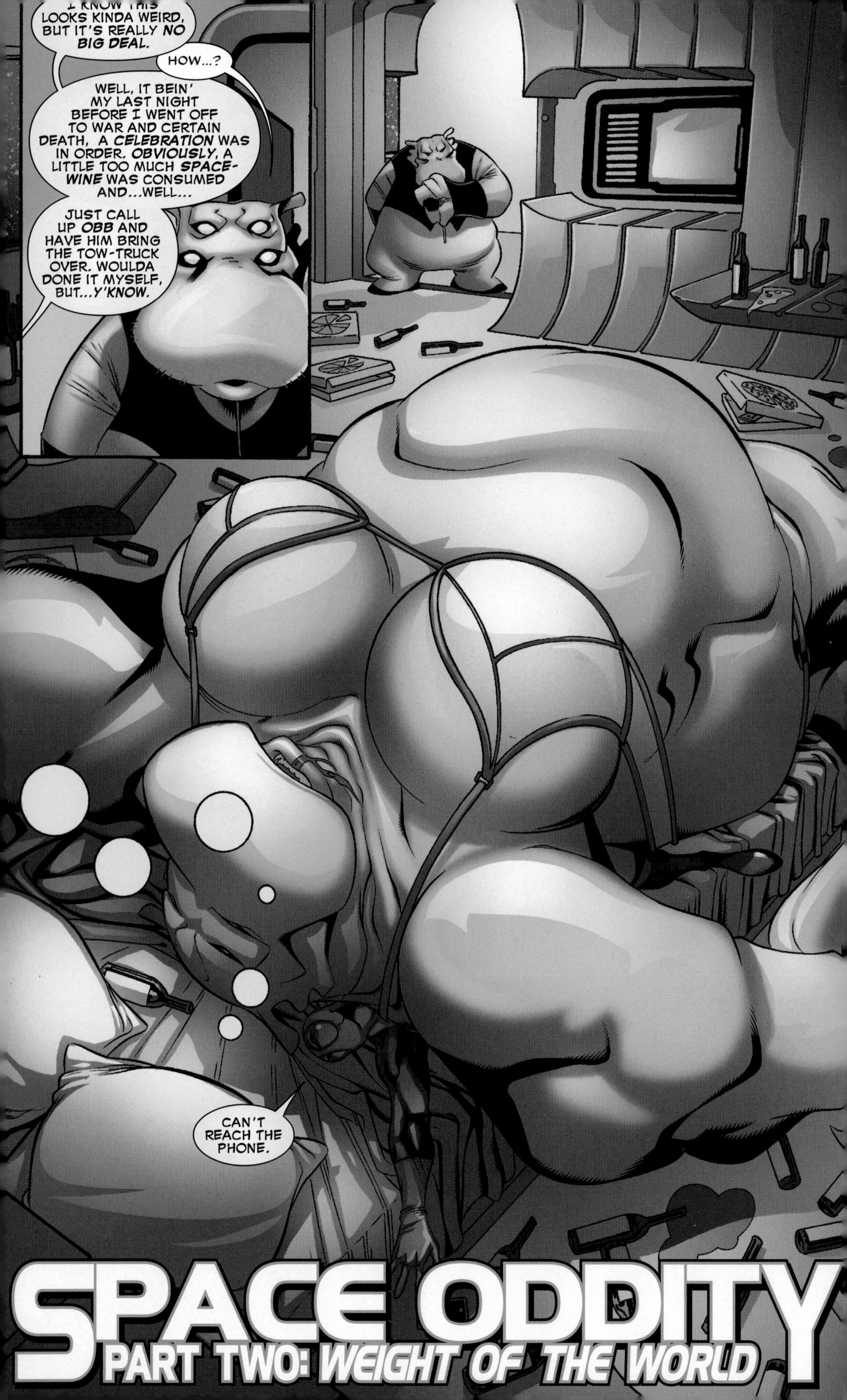
I KNOW THIS LOOKS KINDA WEIRD, BUT IT'S REALLY NO BIG DEAL.
HOW...?
WELL, IT BEIN' MY LAST NIGHT BEFORE I WENT OFF TO WAR AND CERTAIN DEATH, A CELEBRATION WAS IN ORDER. OBVIOUSLY, A LITTLE TOO MUCH SPACE-WINE WAS CONSUMED AND...WELL...
JUST CALL UP OBB AND HAVE HIM BRING THE TOW-TRUCK OVER. WOULDA DONE IT MYSELF, BUT...Y'KNOW.
CAN'T REACH THE PHONE.
SPACE ODDITY
PART TWO: WEIGHT OF THE WORLD

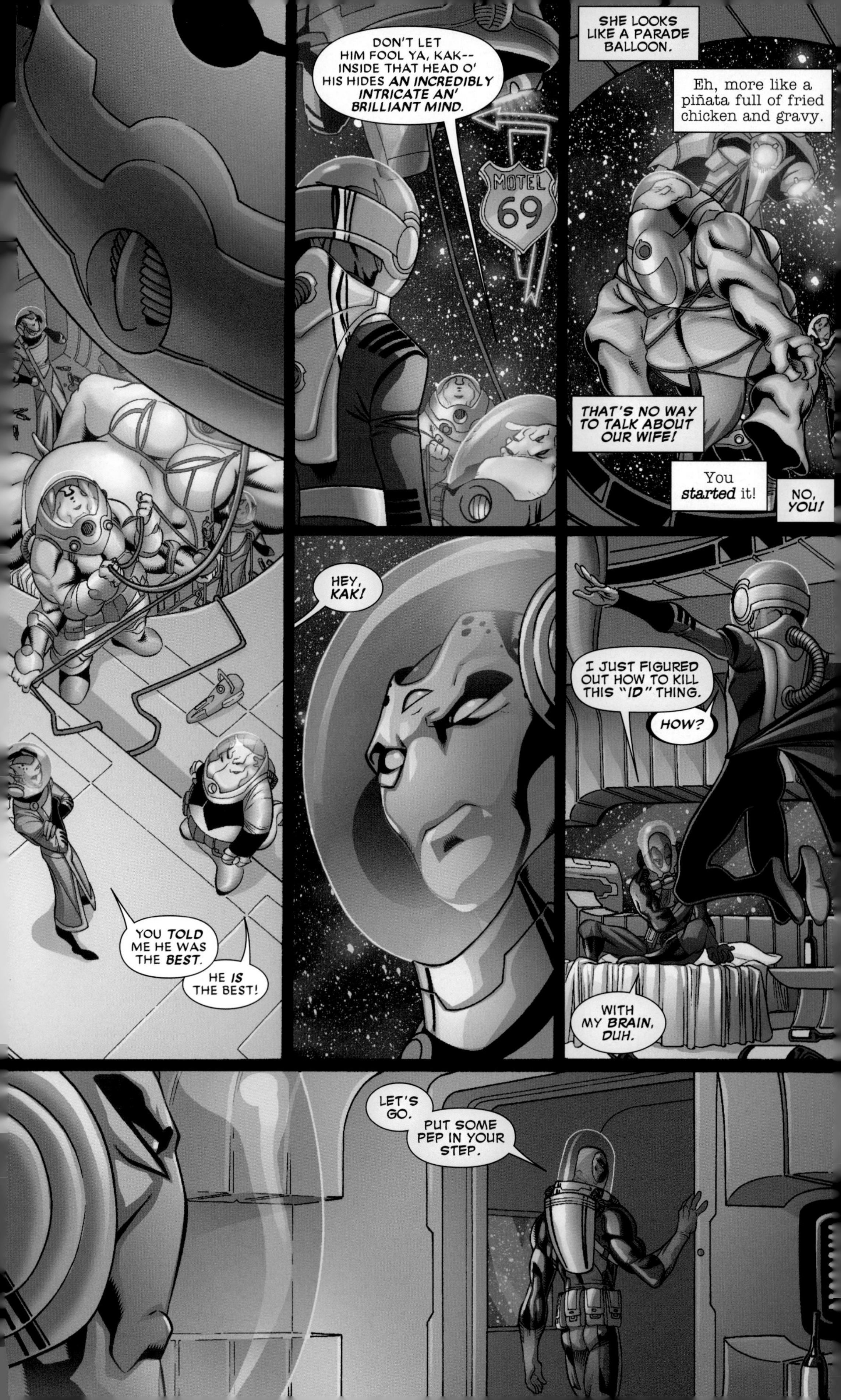

DON'T LET HIM FOOL YA, KAK-- INSIDE THAT HEAD O' HIS HIDES AN INCREDIBLY INTRICATE AN' BRILLIANT MIND.
MOTEL 69
SHE LOOKS LIKE A PARADE BALLOON.
Eh, more like a piñata full of fried chicken and gravy.
THAT'S NO WAY TO TALK ABOUT OUR WIFE!
You started it!
NO, YOU!
YOU TOLD ME HE WAS THE BEST.
HE IS THE BEST!
HEY, KAK!
I JUST FIGURED OUT HOW TO KILL THIS "ID" THING.
HOW?
WITH MY BRAIN, DUH.
LET'S GO.
PUT SOME PEP IN YOUR STEP.

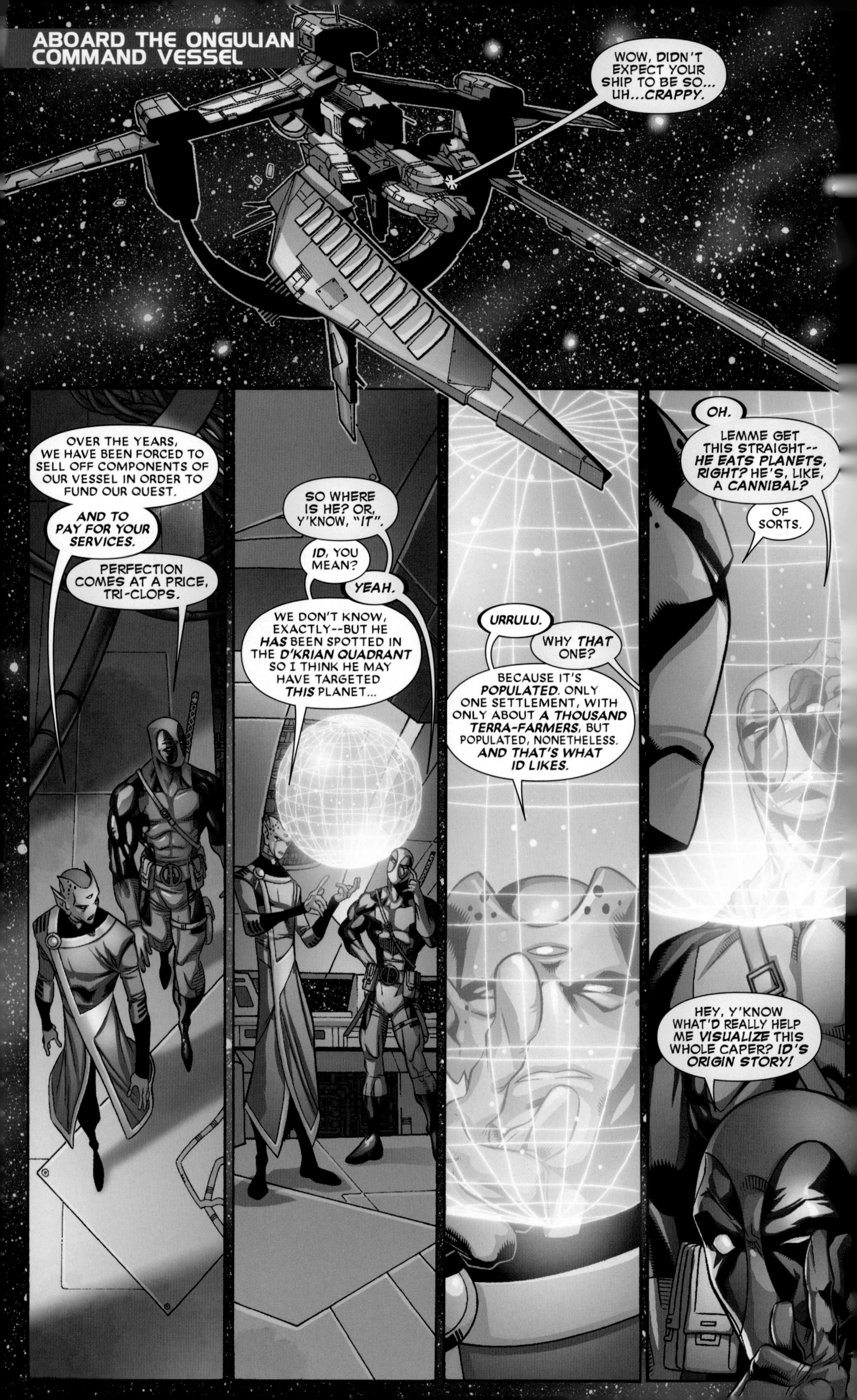
ABOARD THE ONGULIAN COMMAND VESSEL
WOW, DIDN'T EXPECT YOUR SHIP TO BE SO... UH...CRAPPY.
OVER THE YEARS, WE HAVE BEEN FORCED TO SELL OFF COMPONENTS OF OUR VESSEL IN ORDER TO FUND OUR QUEST.
AND TO PAY FOR YOUR SERVICES.
PERFECTION COMES AT A PRICE, TRI-CLOPS.
SO WHERE IS HE? OR, Y'KNOW, "IT".
ID, YOU MEAN?
YEAH.
WE DON'T KNOW, EXACTLY--BUT HE HAS BEEN SPOTTED IN THE D'KRIAN QUADRANT SO I THINK HE MAY HAVE TARGETED THIS PLANET...
URRULU.
WHY THAT ONE?
BECAUSE IT'S POPULATED. ONLY ONE SETTLEMENT, WITH ONLY ABOUT A THOUSAND TERRA-FARMERS, BUT POPULATED, NONETHELESS. AND THAT'S WHAT ID LIKES.
OH.
LEMME GET THIS STRAIGHT-- HE EATS PLANETS, RIGHT? HE'S, LIKE, A CANNIBAL?
OF SORTS.
HEY, Y'KNOW WHAT'D REALLY HELP ME VISUALIZE THIS WHOLE CAPER? ID'S ORIGIN STORY!

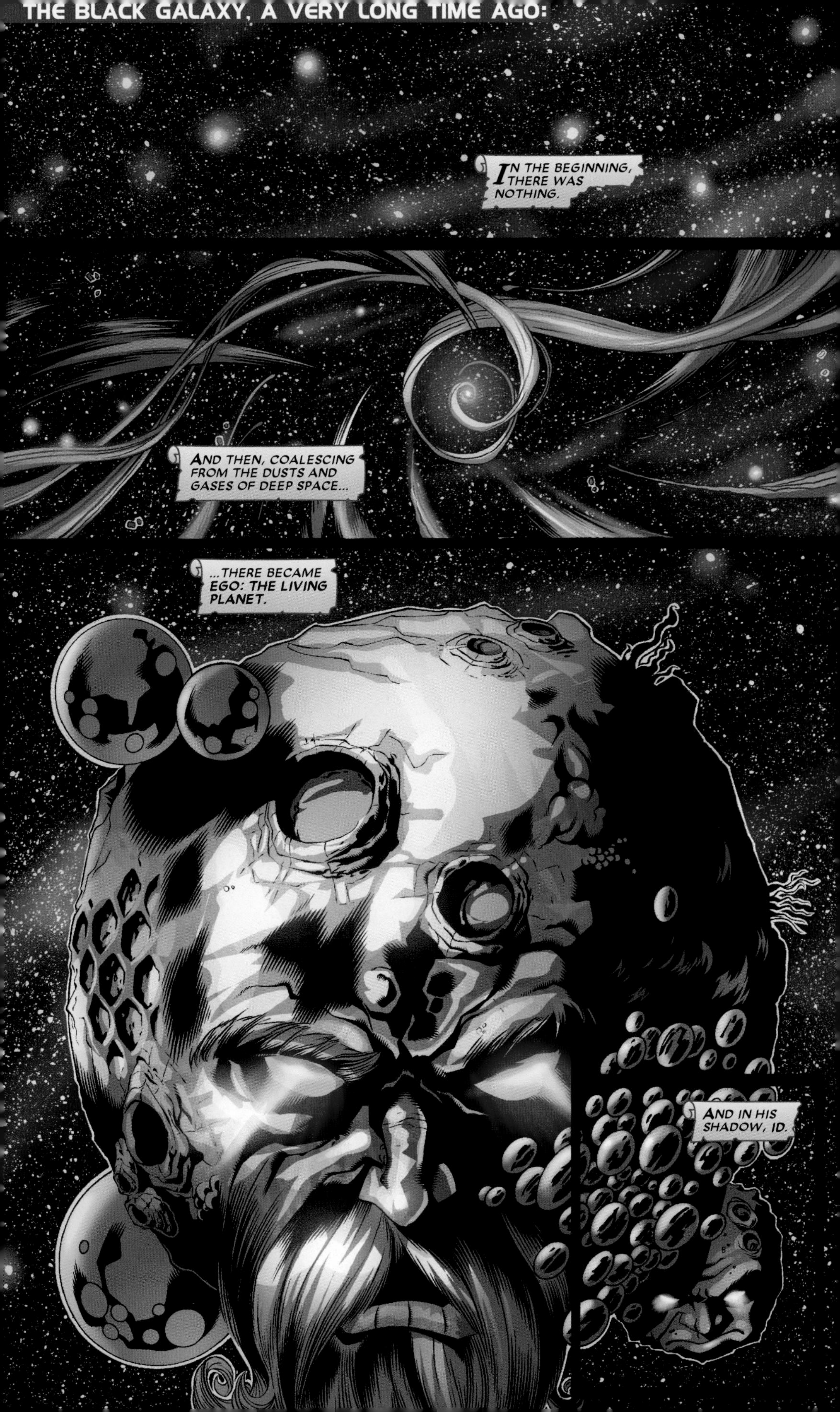
THE BLACK GALAXY, A VERY LONG TIME AGO:
IN THE BEGINNING, THERE WAS NOTHING.
AND THEN, COALESCING FROM THE DUSTS AND GASES OF DEEP SPACE...
...THERE BECAME EGO: THE LIVING PLANET.
AND IN HIS SHADOW, ID.

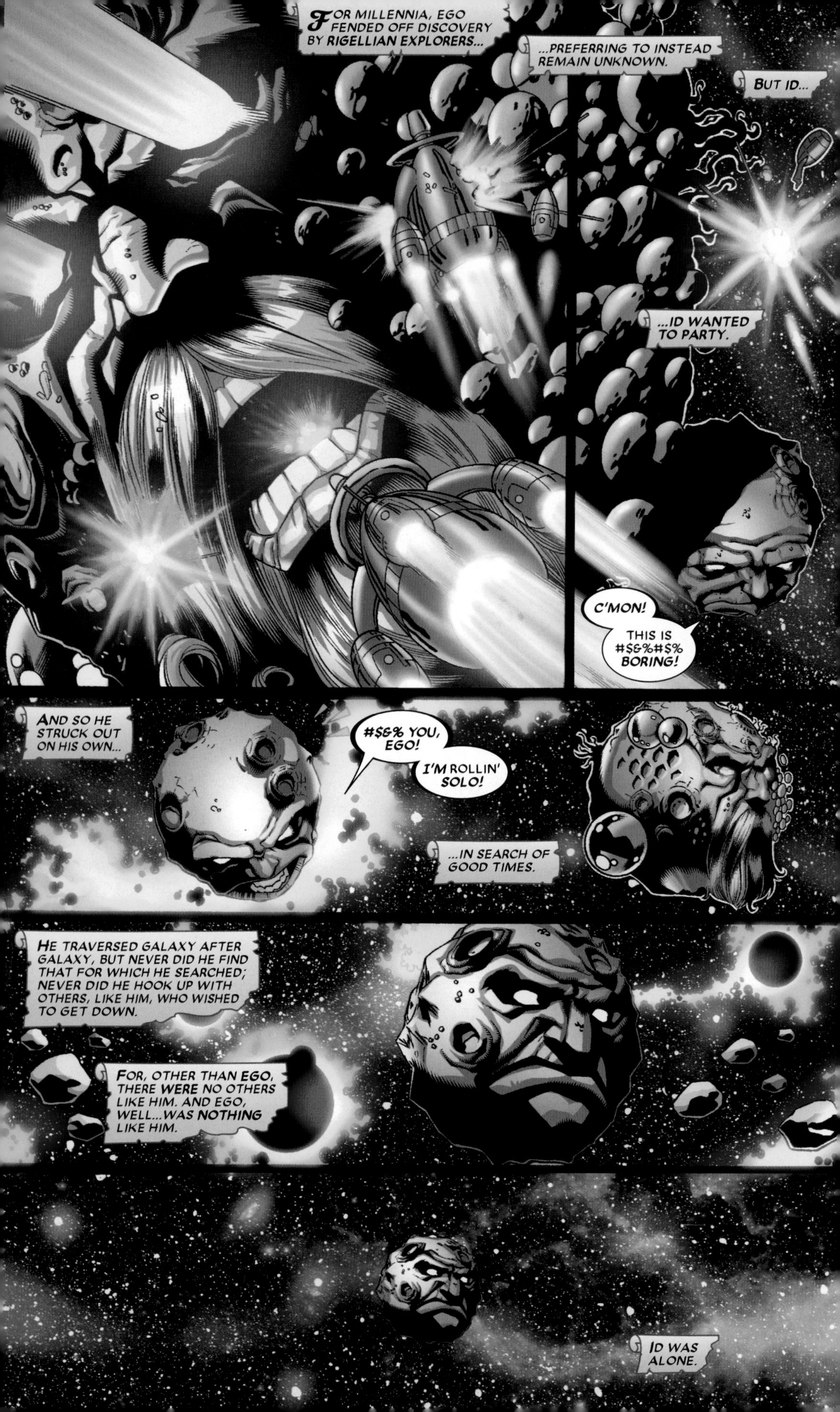
FOR MILLENNIA, EGO FENDED OFF DISCOVERY BY RIGELLIAN EXPLORERS...
...PREFERRING TO INSTEAD REMAIN UNKNOWN.
BUT ID...
...ID WANTED TO PARTY.
C'MON!
THIS IS #$&%#$% BORING!
AND SO HE STRUCK OUT ON HIS OWN...
#$&% YOU, EGO!
I'M ROLLIN' SOLO!
...IN SEARCH OF GOOD TIMES.
HE TRAVERSED GALAXY AFTER GALAXY, BUT NEVER DID HE FIND THAT FOR WHICH HE SEARCHED; NEVER DID HE HOOK UP WITH OTHERS, LIKE HIM, WHO WISHED TO GET DOWN.
FOR, OTHER THAN EGO, THERE WERE NO OTHERS LIKE HIM. AND EGO, WELL...WAS NOTHING LIKE HIM.
ID WAS ALONE.

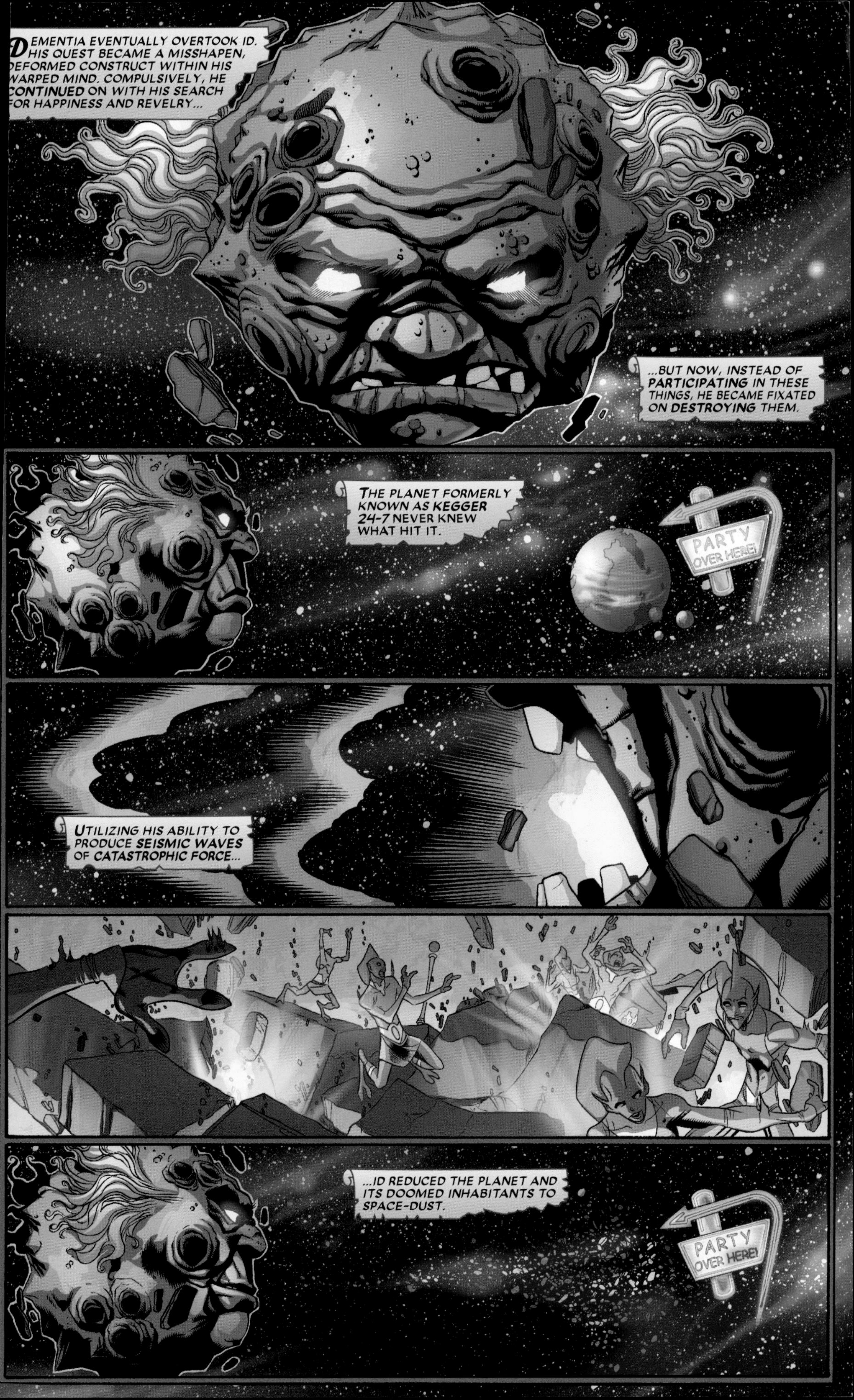
DEMENTIA EVENTUALLY OVERTOOK ID. HIS QUEST BECAME A MISSHAPEN, DEFORMED CONSTRUCT WITHIN HIS WARPED MIND. COMPULSIVELY, HE CONTINUED ON WITH HIS SEARCH FOR HAPPINESS AND REVELRY...
...BUT NOW, INSTEAD OF PARTICIPATING IN THESE THINGS, HE BECAME FIXATED ON DESTROYING THEM.
THE PLANET FORMERLY KNOWN AS KEGGER 24-7 NEVER KNEW WHAT HIT IT.
PARTY OVER HERE!
UTILIZING HIS ABILITY TO PRODUCE SEISMIC WAVES OF CATASTROPHIC FORCE...
...ID REDUCED THE PLANET AND ITS DOOMED INHABITANTS TO SPACE-DUST.
PARTY OVER HERE!

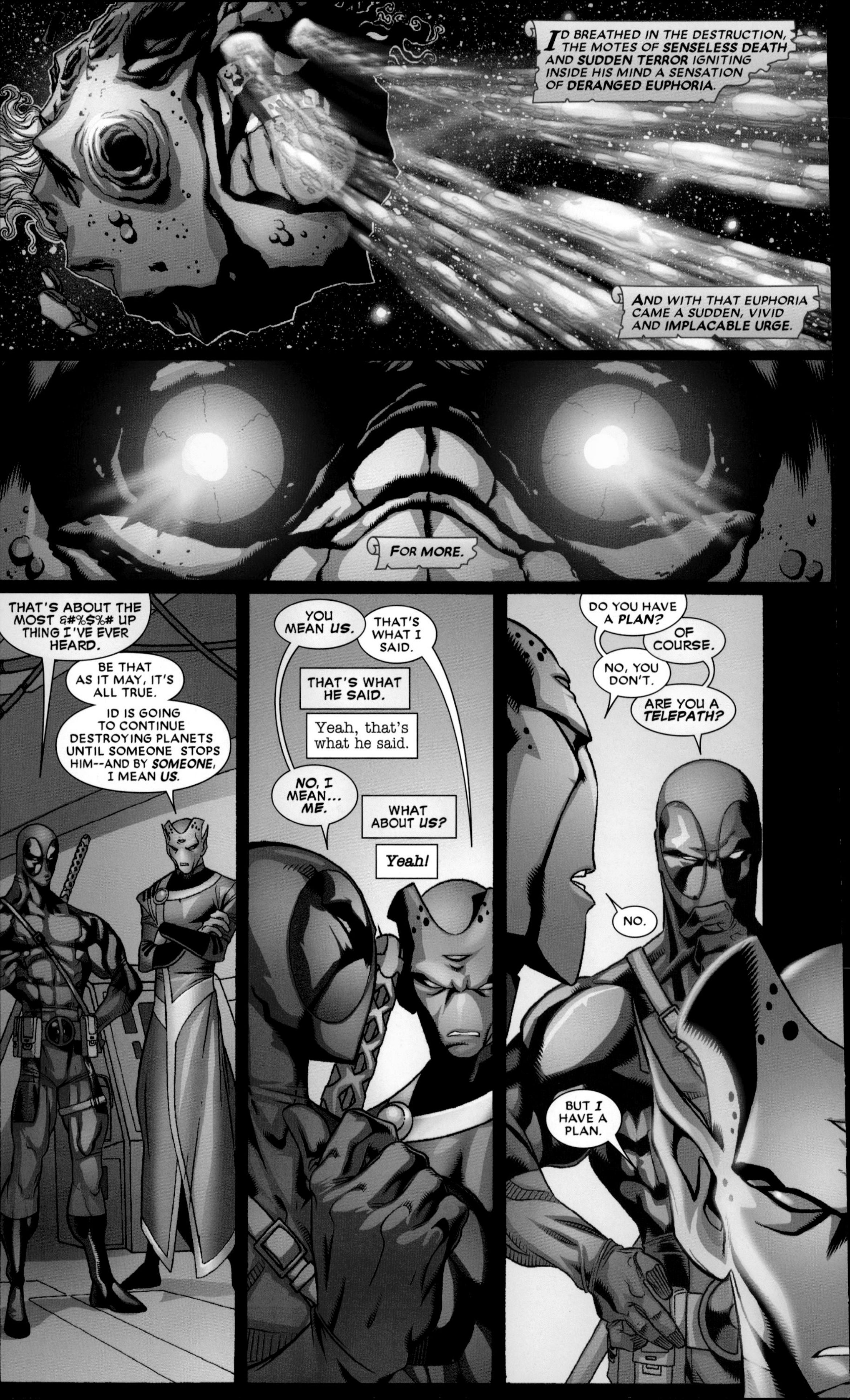
ID BREATHED IN THE DESTRUCTION, THE MOTES OF SENSELESS DEATH AND SUDDEN TERROR IGNITING INSIDE HIS MIND A SENSATION OF DERANGED EUPHORIA.
AND WITH THAT EUPHORIA CAME A SUDDEN, VIVID AND IMPLACABLE URGE.
FOR MORE.
THAT'S ABOUT THE MOST &#%$%# UP THING I'VE EVER HEARD.
BE THAT AS IT MAY, IT'S ALL TRUE.
ID IS GOING TO CONTINUE DESTROYING PLANETS UNTIL SOMEONE STOPS HIM--AND BY SOMEONE, I MEAN US.
YOU MEAN US.
THAT'S WHAT I SAID.
THAT'S WHAT HE SAID.
Yeah, that's what he said.
NO, I MEAN... ME.
WHAT ABOUT US?
Yeah!
DO YOU HAVE A PLAN?
OF COURSE.
NO, YOU DON'T.
ARE YOU A TELEPATH?
NO.
BUT I HAVE A PLAN.

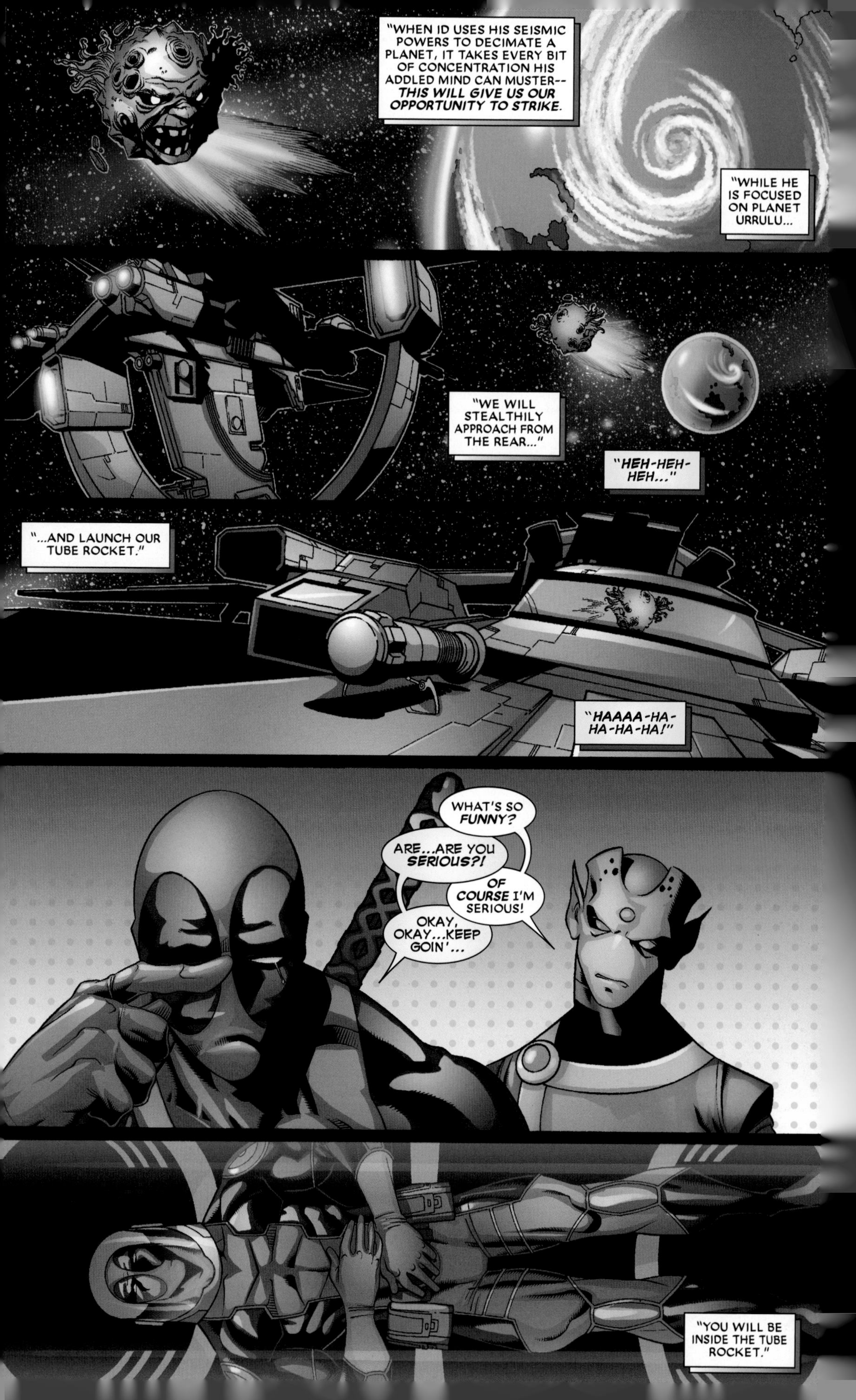
"WHEN ID USES HIS SEISMIC POWERS TO DECIMATE A PLANET, IT TAKES EVERY BIT OF CONCENTRATION HIS ADDLED MIND CAN MUSTER-- *THIS WILL GIVE US OUR OPPORTUNITY TO STRIKE.*
"WHILE HE IS FOCUSED ON PLANET URRULU...
"WE WILL STEALTHILY APPROACH FROM THE REAR..."
"*HEH-HEH-HEH...*"
"...AND LAUNCH OUR TUBE ROCKET."
"*HAAAA-HA-HA-HA-HA!*"
WHAT'S SO *FUNNY?*
ARE...ARE YOU *SERIOUS?!*
OF *COURSE* I'M SERIOUS!
OKAY, OKAY...KEEP GOIN'...
"YOU WILL BE INSIDE THE TUBE ROCKET."

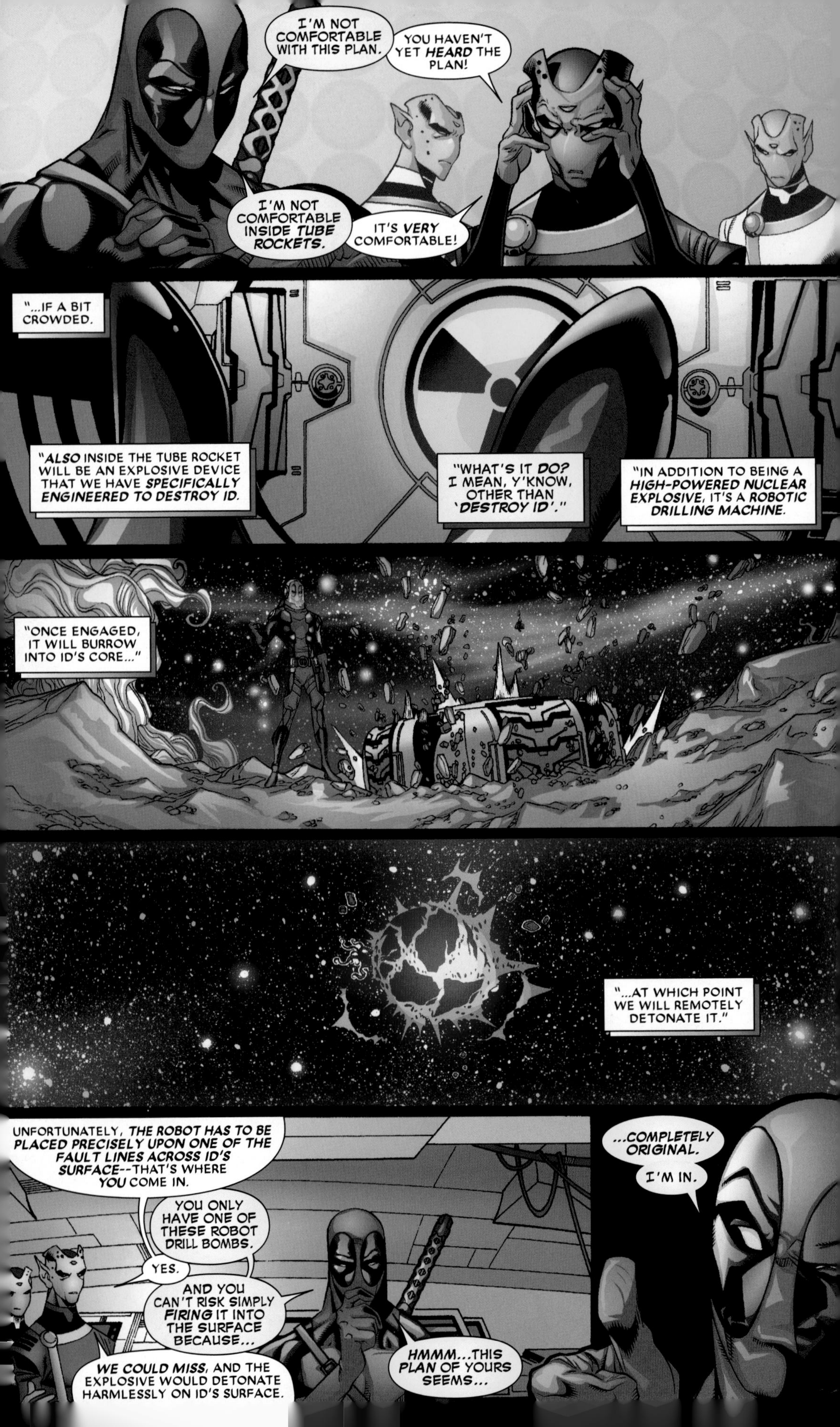
I'M NOT COMFORTABLE WITH THIS PLAN.
YOU HAVEN'T YET HEARD THE PLAN!
I'M NOT COMFORTABLE INSIDE TUBE ROCKETS.
IT'S VERY COMFORTABLE!
"...IF A BIT CROWDED.
"ALSO INSIDE THE TUBE ROCKET WILL BE AN EXPLOSIVE DEVICE THAT WE HAVE SPECIFICALLY ENGINEERED TO DESTROY ID.
"WHAT'S IT DO? I MEAN, Y'KNOW, OTHER THAN 'DESTROY ID'."
"IN ADDITION TO BEING A HIGH-POWERED NUCLEAR EXPLOSIVE, IT'S A ROBOTIC DRILLING MACHINE.
"ONCE ENGAGED, IT WILL BURROW INTO ID'S CORE..."
"...AT WHICH POINT WE WILL REMOTELY DETONATE IT."
UNFORTUNATELY, THE ROBOT HAS TO BE PLACED PRECISELY UPON ONE OF THE FAULT LINES ACROSS ID'S SURFACE--THAT'S WHERE YOU COME IN.
YOU ONLY HAVE ONE OF THESE ROBOT DRILL BOMBS.
YES.
AND YOU CAN'T RISK SIMPLY FIRING IT INTO THE SURFACE BECAUSE...
WE COULD MISS, AND THE EXPLOSIVE WOULD DETONATE HARMLESSLY ON ID'S SURFACE.
HMMM...THIS PLAN OF YOURS SEEMS...
...COMPLETELY ORIGINAL.
I'M IN.

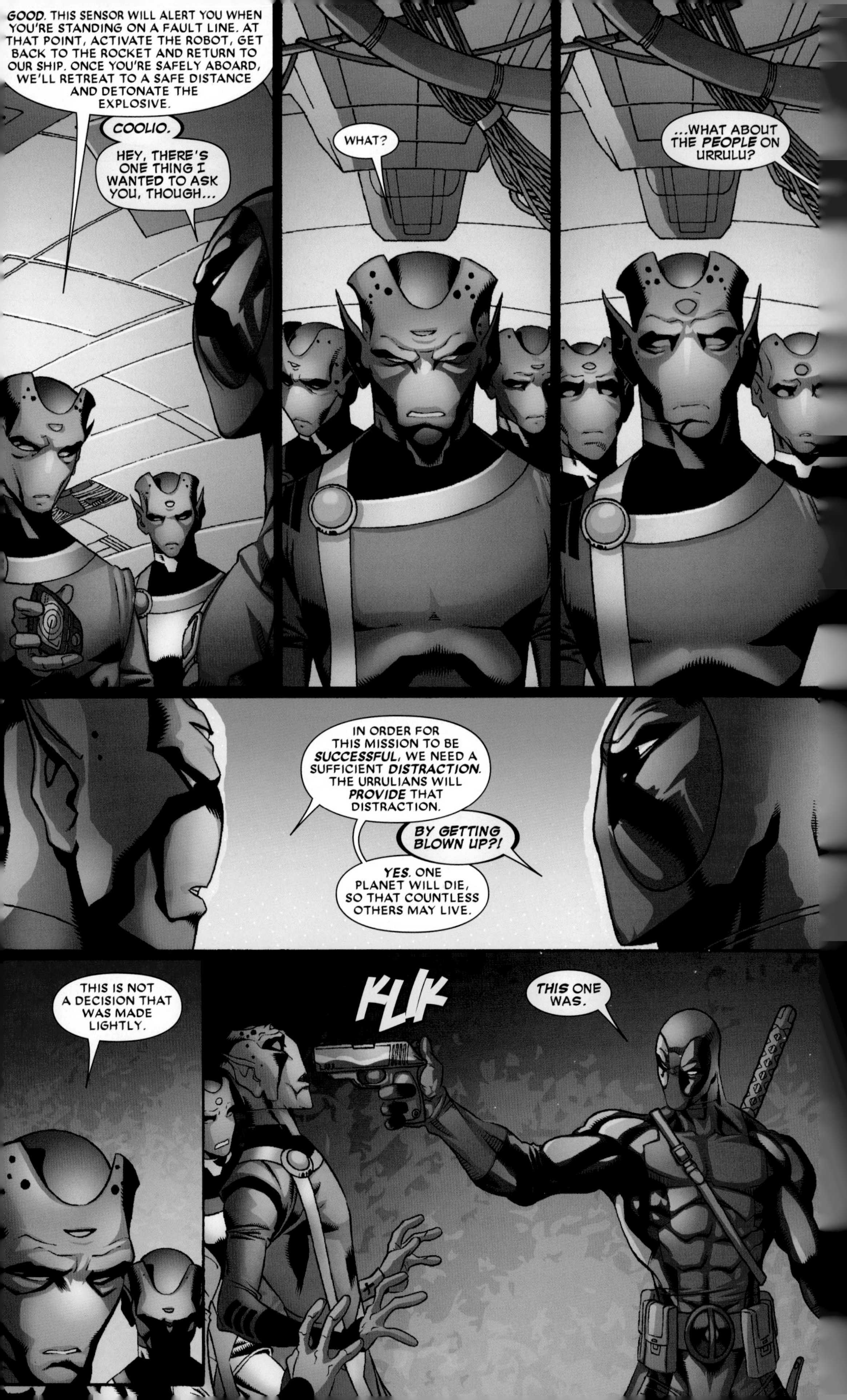
GOOD. THIS SENSOR WILL ALERT YOU WHEN YOU'RE STANDING ON A FAULT LINE. AT THAT POINT, ACTIVATE THE ROBOT, GET BACK TO THE ROCKET AND RETURN TO OUR SHIP. ONCE YOU'RE SAFELY ABOARD, WE'LL RETREAT TO A SAFE DISTANCE AND DETONATE THE EXPLOSIVE.
COOLIO.
HEY, THERE'S ONE THING I WANTED TO ASK YOU, THOUGH...
WHAT?
...WHAT ABOUT THE PEOPLE ON URRULU?
IN ORDER FOR THIS MISSION TO BE SUCCESSFUL, WE NEED A SUFFICIENT DISTRACTION. THE URRULIANS WILL PROVIDE THAT DISTRACTION.
BY GETTING BLOWN UP?!
YES. ONE PLANET WILL DIE, SO THAT COUNTLESS OTHERS MAY LIVE.
THIS IS NOT A DECISION THAT WAS MADE LIGHTLY.
KLIK
THIS ONE WAS.

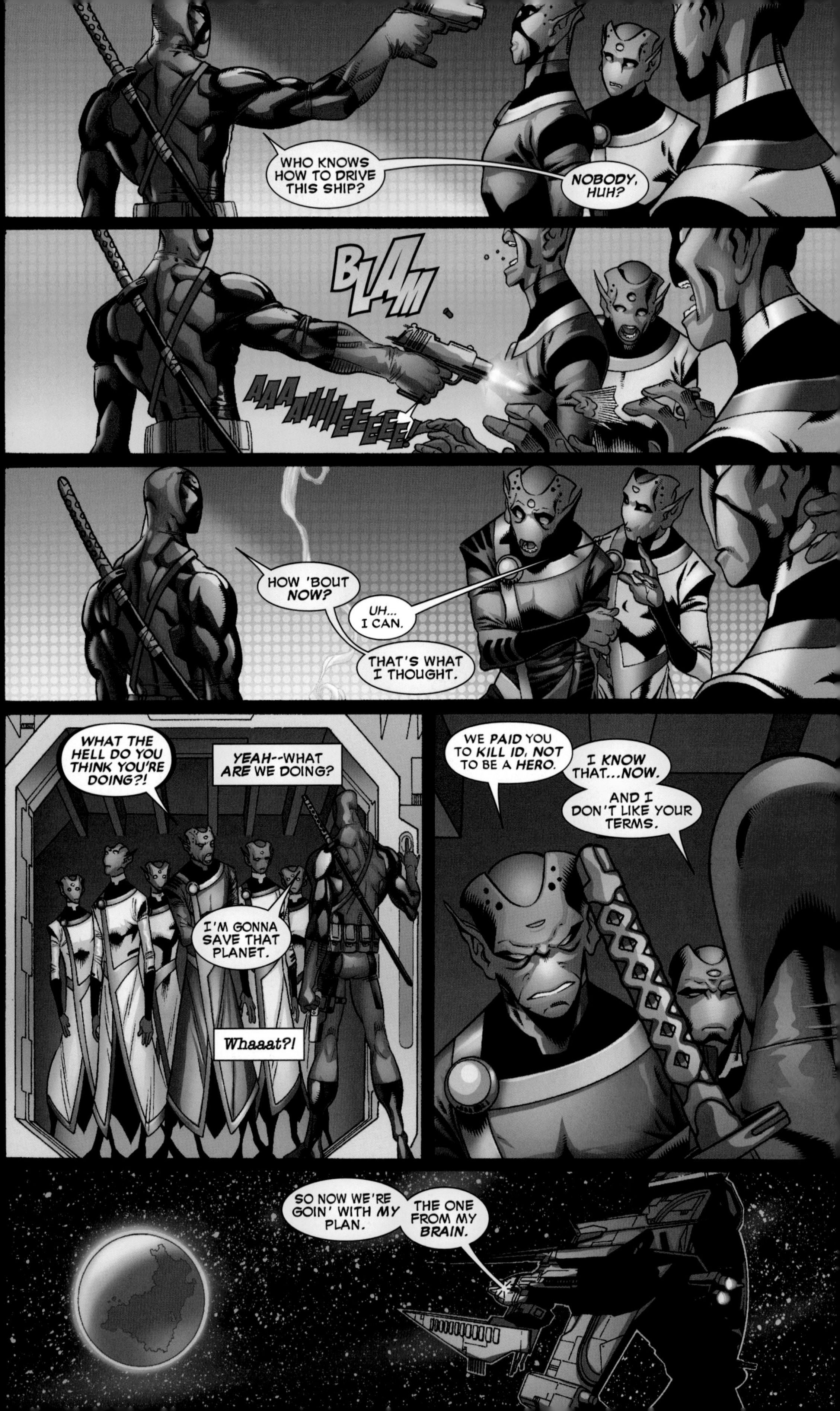
WHO KNOWS HOW TO DRIVE THIS SHIP?
NOBODY, HUH?
BLAM
AAAAIIIIEEEEEE!
HOW 'BOUT NOW?
UH... I CAN.
THAT'S WHAT I THOUGHT.
WHAT THE HELL DO YOU THINK YOU'RE DOING?!
YEAH--WHAT ARE WE DOING?
I'M GONNA SAVE THAT PLANET.
Whaaat?!
WE PAID YOU TO KILL ID, NOT TO BE A HERO.
I KNOW THAT...NOW.
AND I DON'T LIKE YOUR TERMS.
SO NOW WE'RE GOIN' WITH MY PLAN.
THE ONE FROM MY BRAIN.

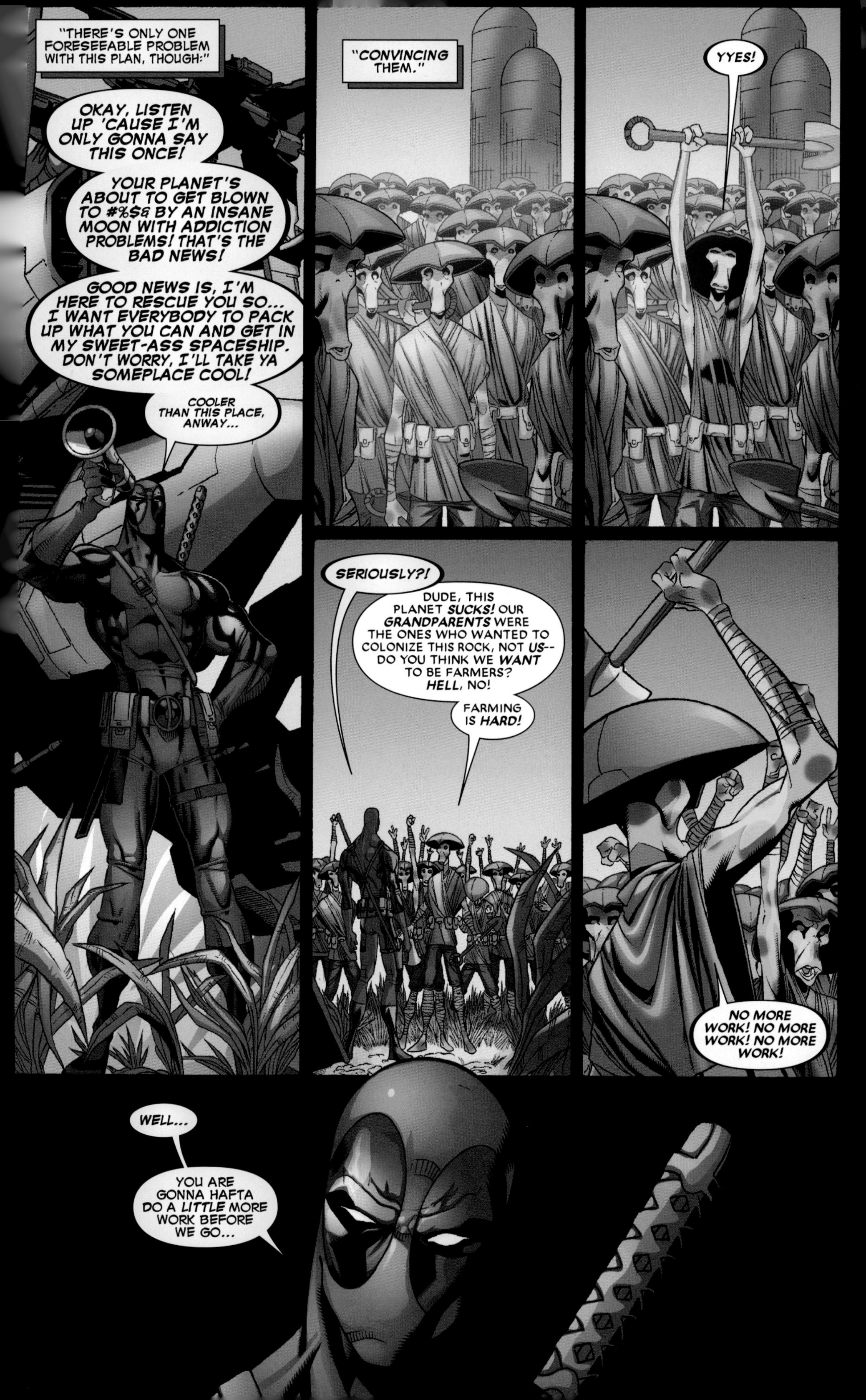
"THERE'S ONLY ONE FORESEEABLE PROBLEM WITH THIS PLAN, THOUGH:"
OKAY, LISTEN UP 'CAUSE I'M ONLY GONNA SAY THIS ONCE!
YOUR PLANET'S ABOUT TO GET BLOWN TO #%$& BY AN INSANE MOON WITH ADDICTION PROBLEMS! THAT'S THE BAD NEWS!
GOOD NEWS IS, I'M HERE TO RESCUE YOU SO... I WANT EVERYBODY TO PACK UP WHAT YOU CAN AND GET IN MY SWEET-ASS SPACESHIP. DON'T WORRY, I'LL TAKE YA SOMEPLACE COOL!
COOLER THAN THIS PLACE, ANWAY...
"CONVINCING THEM."
YYES!
SERIOUSLY?!
DUDE, THIS PLANET SUCKS! OUR GRANDPARENTS WERE THE ONES WHO WANTED TO COLONIZE THIS ROCK, NOT US-- DO YOU THINK WE WANT TO BE FARMERS? HELL, NO!
FARMING IS HARD!
NO MORE WORK! NO MORE WORK! NO MORE WORK!
WELL...
YOU ARE GONNA HAFTA DO A LITTLE MORE WORK BEFORE WE GO...

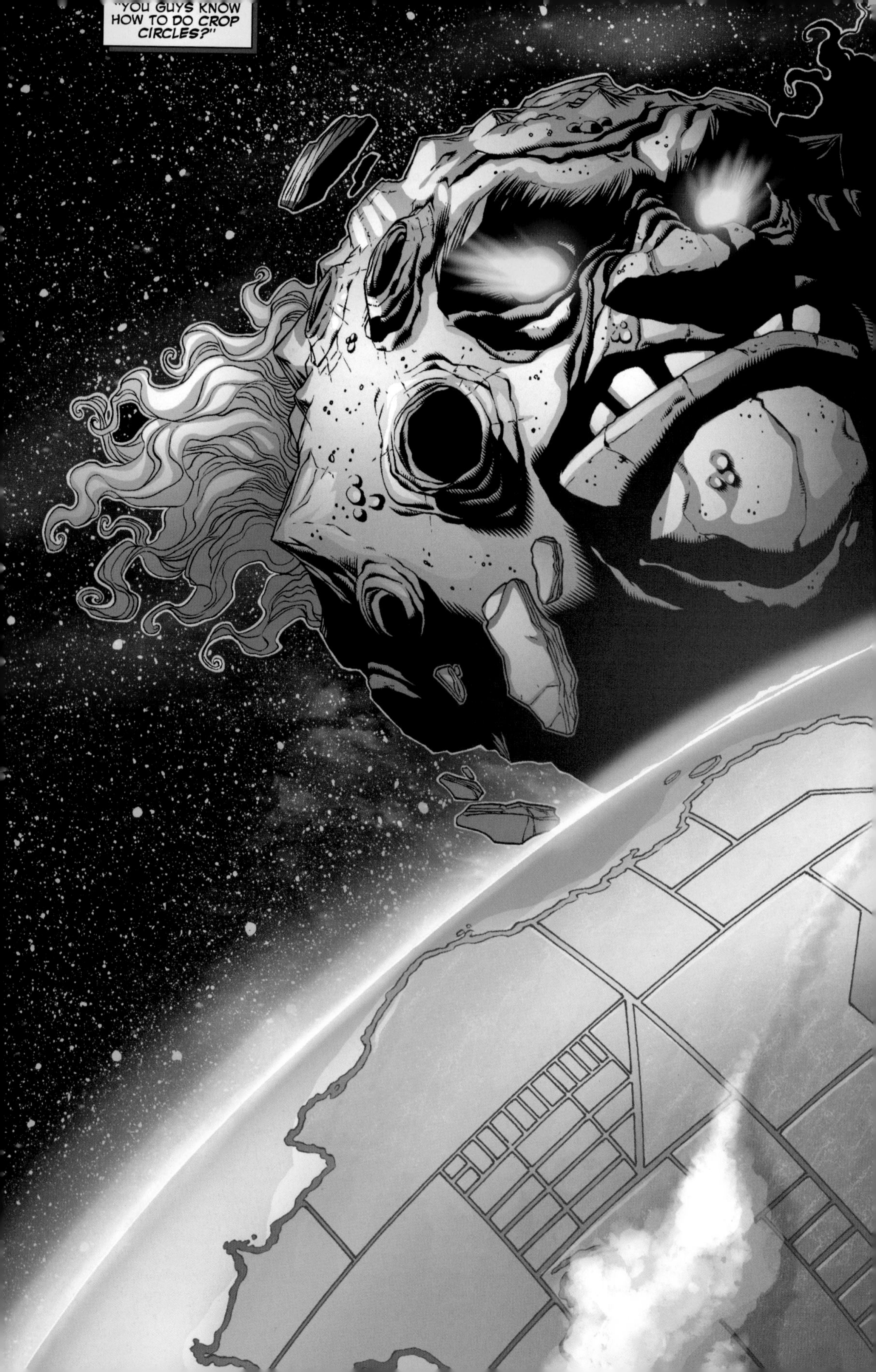
"YOU GUYS KNOW HOW TO DO CROP CIRCLES?"

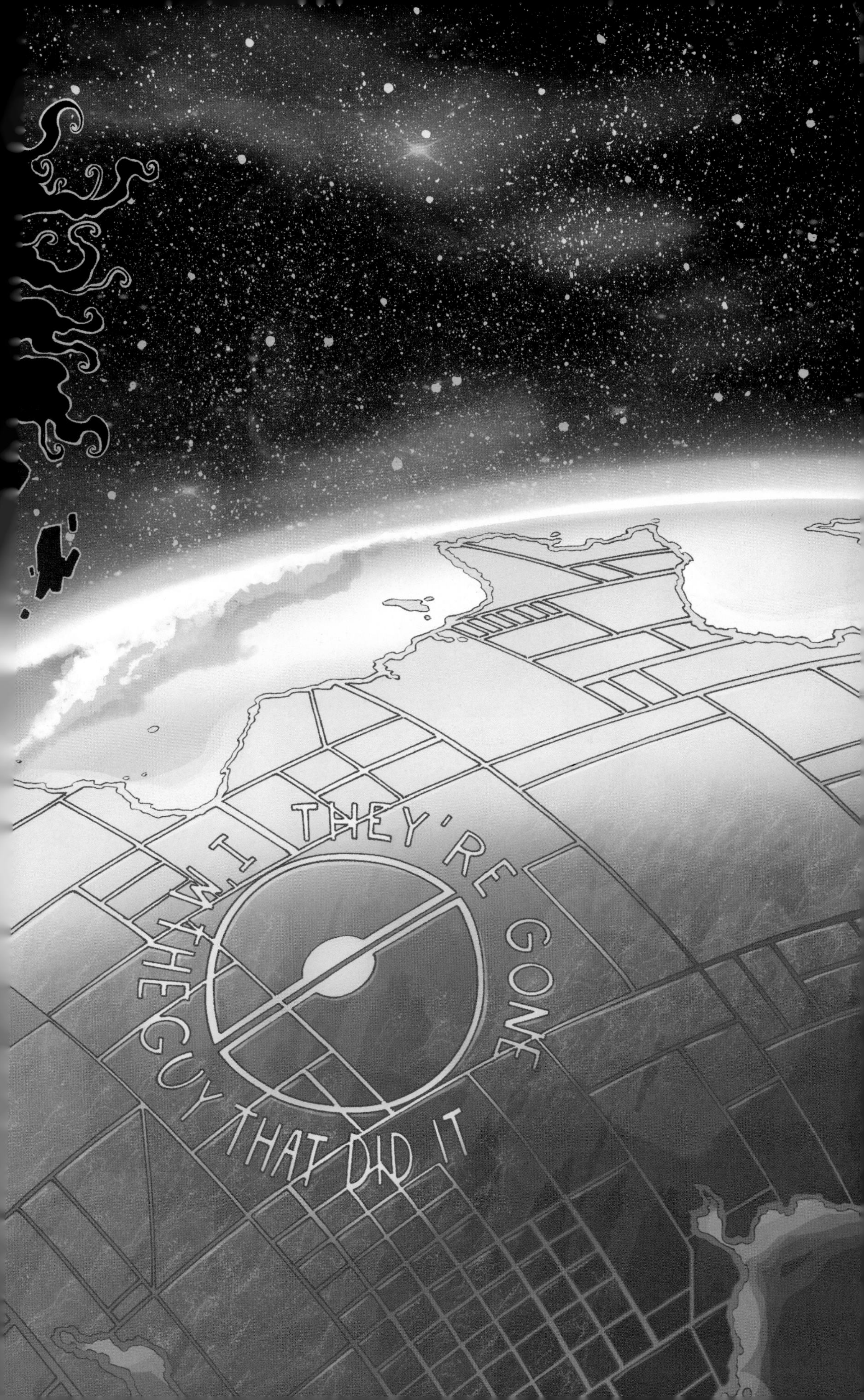
THEY'RE GONE
I'M THE GUY THAT DID IT

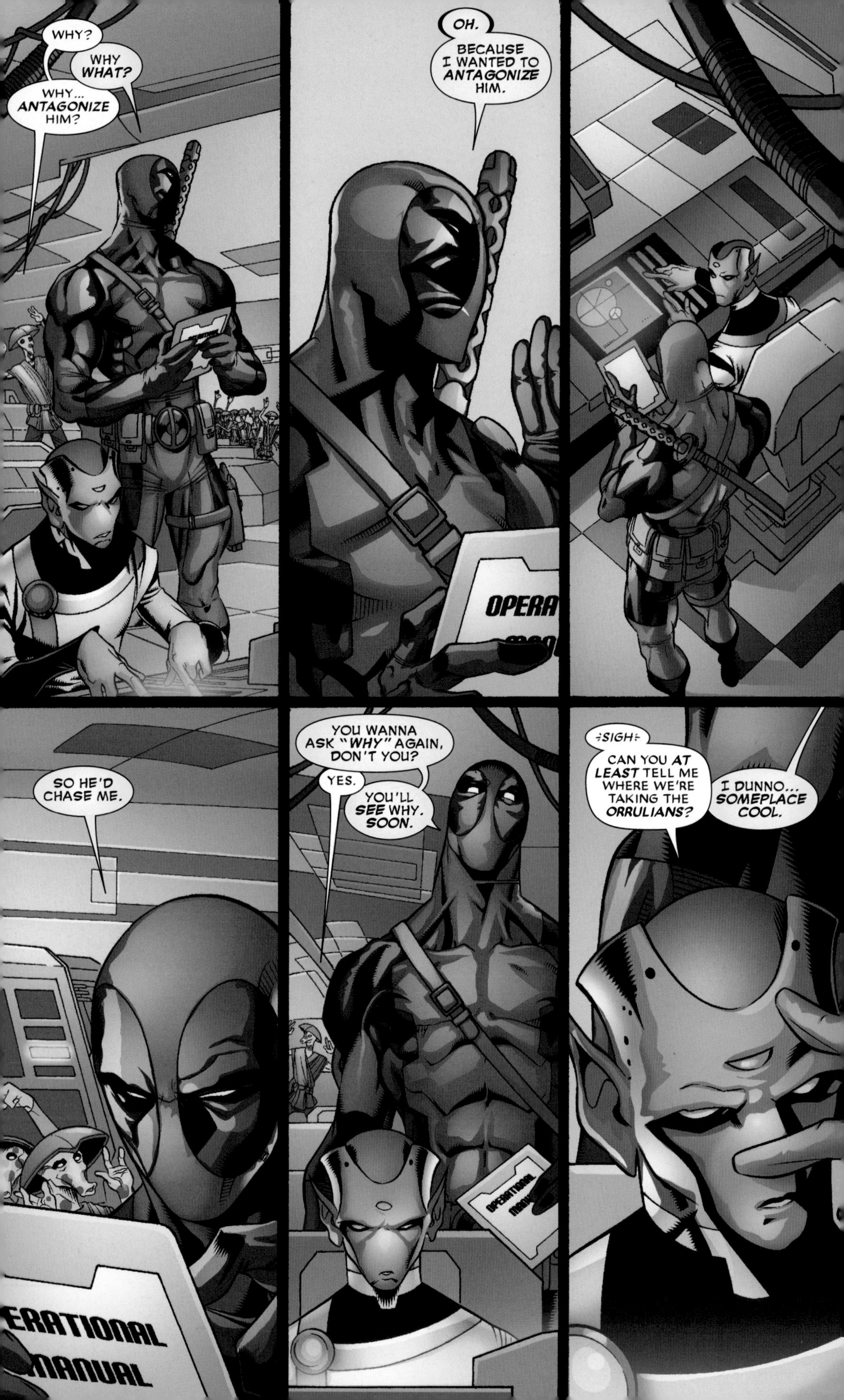
WHY?
WHY WHAT?
WHY... ANTAGONIZE HIM?
OH.
BECAUSE I WANTED TO ANTAGONIZE HIM.
OPERA
SO HE'D CHASE ME.
ERATIONAL MANUAL
YOU WANNA ASK "WHY" AGAIN, DON'T YOU?
YES.
YOU'LL SEE WHY. SOON.
OPERATIONAL MANUAL
=SIGH=
CAN YOU AT LEAST TELL ME WHERE WE'RE TAKING THE ORRULIANS?
I DUNNO... SOMEPLACE COOL.

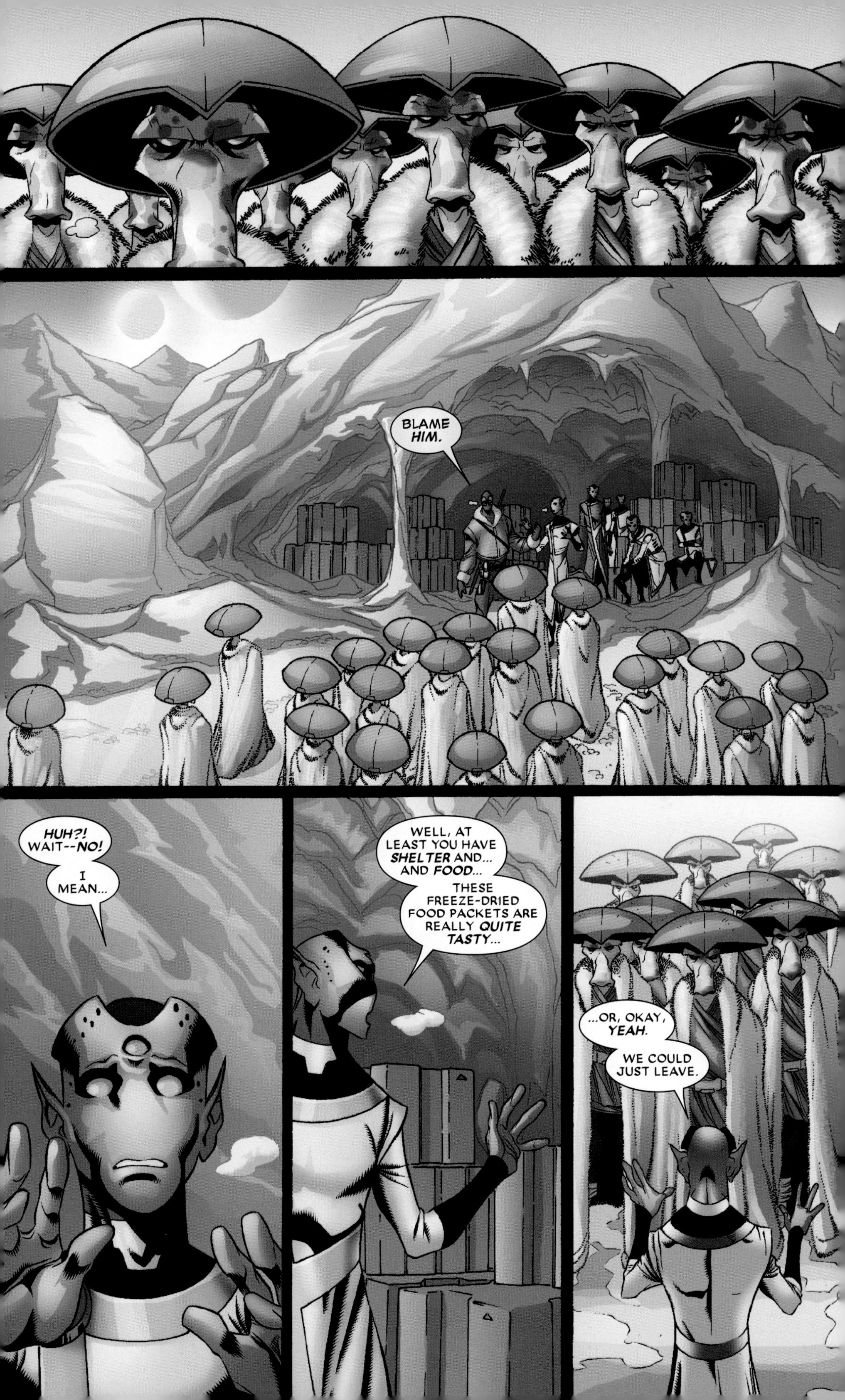
BLAME HIM.
HUH?! WAIT--NO!
I MEAN...
WELL, AT LEAST YOU HAVE SHELTER AND... AND FOOD...
THESE FREEZE-DRIED FOOD PACKETS ARE REALLY QUITE TASTY...
...OR, OKAY, YEAH.
WE COULD JUST LEAVE.

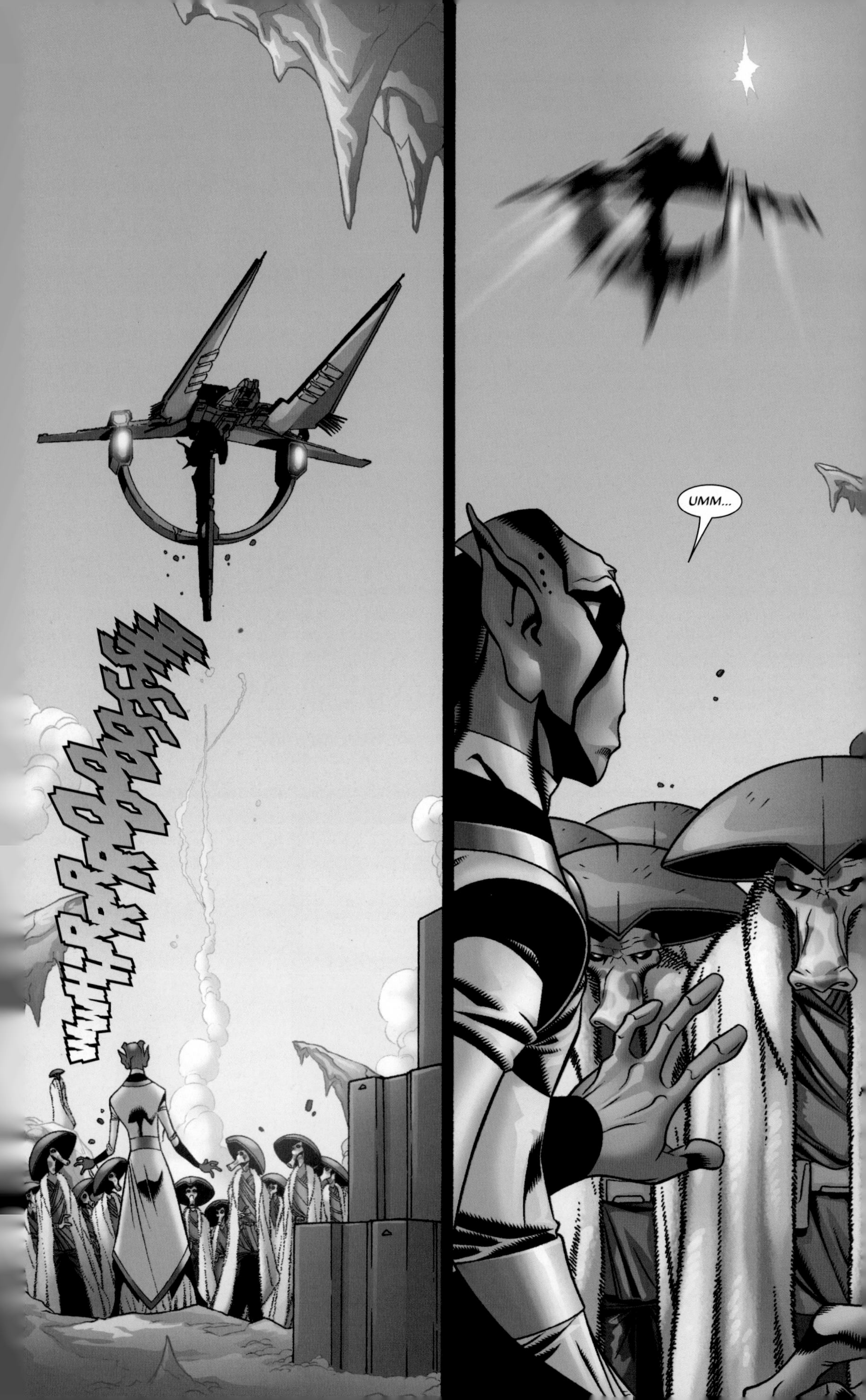
WHHRR-BOOOSHH
UMM...

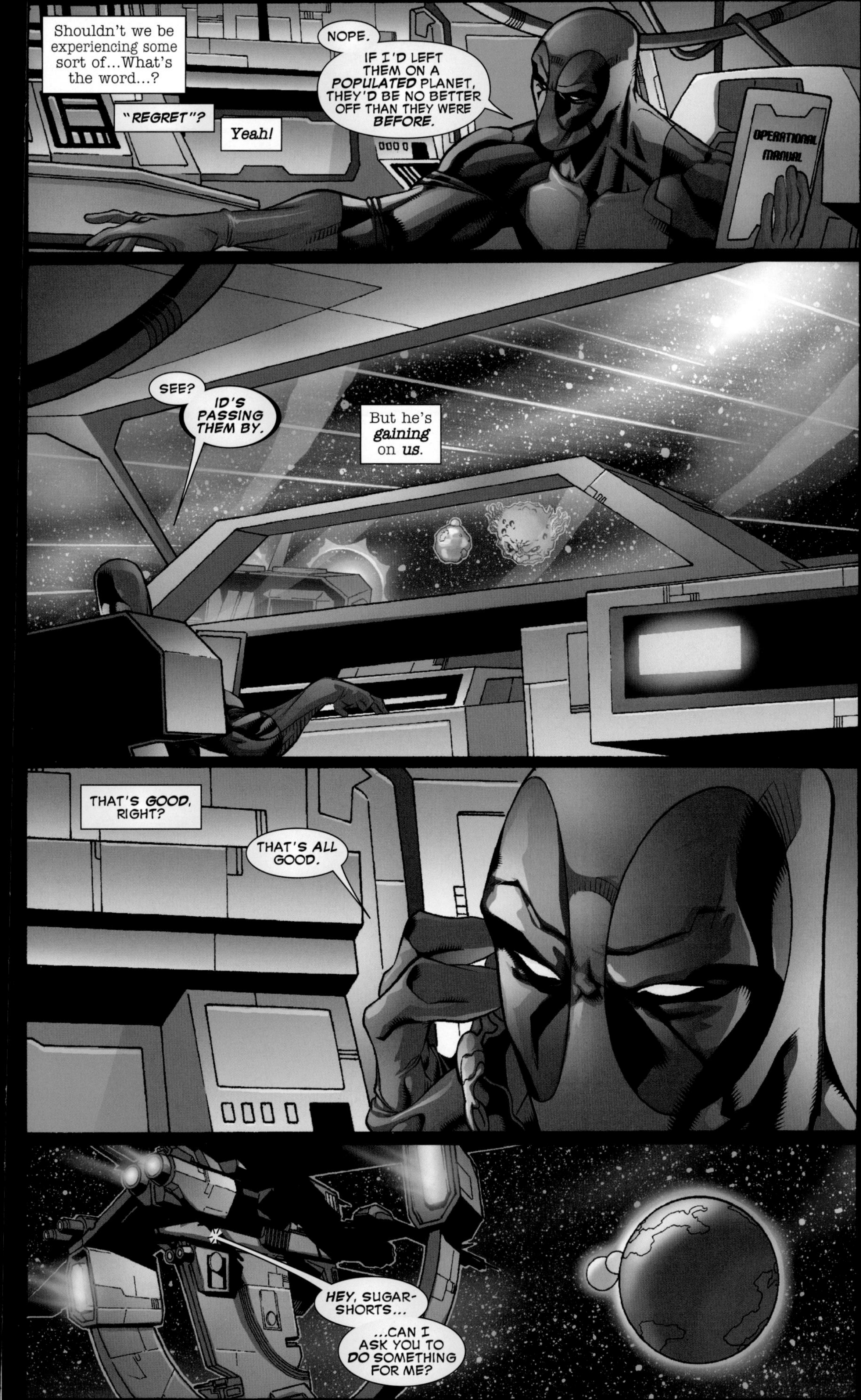
Shouldn't we be experiencing some sort of...What's the word...?
NOPE.
IF I'D LEFT THEM ON A POPULATED PLANET, THEY'D BE NO BETTER OFF THAN THEY WERE BEFORE.
"REGRET"?
Yeah!
OPERATIONAL MANUAL
SEE?
ID'S PASSING THEM BY.
But he's gaining on us.
THAT'S GOOD, RIGHT?
THAT'S ALL GOOD.
HEY, SUGAR-SHORTS...
...CAN I ASK YOU TO DO SOMETHING FOR ME?

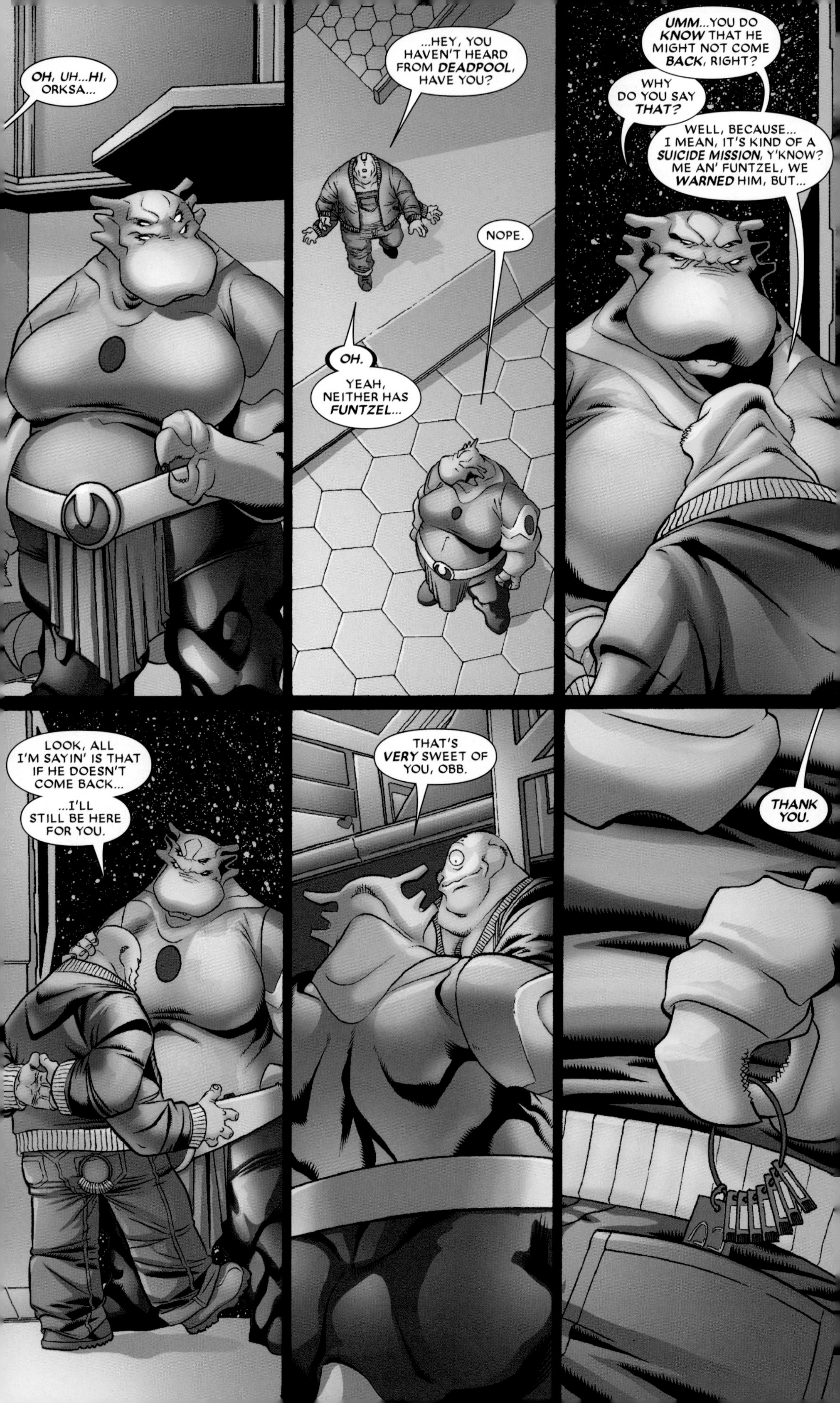
OH, UH...HI, ORKSA...
...HEY, YOU HAVEN'T HEARD FROM DEADPOOL, HAVE YOU?
NOPE.
OH.
YEAH, NEITHER HAS FUNTZEL...
UMM...YOU DO KNOW THAT HE MIGHT NOT COME BACK, RIGHT?
WHY DO YOU SAY THAT?
WELL, BECAUSE... I MEAN, IT'S KIND OF A SUICIDE MISSION, Y'KNOW? ME AN' FUNTZEL, WE WARNED HIM, BUT...
LOOK, ALL I'M SAYIN' IS THAT IF HE DOESN'T COME BACK...
...I'LL STILL BE HERE FOR YOU.
THAT'S VERY SWEET OF YOU, OBB.
THANK YOU.

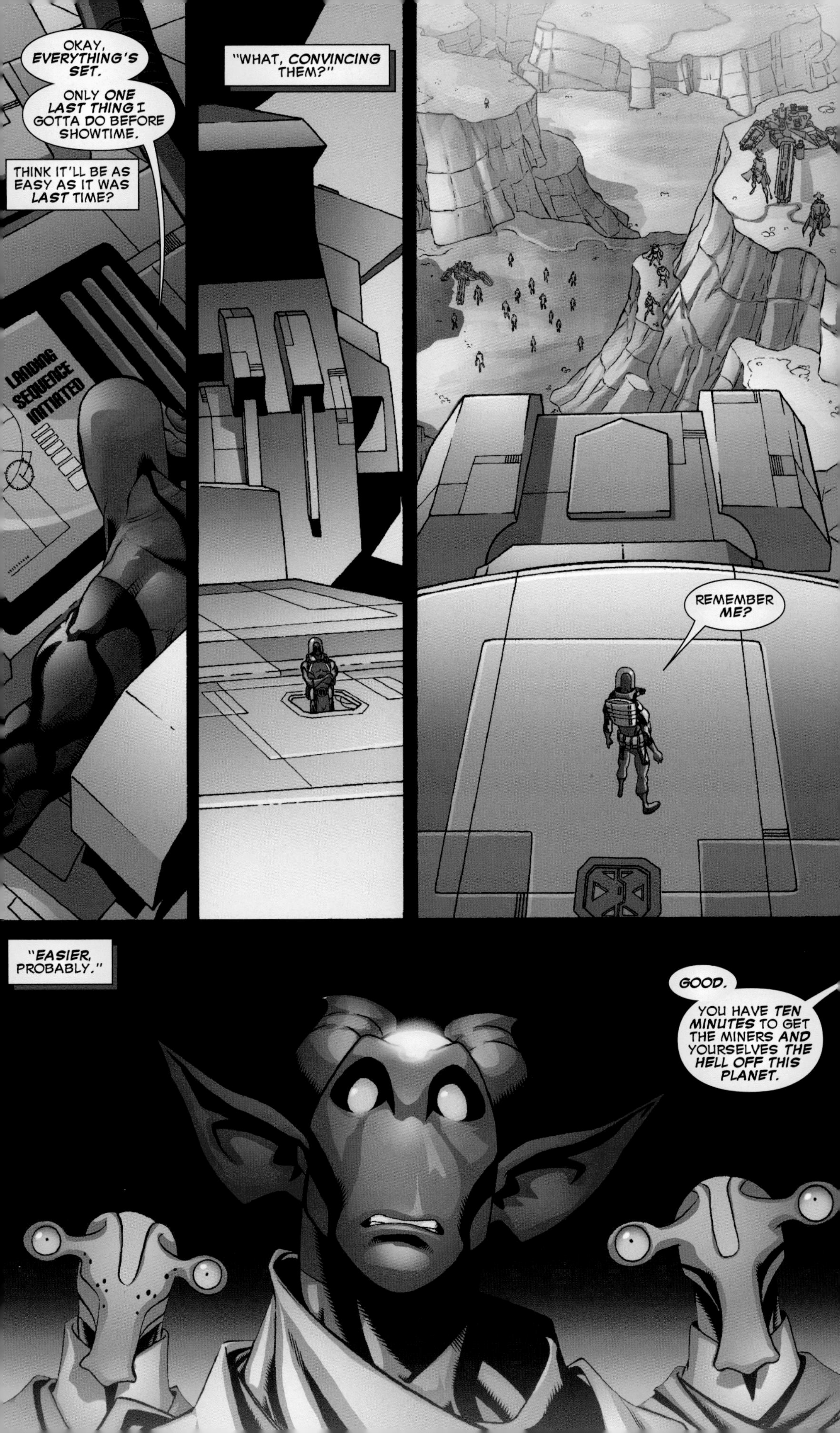
OKAY, EVERYTHING'S SET.
ONLY ONE LAST THING I GOTTA DO BEFORE SHOWTIME.
THINK IT'LL BE AS EASY AS IT WAS LAST TIME?
LANDING SEQUENCE INITIATED
"WHAT, CONVINCING THEM?"
REMEMBER ME?
"EASIER, PROBABLY."
GOOD.
YOU HAVE TEN MINUTES TO GET THE MINERS AND YOURSELVES THE HELL OFF THIS PLANET.

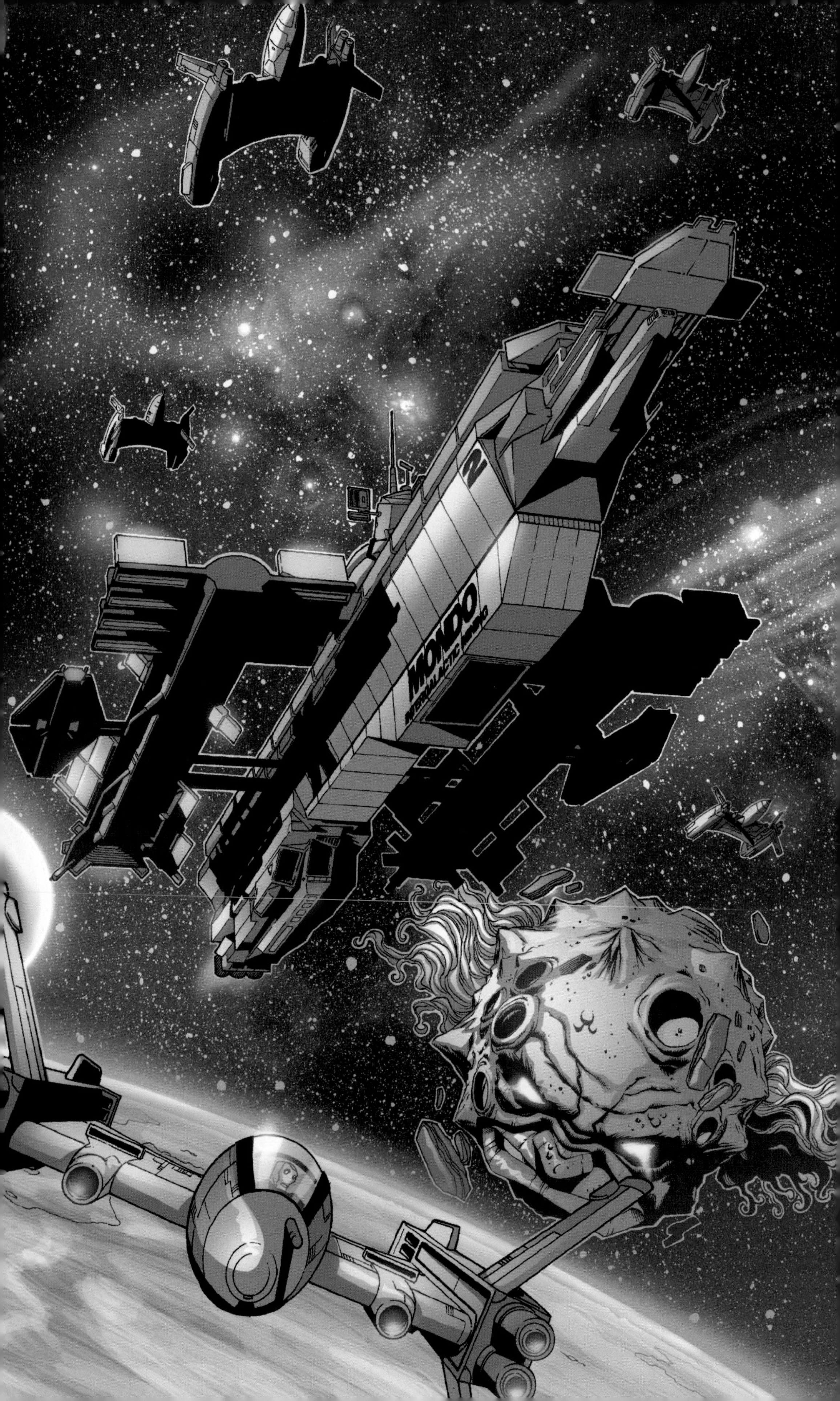
MONDO
INTERGALACTIC

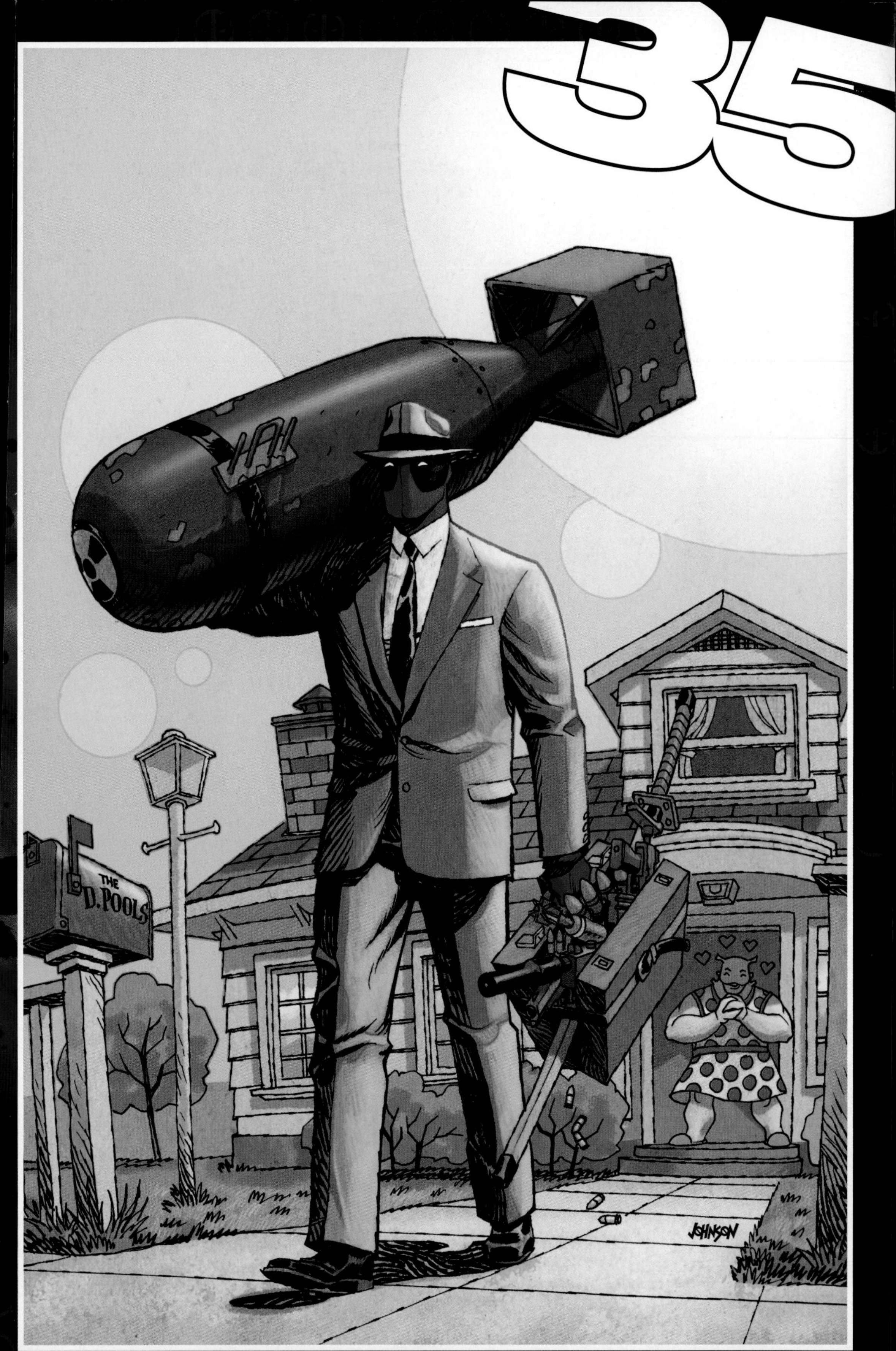
35
THE
D. POOLS
JOHNSON

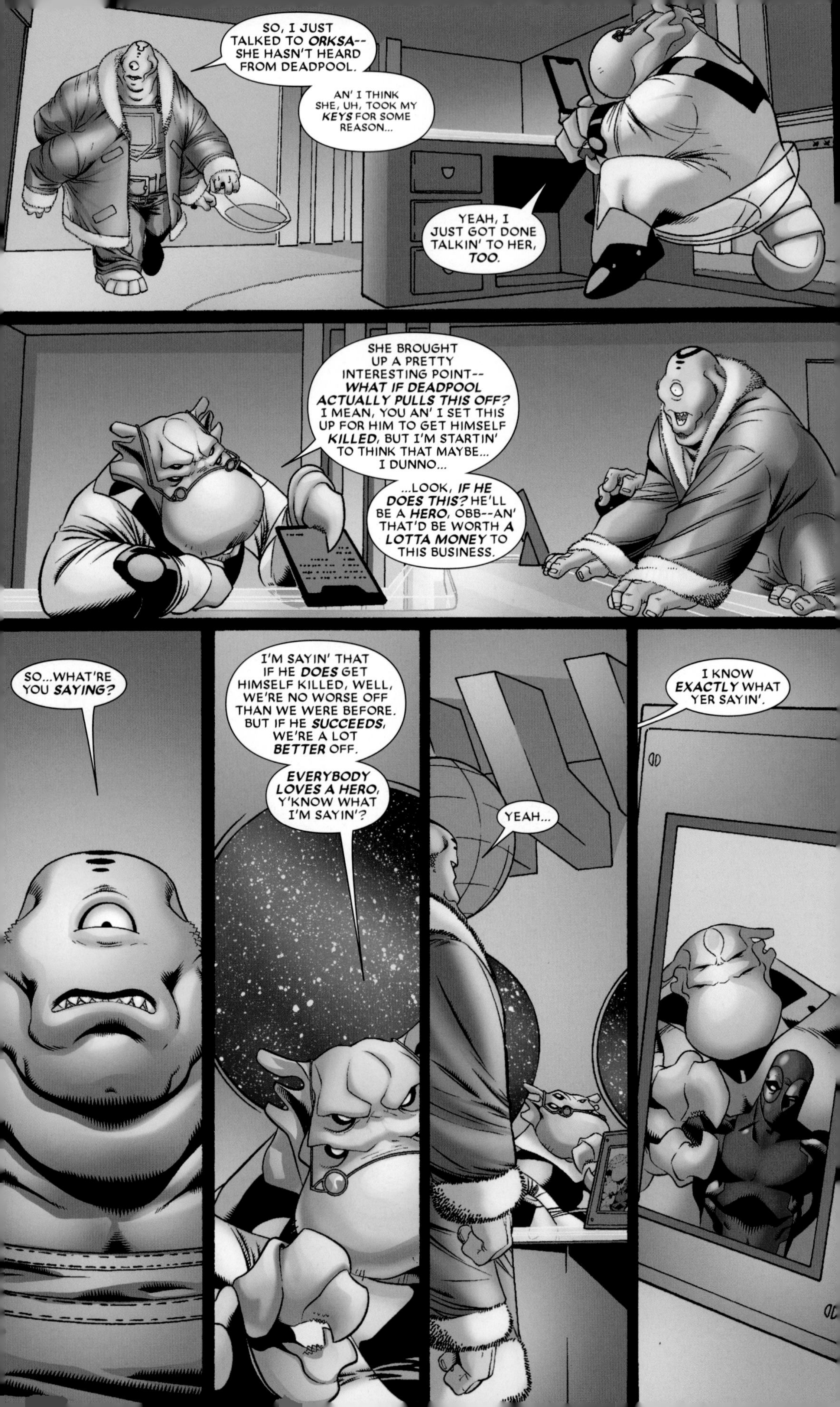
SO, I JUST TALKED TO ORKSA-- SHE HASN'T HEARD FROM DEADPOOL.
AN' I THINK SHE, UH, TOOK MY KEYS FOR SOME REASON...
YEAH, I JUST GOT DONE TALKIN' TO HER, TOO.
SHE BROUGHT UP A PRETTY INTERESTING POINT-- WHAT IF DEADPOOL ACTUALLY PULLS THIS OFF? I MEAN, YOU AN' I SET THIS UP FOR HIM TO GET HIMSELF KILLED, BUT I'M STARTIN' TO THINK THAT MAYBE... I DUNNO...
...LOOK, IF HE DOES THIS? HE'LL BE A HERO, OBB--AN' THAT'D BE WORTH A LOTTA MONEY TO THIS BUSINESS.
SO...WHAT'RE YOU SAYING?
I'M SAYIN' THAT IF HE DOES GET HIMSELF KILLED, WELL, WE'RE NO WORSE OFF THAN WE WERE BEFORE. BUT IF HE SUCCEEDS, WE'RE A LOT BETTER OFF.
EVERYBODY LOVES A HERO, Y'KNOW WHAT I'M SAYIN'?
YEAH...
I KNOW EXACTLY WHAT YER SAYIN'.

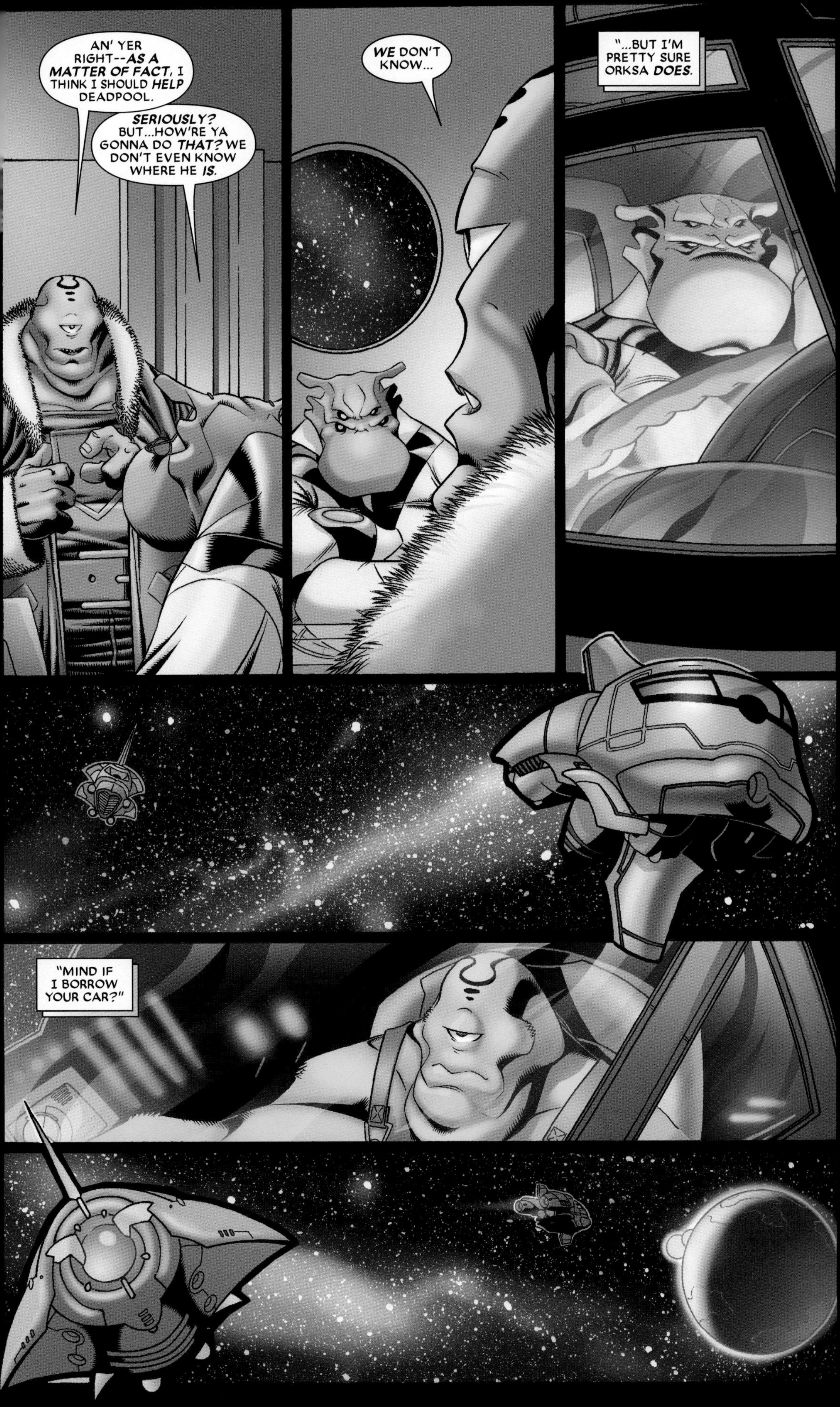
AN' YER RIGHT--AS A MATTER OF FACT, I THINK I SHOULD HELP DEADPOOL.
SERIOUSLY? BUT...HOW'RE YA GONNA DO THAT? WE DON'T EVEN KNOW WHERE HE IS.
WE DON'T KNOW...
"...BUT I'M PRETTY SURE ORKSA DOES.
"MIND IF I BORROW YOUR CAR?"

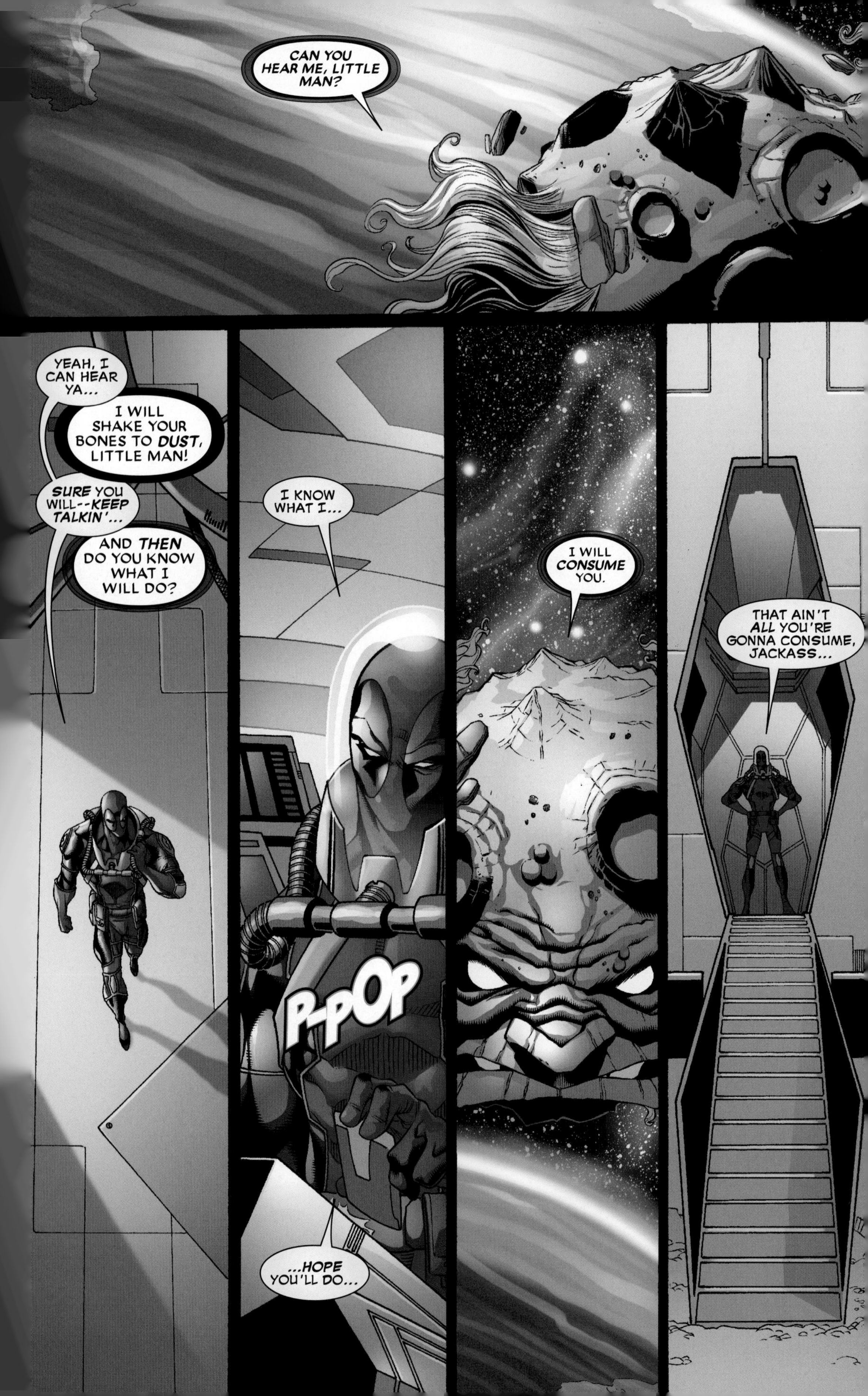
CAN YOU HEAR ME, LITTLE MAN?
YEAH, I CAN HEAR YA...
I WILL SHAKE YOUR BONES TO DUST, LITTLE MAN!
SURE YOU WILL--KEEP TALKIN'...
AND THEN DO YOU KNOW WHAT I WILL DO?
I KNOW WHAT I...
P-POP
...HOPE YOU'LL DO...
I WILL CONSUME YOU.
THAT AIN'T ALL YOU'RE GONNA CONSUME, JACKASS...

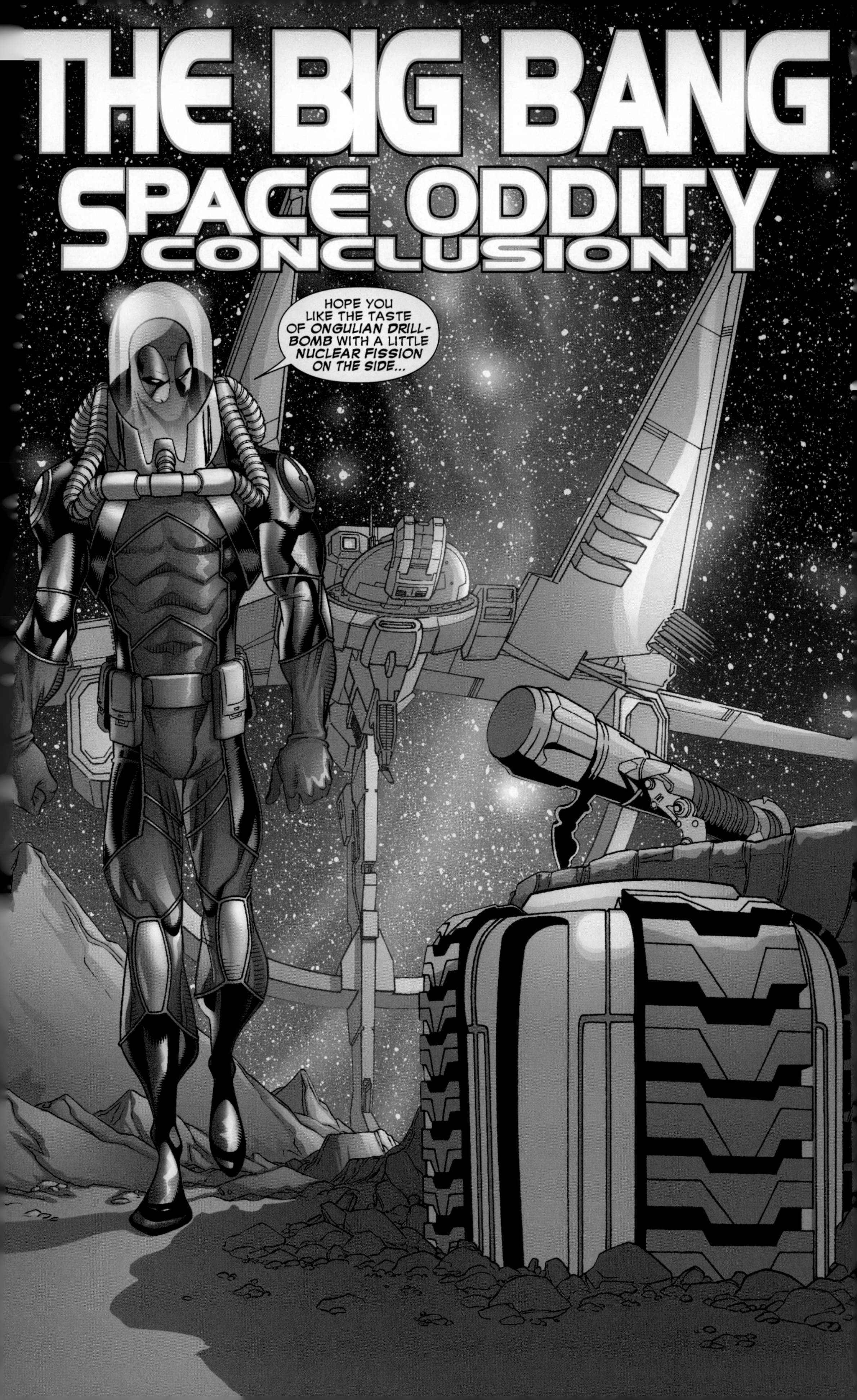
THE BIG BANG
SPACE ODDITY CONCLUSION
HOPE YOU LIKE THE TASTE OF ONGULIAN DRILL-BOMB WITH A LITTLE NUCLEAR FISSION ON THE SIDE...

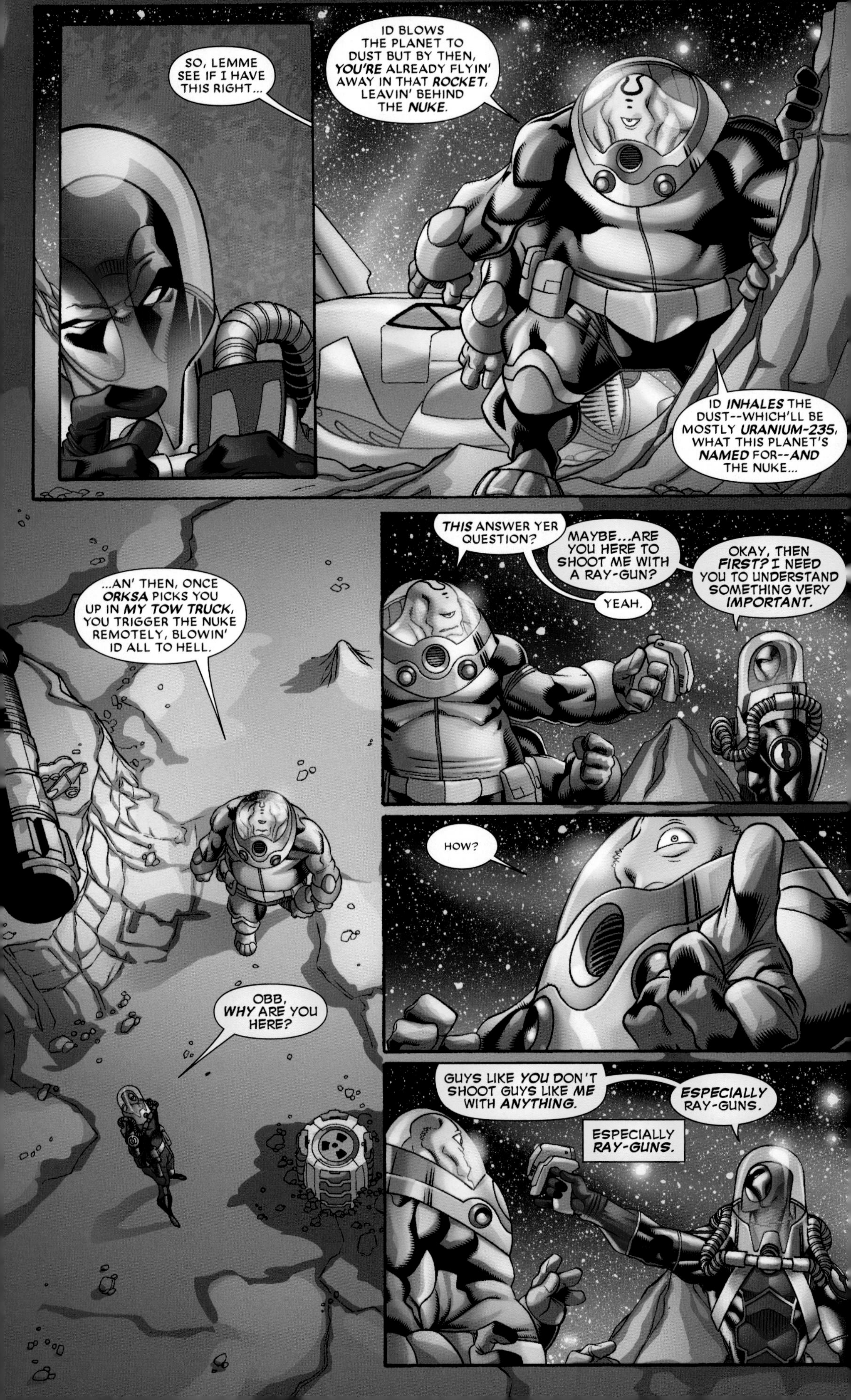

SO, LEMME SEE IF I HAVE THIS RIGHT...
ID BLOWS THE PLANET TO DUST BUT BY THEN, YOU'RE ALREADY FLYIN' AWAY IN THAT ROCKET, LEAVIN' BEHIND THE NUKE.
ID INHALES THE DUST--WHICH'LL BE MOSTLY URANIUM-235, WHAT THIS PLANET'S NAMED FOR--AND THE NUKE...
...AN' THEN, ONCE ORKSA PICKS YOU UP IN MY TOW TRUCK, YOU TRIGGER THE NUKE REMOTELY, BLOWIN' ID ALL TO HELL.
OBB, WHY ARE YOU HERE?
THIS ANSWER YER QUESTION?
MAYBE...ARE YOU HERE TO SHOOT ME WITH A RAY-GUN?
YEAH.
OKAY, THEN FIRST? I NEED YOU TO UNDERSTAND SOMETHING VERY IMPORTANT.
HOW?
GUYS LIKE YOU DON'T SHOOT GUYS LIKE ME WITH ANYTHING.
ESPECIALLY RAY-GUNS.
ESPECIALLY RAY-GUNS.

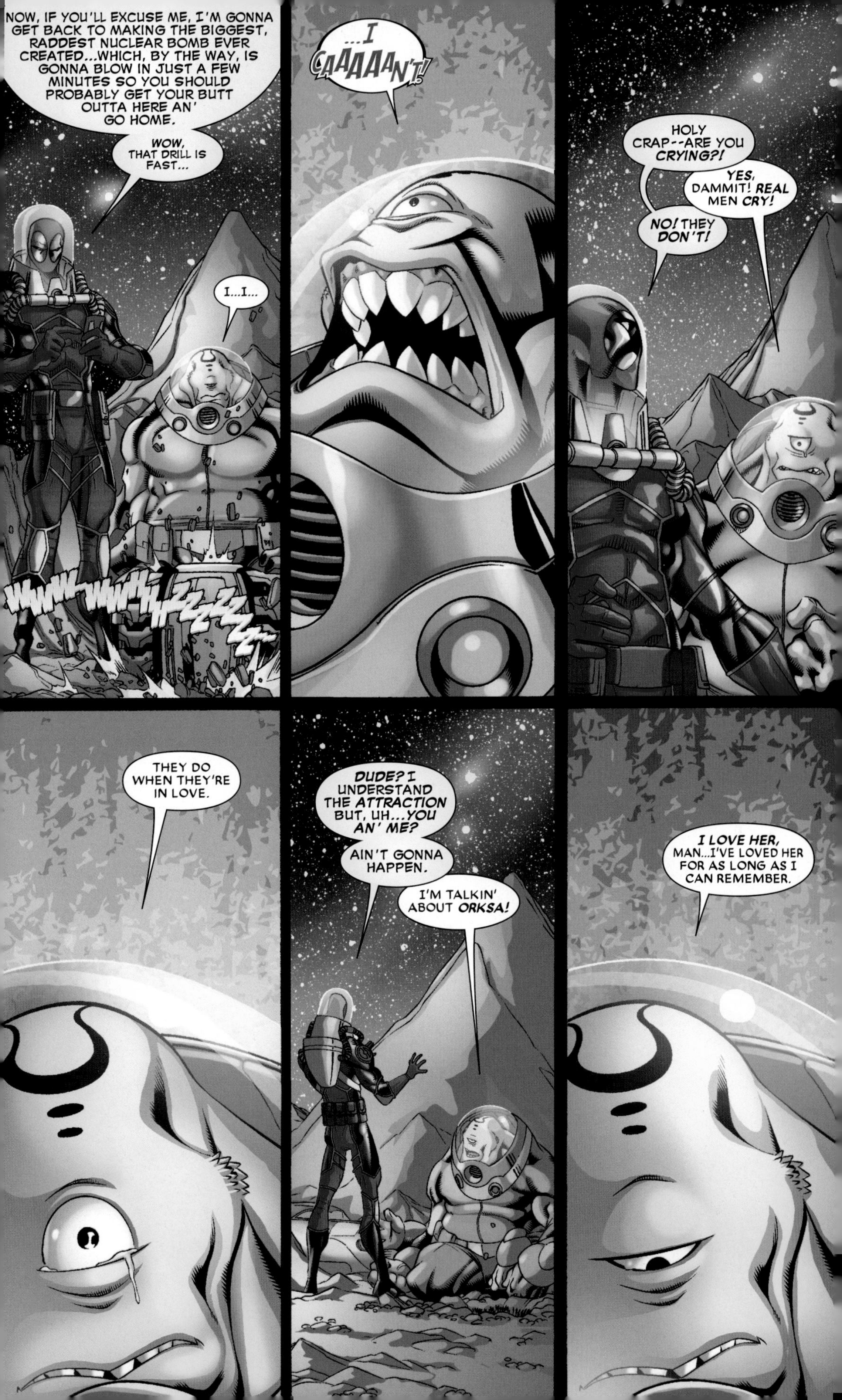
NOW, IF YOU'LL EXCUSE ME, I'M GONNA GET BACK TO MAKING THE BIGGEST, RADDEST NUCLEAR BOMB EVER CREATED...WHICH, BY THE WAY, IS GONNA BLOW IN JUST A FEW MINUTES SO YOU SHOULD PROBABLY GET YOUR BUTT OUTTA HERE AN' GO HOME.
WOW, THAT DRILL IS FAST...
I...I...
WWWHWWWHHZZZZZZ
...I CAAAAAN'T!
HOLY CRAP--ARE YOU CRYING?!
YES, DAMMIT! REAL MEN CRY!
NO! THEY DON'T!
THEY DO WHEN THEY'RE IN LOVE.
DUDE? I UNDERSTAND THE ATTRACTION BUT, UH...YOU AN' ME?
AIN'T GONNA HAPPEN.
I'M TALKIN' ABOUT ORKSA!
I LOVE HER, MAN...I'VE LOVED HER FOR AS LONG AS I CAN REMEMBER.

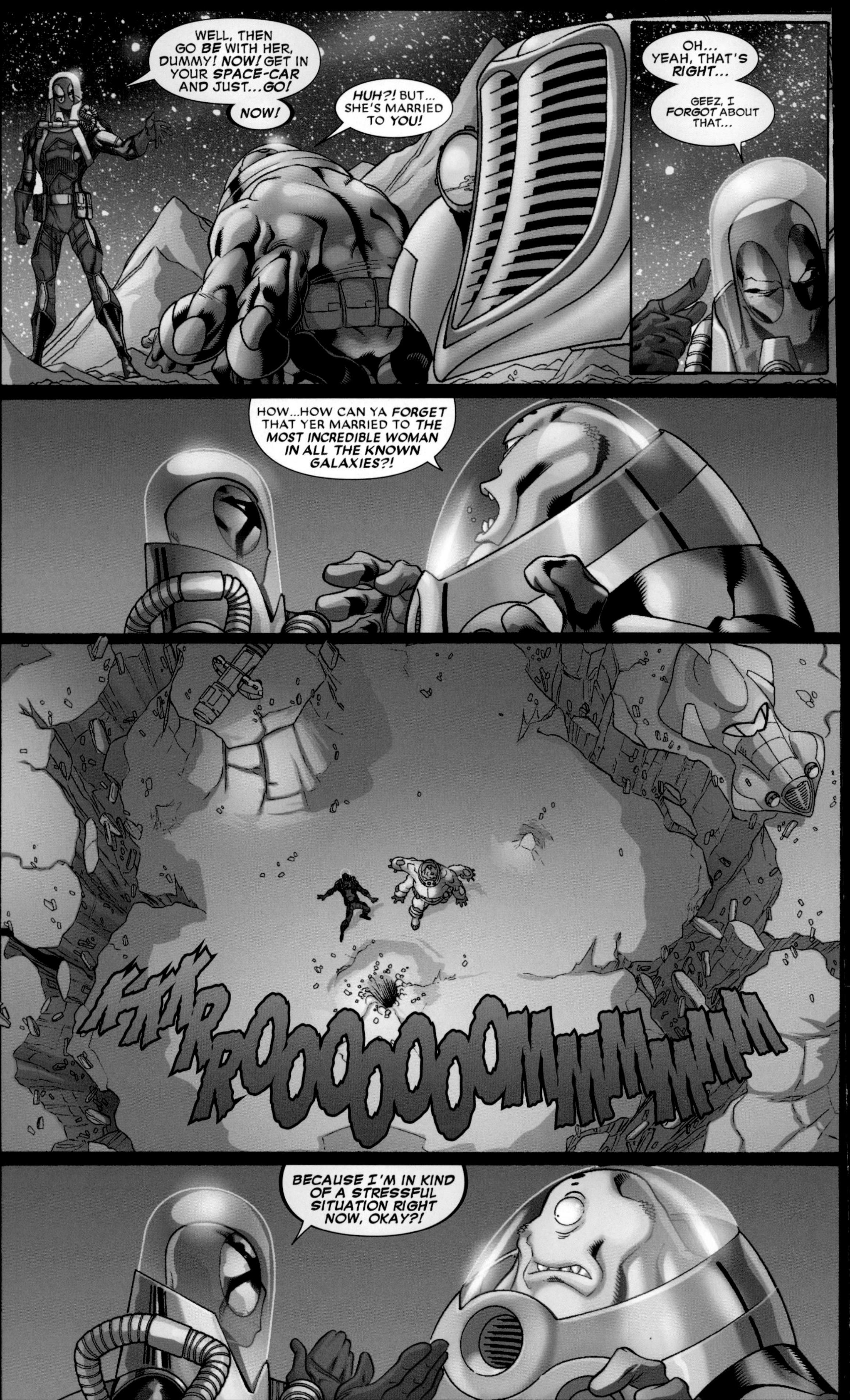
WELL, THEN GO BE WITH HER, DUMMY! NOW! GET IN YOUR SPACE-CAR AND JUST...GO!
NOW!
HUH?! BUT... SHE'S MARRIED TO YOU!
OH... YEAH, THAT'S RIGHT...
GEEZ, I FORGOT ABOUT THAT...
HOW...HOW CAN YA FORGET THAT YER MARRIED TO THE MOST INCREDIBLE WOMAN IN ALL THE KNOWN GALAXIES?!
KA-RROOOOOOOMMMMMMMM
BECAUSE I'M IN KIND OF A STRESSFUL SITUATION RIGHT NOW, OKAY?!

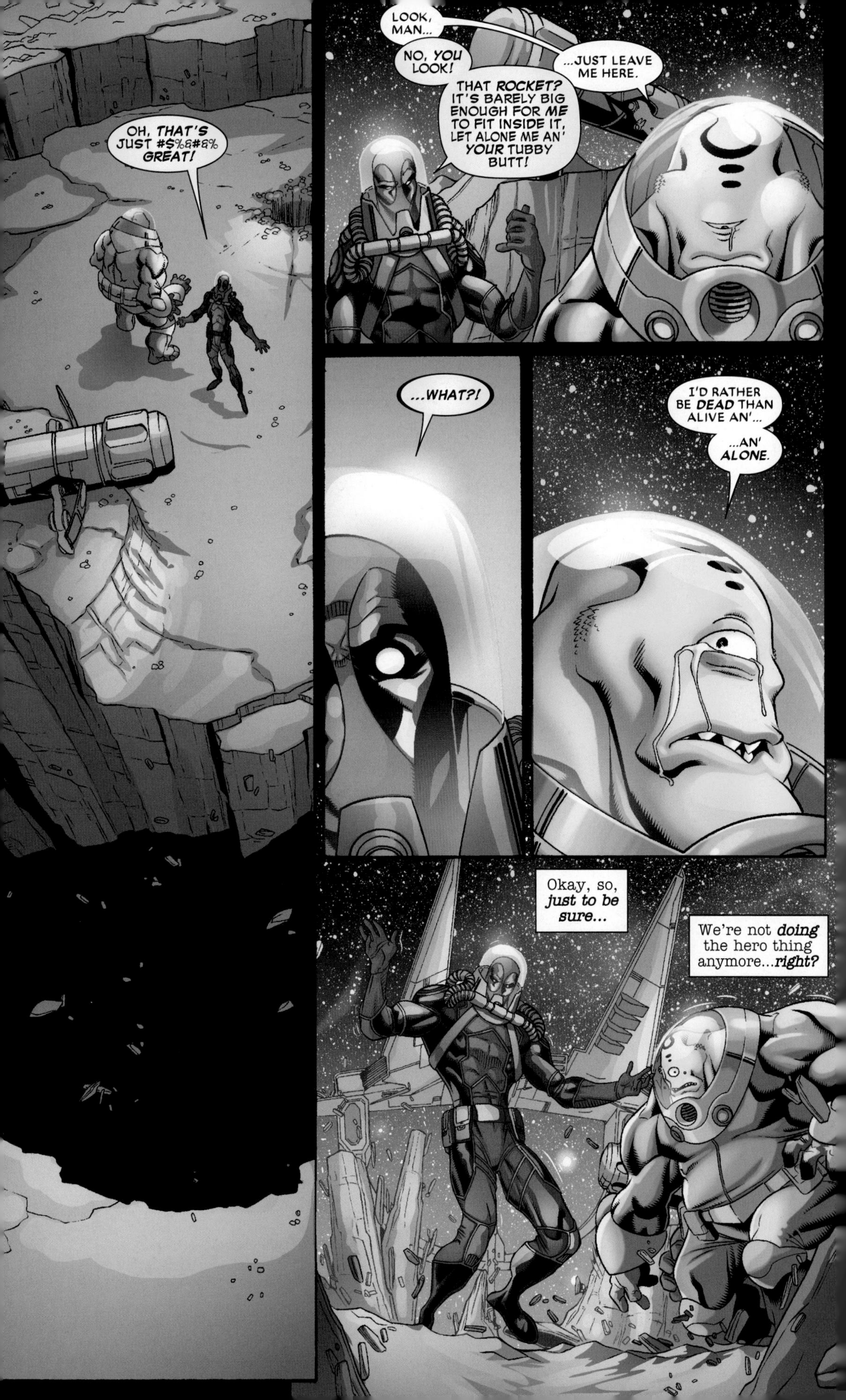

OH, THAT'S JUST #$%&#&% GREAT!
LOOK, MAN...
NO, YOU LOOK!
THAT ROCKET? IT'S BARELY BIG ENOUGH FOR ME TO FIT INSIDE IT, LET ALONE ME AN' YOUR TUBBY BUTT!
...JUST LEAVE ME HERE.
...WHAT?!
I'D RATHER BE DEAD THAN ALIVE AN'...
...AN' ALONE.
Okay, so, just to be sure...
We're not doing the hero thing anymore...right?

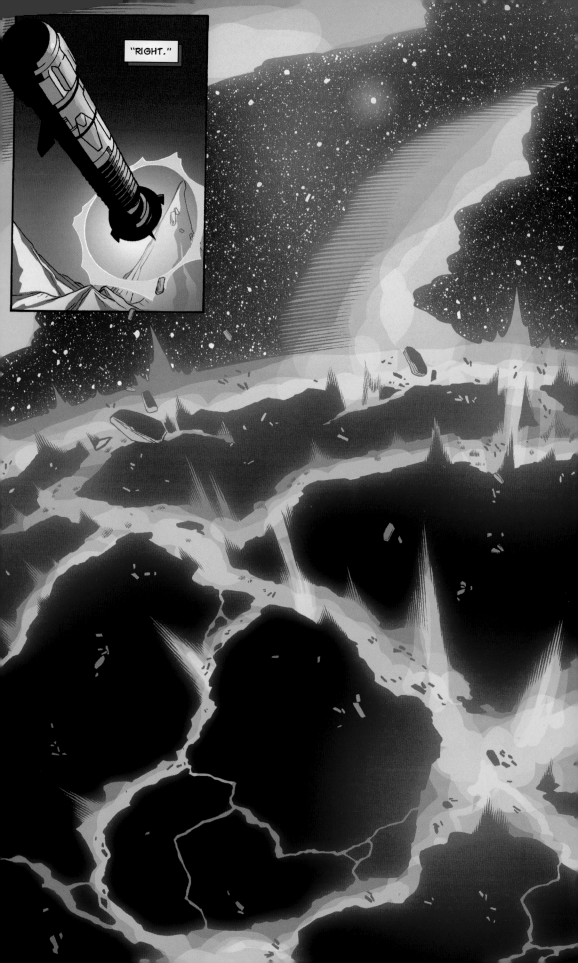

"RIGHT."

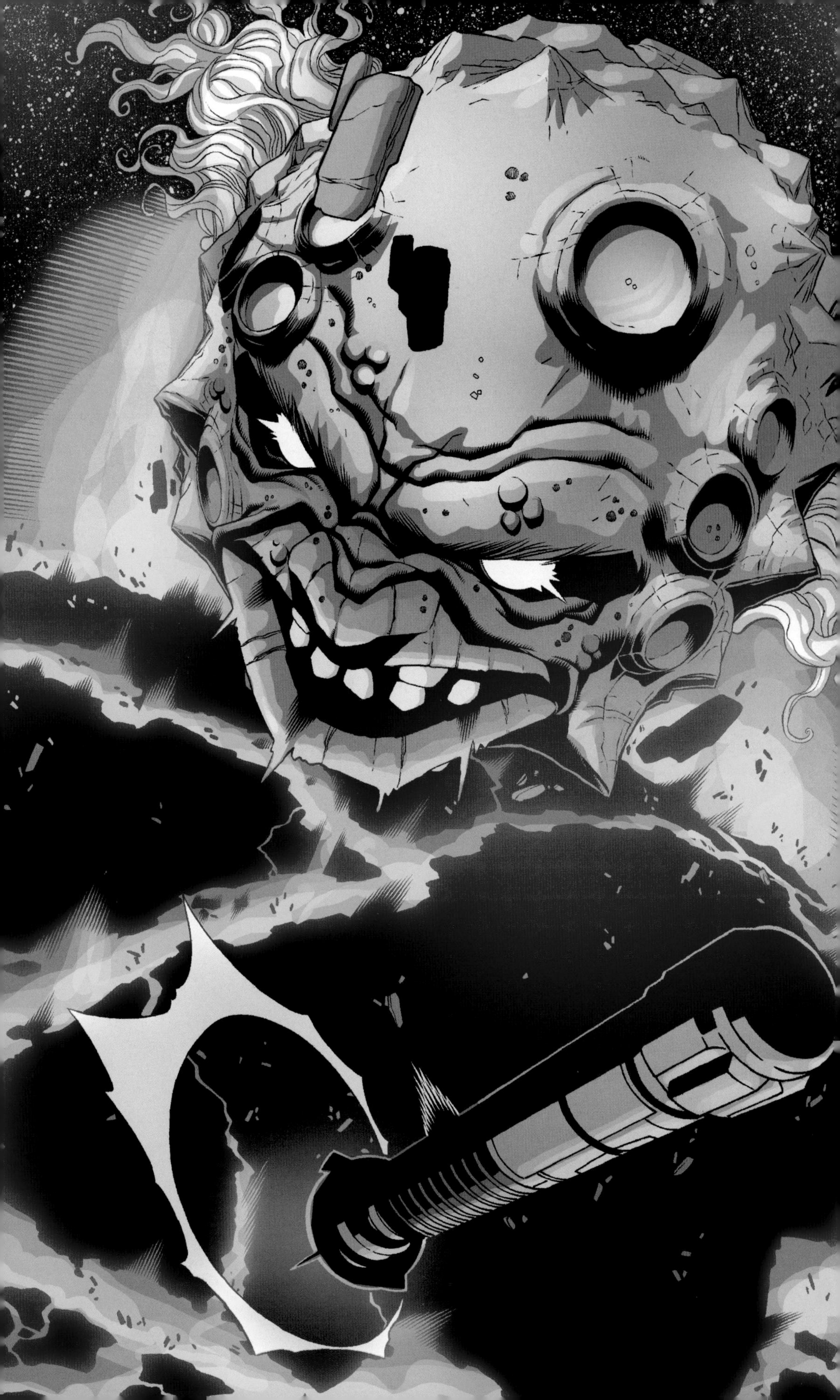

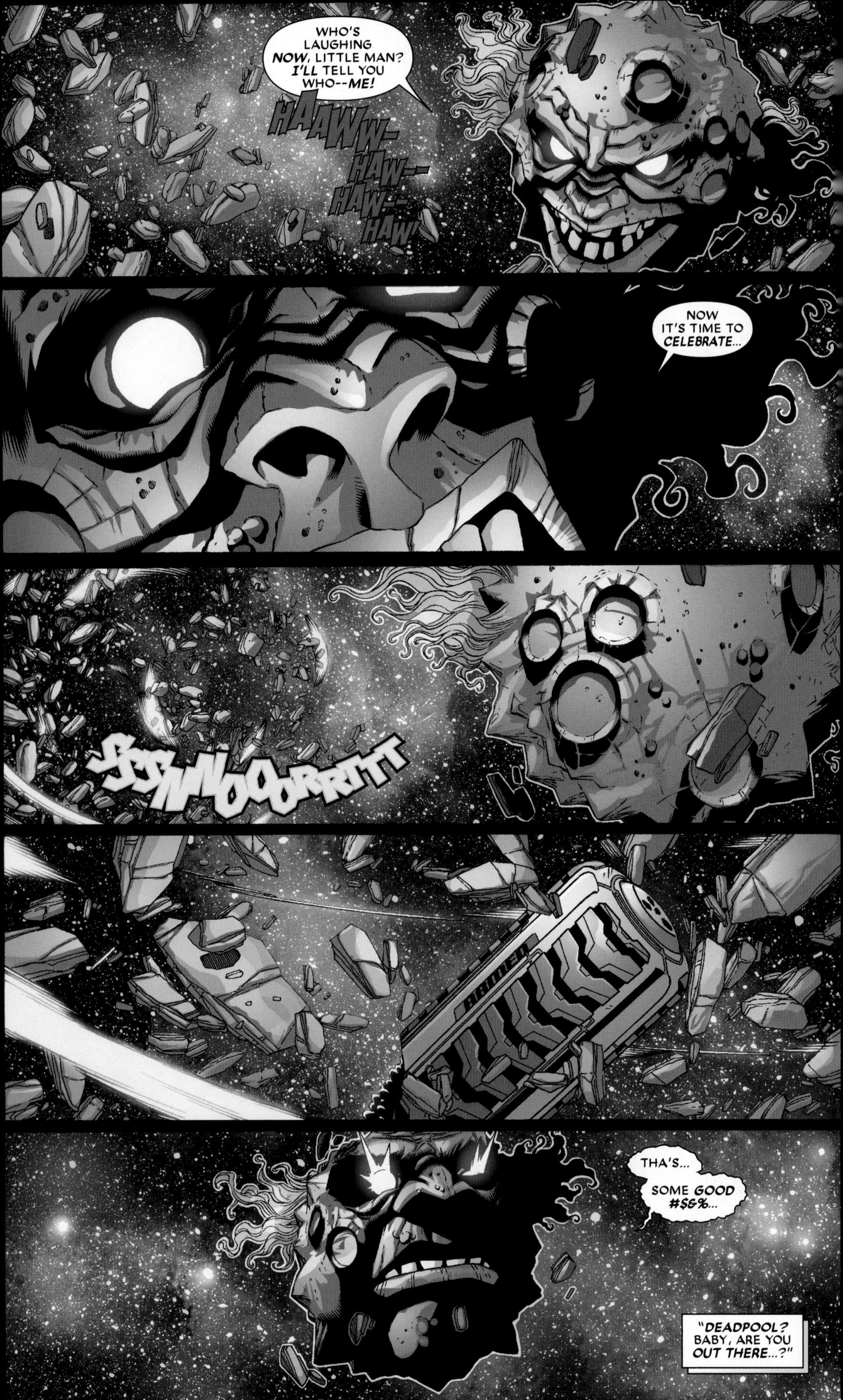
WHO'S LAUGHING NOW, LITTLE MAN? I'LL TELL YOU WHO--ME!
HAAWW-HAW--HAW--HAW!
NOW IT'S TIME TO CELEBRATE...
SSSNNOOORRRITT
THA'S...
SOME GOOD #$&%...
"DEADPOOL? BABY, ARE YOU OUT THERE...?"

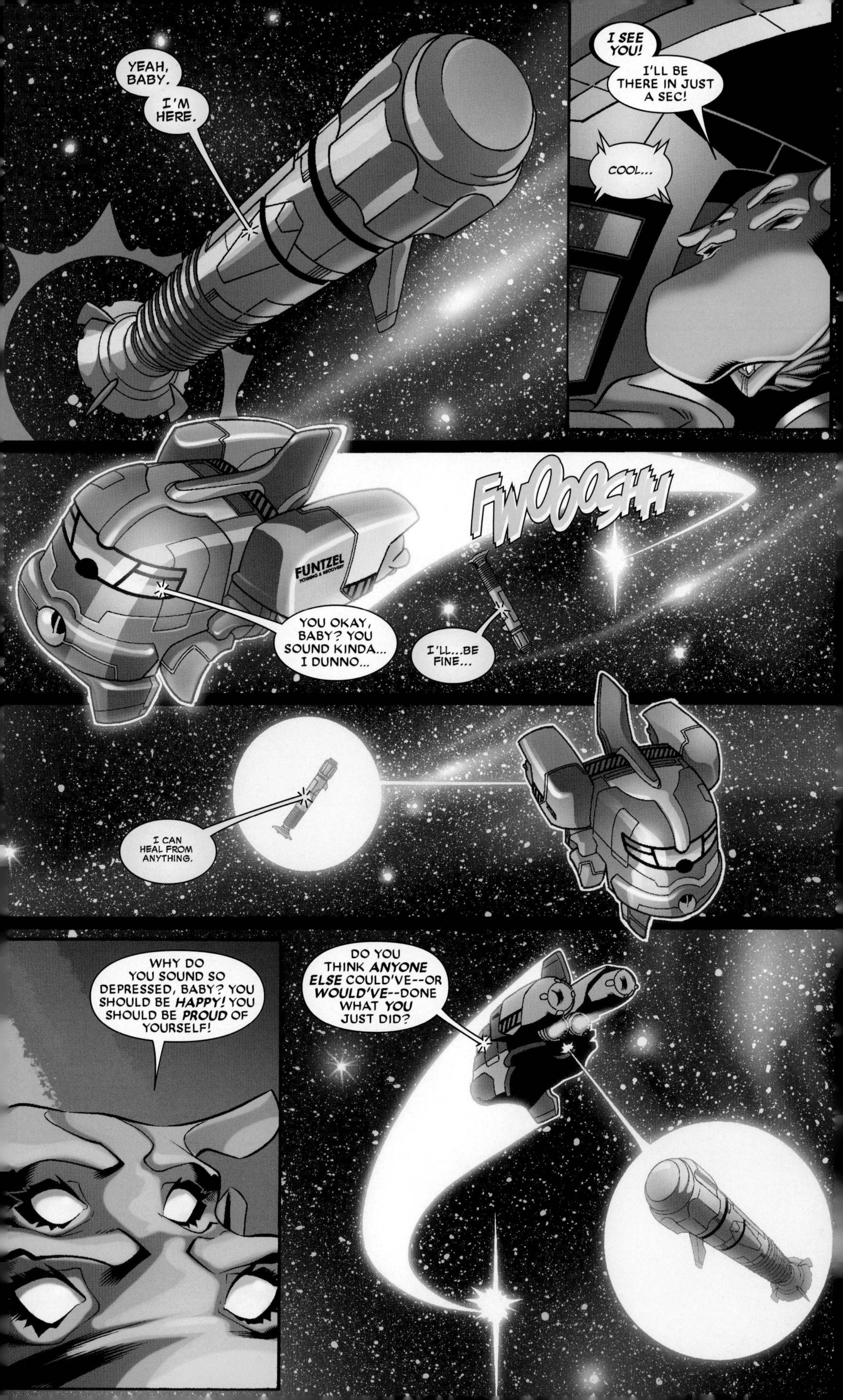
YEAH, BABY.
I'M HERE.
I SEE YOU!
I'LL BE THERE IN JUST A SEC!
COOL...
FWOOOSHH
FUNTZEL TOWING & RECOVERY
YOU OKAY, BABY? YOU SOUND KINDA... I DUNNO...
I'LL...BE FINE...
I CAN HEAL FROM ANYTHING.
WHY DO YOU SOUND SO DEPRESSED, BABY? YOU SHOULD BE *HAPPY!* YOU SHOULD BE *PROUD* OF YOURSELF!
DO YOU THINK *ANYONE ELSE* COULD'VE--OR *WOULD'VE*--DONE WHAT *YOU* JUST DID?

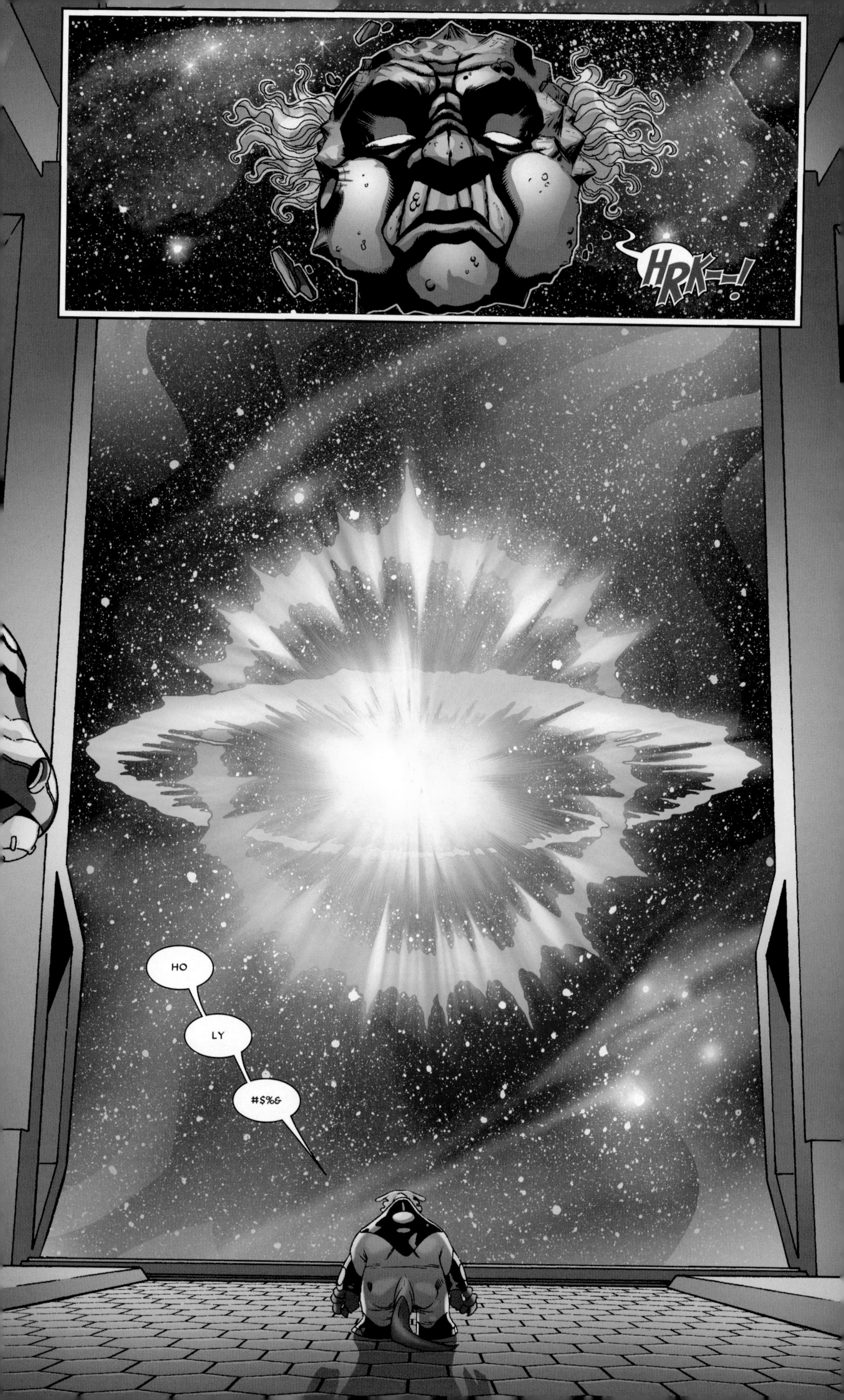
HRK--!
HO
LY
#$%&

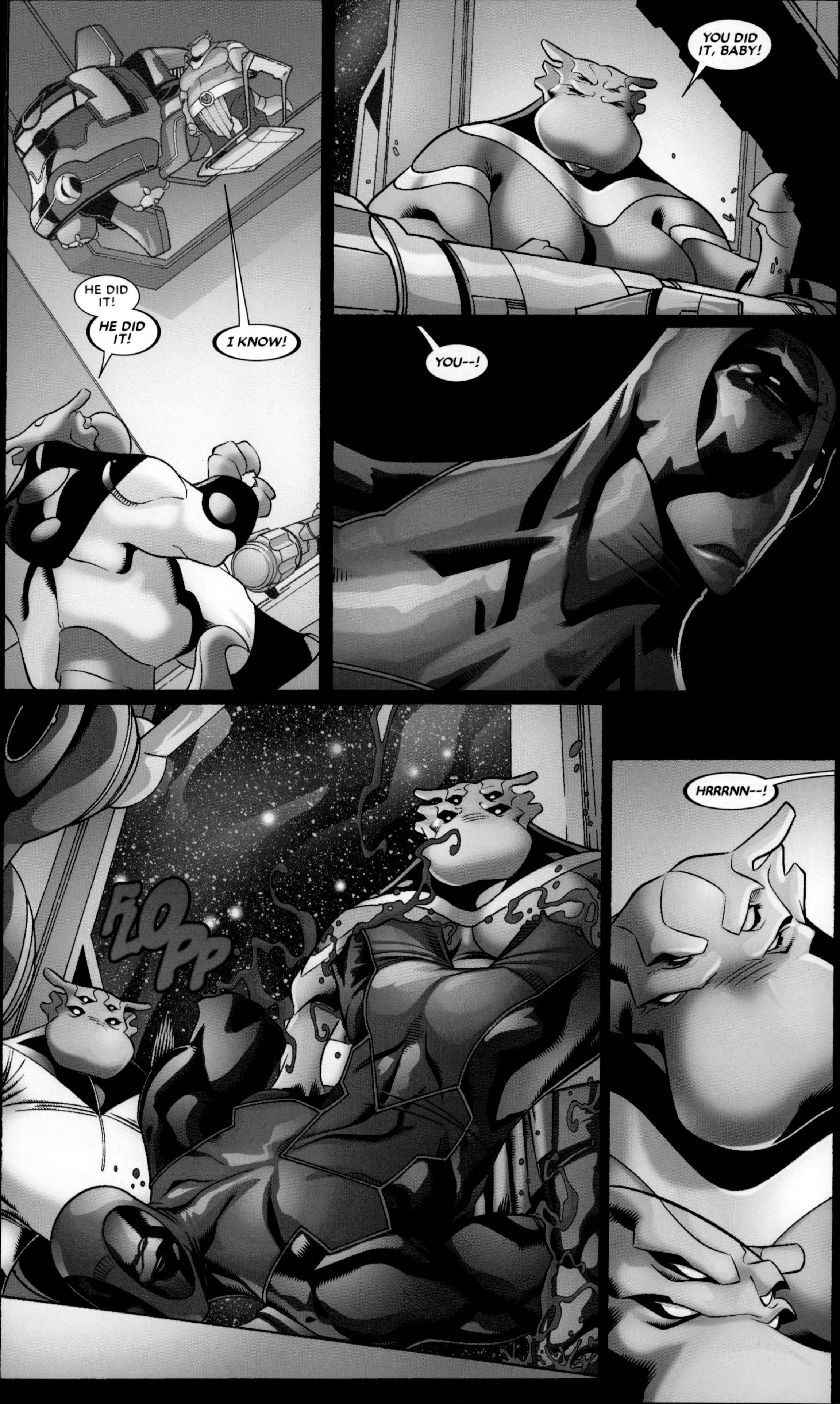

HE DID IT!
HE DID IT!
I KNOW!
YOU DID IT, BABY!
YOU--!
FLOPP
HRRRNN--!

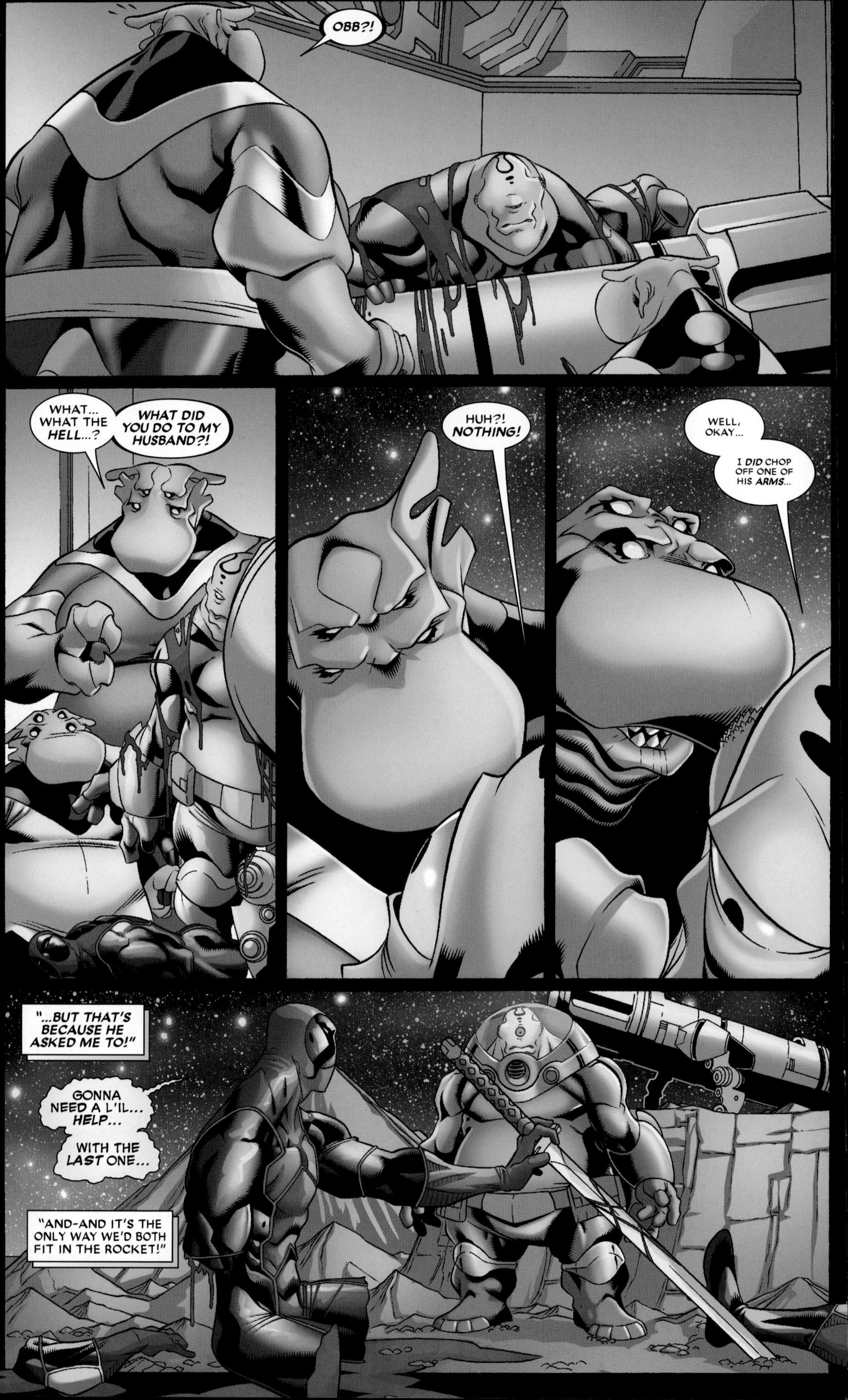
OBB?!
WHAT... WHAT THE HELL...?
WHAT DID YOU DO TO MY HUSBAND?!
HUH?! NOTHING!
WELL, OKAY...
I DID CHOP OFF ONE OF HIS ARMS...
"...BUT THAT'S BECAUSE HE ASKED ME TO!"
GONNA NEED A L'IL... HELP...
WITH THE LAST ONE...
"AND-AND IT'S THE ONLY WAY WE'D BOTH FIT IN THE ROCKET!"

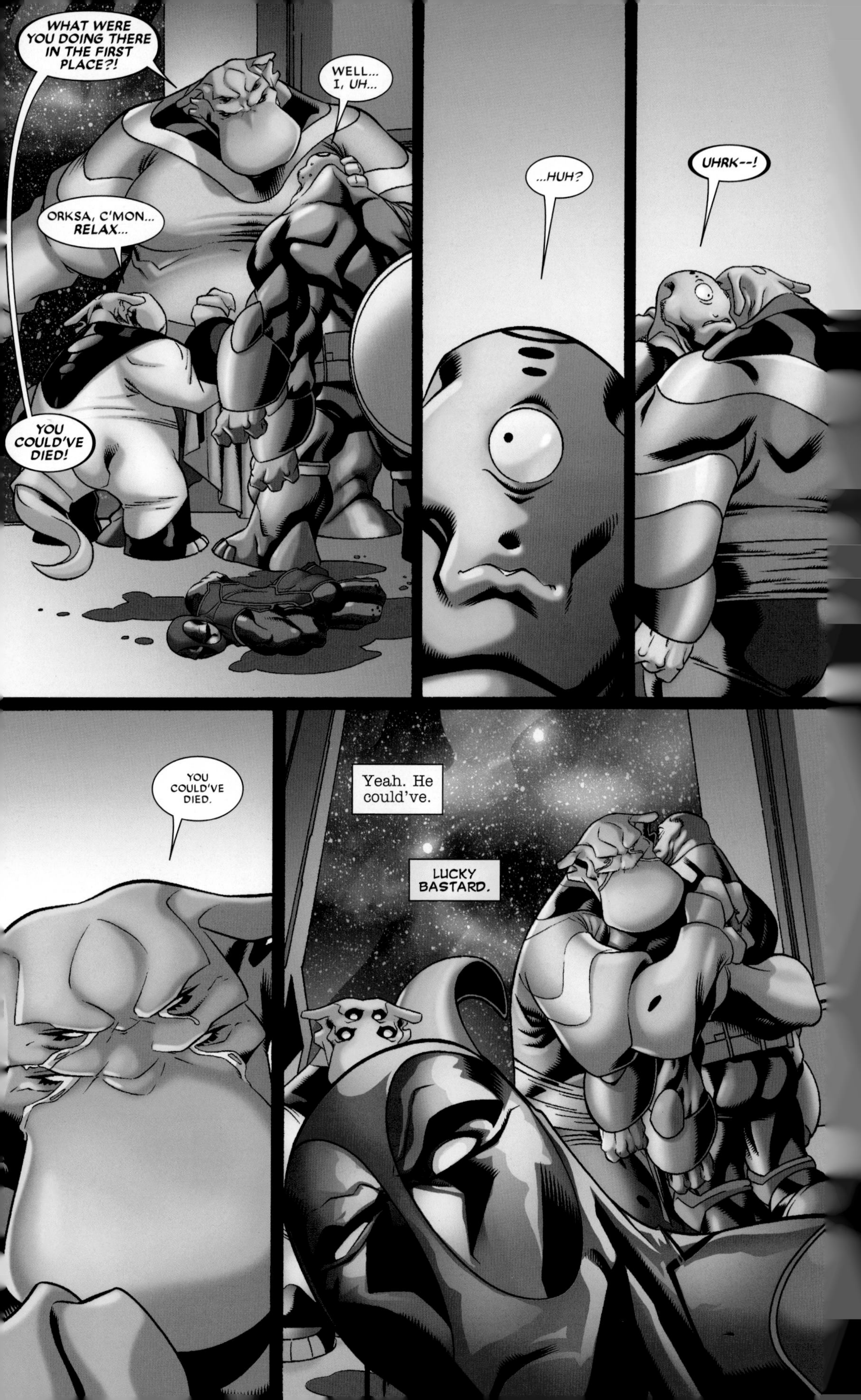
WHAT WERE YOU DOING THERE IN THE FIRST PLACE?!
WELL... I, UH...
ORKSA, C'MON... RELAX...
YOU COULD'VE DIED!
...HUH?
UHRK--!
YOU COULD'VE DIED.
Yeah. He could've.
LUCKY BASTARD.

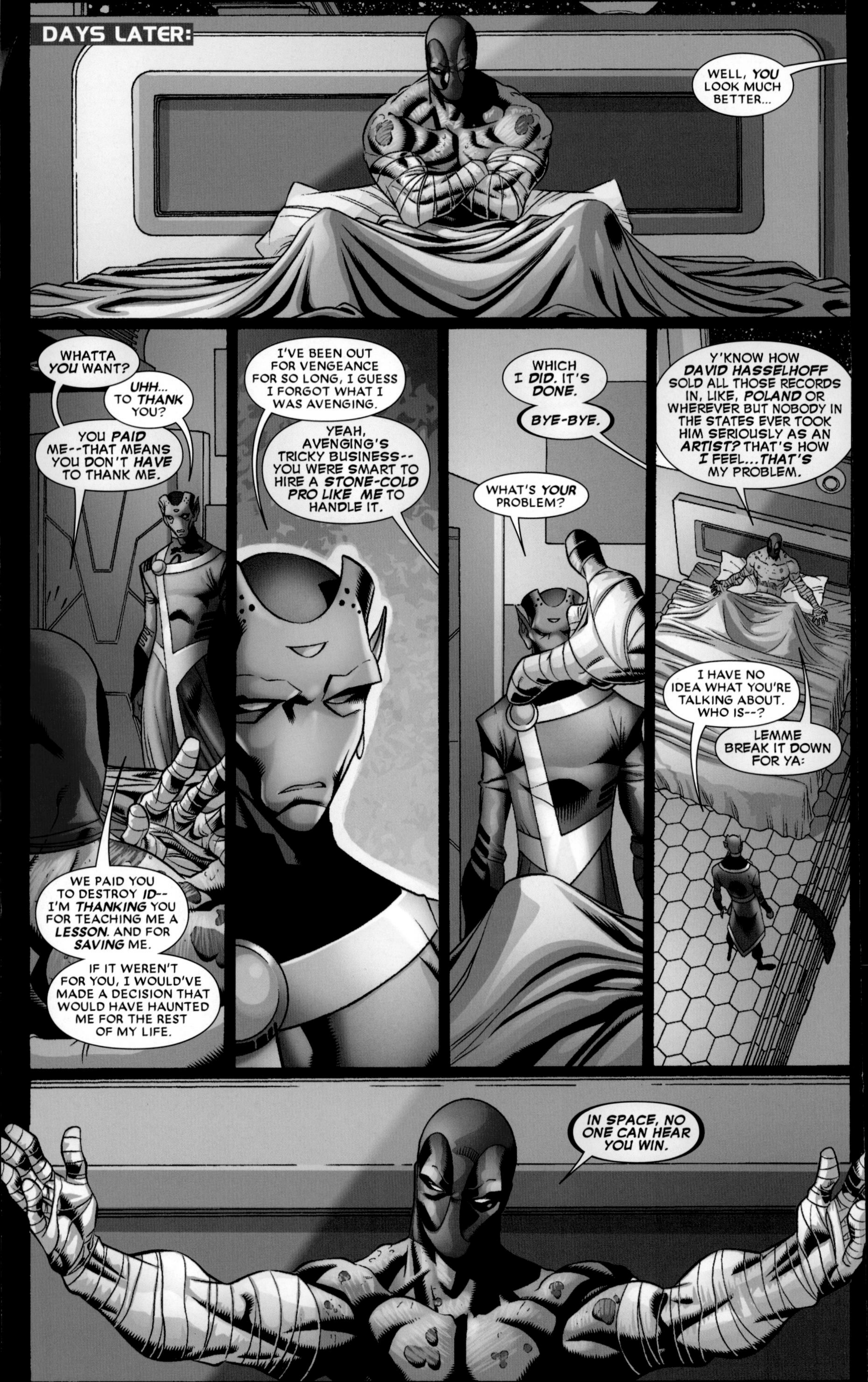
DAYS LATER:
WELL, YOU LOOK MUCH BETTER...
WHATTA YOU WANT?
UHH... TO THANK YOU?
YOU PAID ME--THAT MEANS YOU DON'T HAVE TO THANK ME.
WE PAID YOU TO DESTROY ID-- I'M THANKING YOU FOR TEACHING ME A LESSON. AND FOR SAVING ME.
IF IT WEREN'T FOR YOU, I WOULD'VE MADE A DECISION THAT WOULD HAVE HAUNTED ME FOR THE REST OF MY LIFE.
I'VE BEEN OUT FOR VENGEANCE FOR SO LONG, I GUESS I FORGOT WHAT I WAS AVENGING.
YEAH, AVENGING'S TRICKY BUSINESS-- YOU WERE SMART TO HIRE A STONE-COLD PRO LIKE ME TO HANDLE IT.
WHICH I DID. IT'S DONE.
BYE-BYE.
WHAT'S YOUR PROBLEM?
Y'KNOW HOW DAVID HASSELHOFF SOLD ALL THOSE RECORDS IN, LIKE, POLAND OR WHEREVER BUT NOBODY IN THE STATES EVER TOOK HIM SERIOUSLY AS AN ARTIST? THAT'S HOW I FEEL...THAT'S MY PROBLEM.
I HAVE NO IDEA WHAT YOU'RE TALKING ABOUT. WHO IS--?
LEMME BREAK IT DOWN FOR YA:
IN SPACE, NO ONE CAN HEAR YOU WIN.

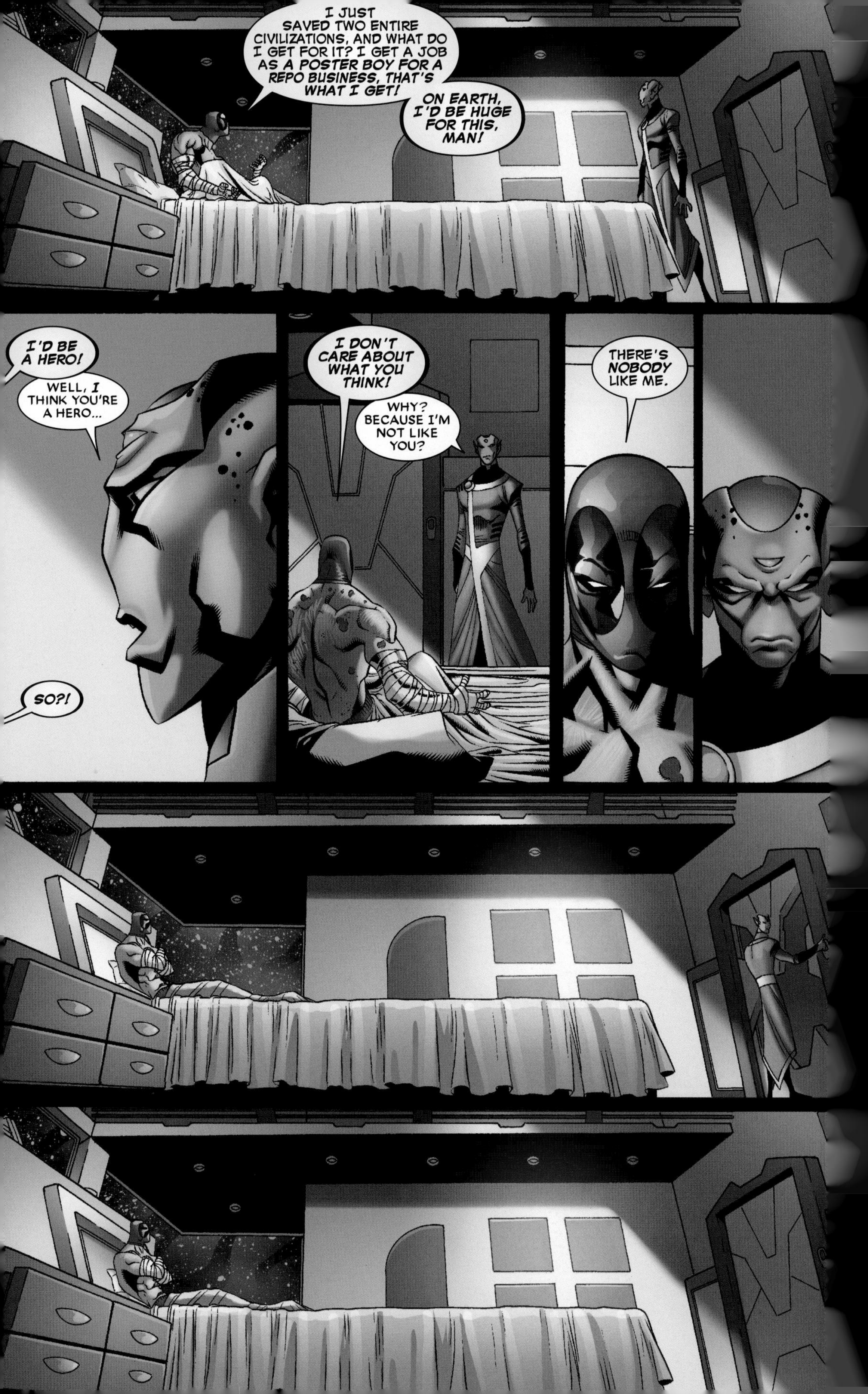
I JUST SAVED TWO ENTIRE CIVILIZATIONS, AND WHAT DO I GET FOR IT? I GET A JOB AS A POSTER BOY FOR A REPO BUSINESS, THAT'S WHAT I GET!
ON EARTH, I'D BE HUGE FOR THIS, MAN!
I'D BE A HERO!
WELL, I THINK YOU'RE A HERO...
SO?!
I DON'T CARE ABOUT WHAT YOU THINK!
WHY? BECAUSE I'M NOT LIKE YOU?
THERE'S NOBODY LIKE ME.

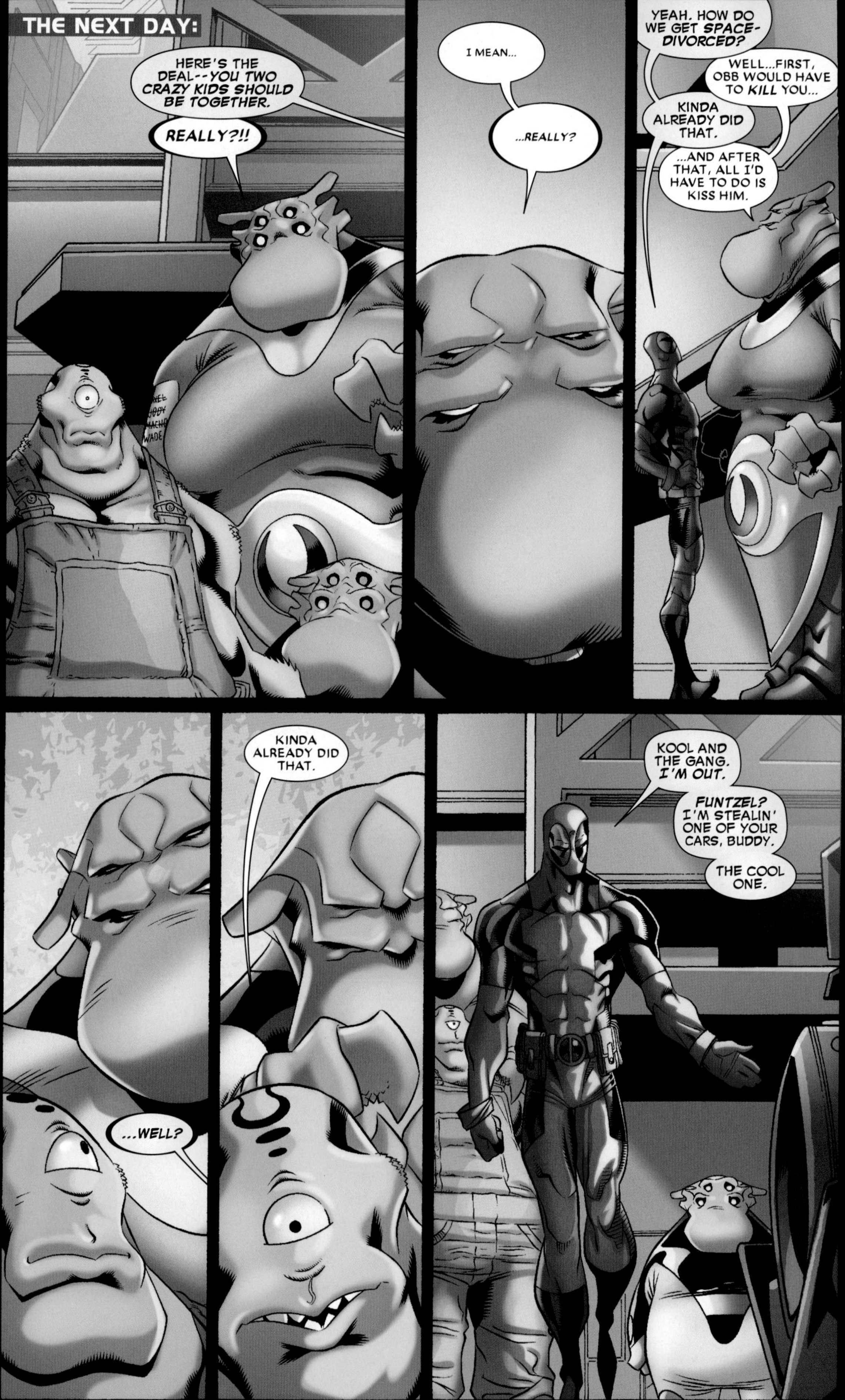
THE NEXT DAY:
HERE'S THE DEAL--YOU TWO CRAZY KIDS SHOULD BE TOGETHER.
REALLY?!!
I MEAN...
...REALLY?
YEAH. HOW DO WE GET SPACE-DIVORCED?
WELL...FIRST, OBB WOULD HAVE TO KILL YOU...
KINDA ALREADY DID THAT.
...AND AFTER THAT, ALL I'D HAVE TO DO IS KISS HIM.
KINDA ALREADY DID THAT.
...WELL?
KOOL AND THE GANG. I'M OUT.
FUNTZEL? I'M STEALIN' ONE OF YOUR CARS, BUDDY.
THE COOL ONE.

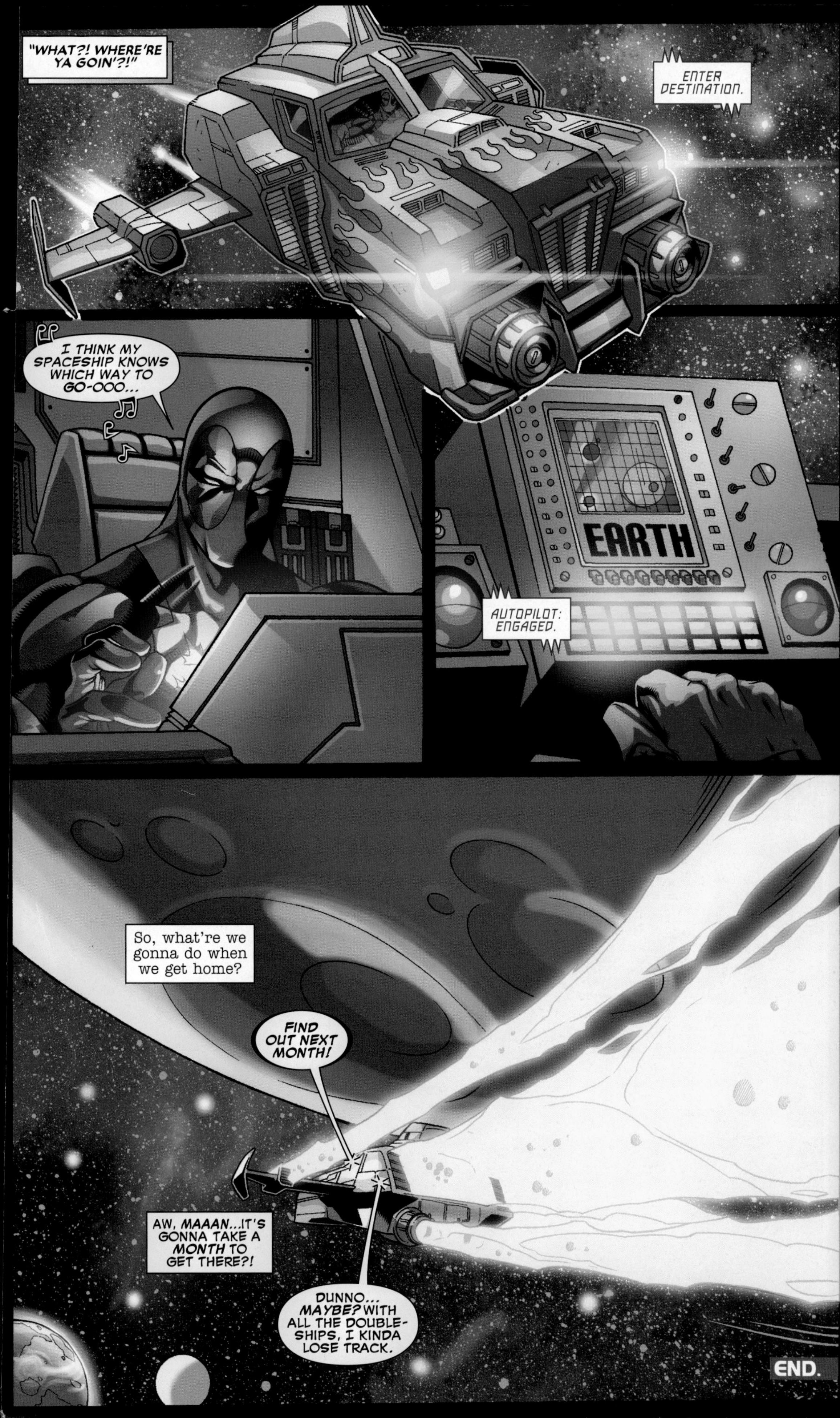
"WHAT?! WHERE'RE YA GOIN'?!"
ENTER DESTINATION.
I THINK MY SPACESHIP KNOWS WHICH WAY TO GO-OOO...
EARTH
AUTOPILOT: ENGAGED.
So, what're we gonna do when we get home?
FIND OUT NEXT MONTH!
AW, MAAAN...IT'S GONNA TAKE A MONTH TO GET THERE?!
DUNNO... MAYBE? WITH ALL THE DOUBLE-SHIPS, I KINDA LOSE TRACK.
END.

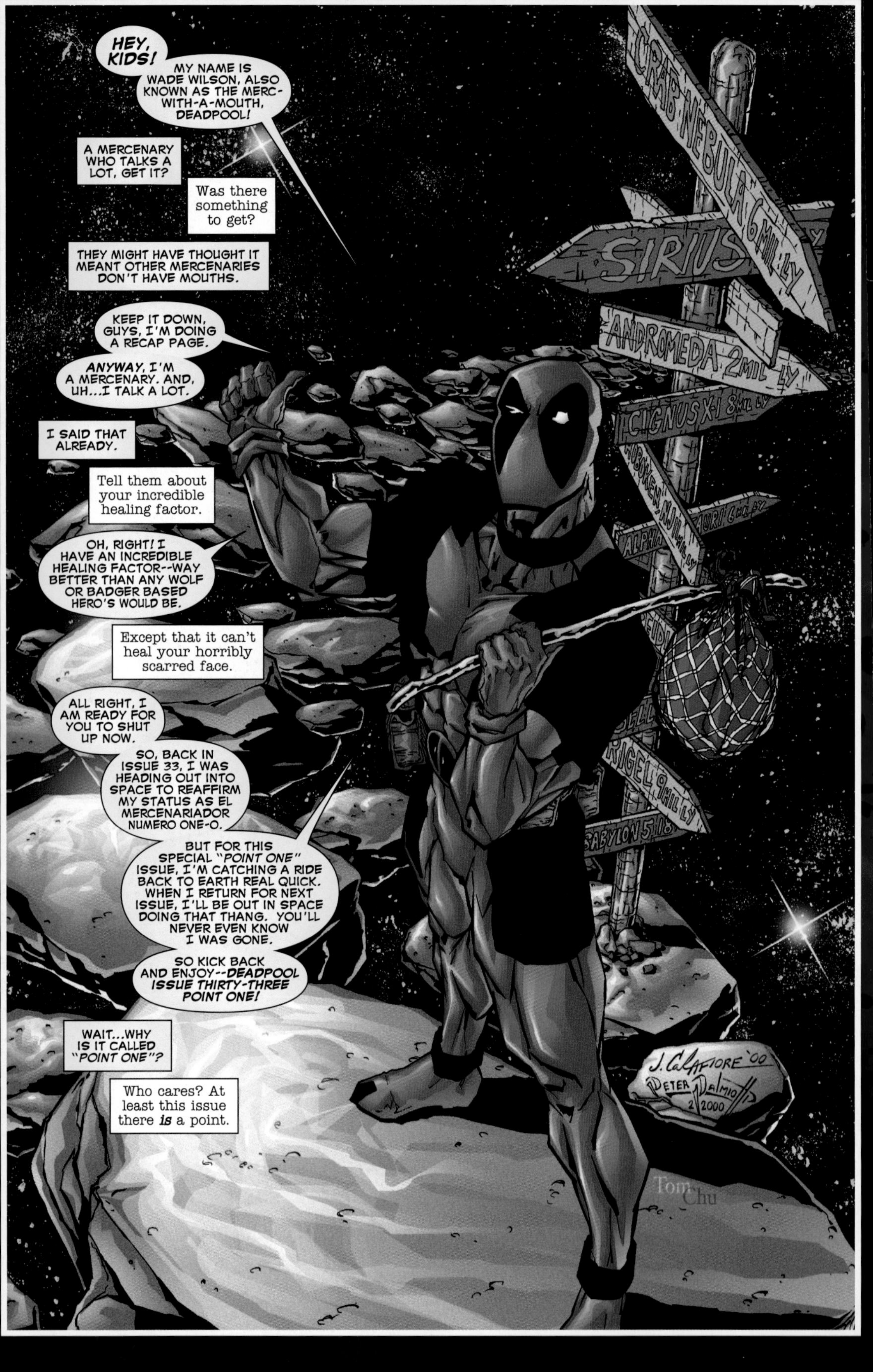

HEY, KIDS!
MY NAME IS WADE WILSON, ALSO KNOWN AS THE MERC-WITH-A-MOUTH, DEADPOOL!
A MERCENARY WHO TALKS A LOT, GET IT?
Was there something to get?
THEY MIGHT HAVE THOUGHT IT MEANT OTHER MERCENARIES DON'T HAVE MOUTHS.
KEEP IT DOWN, GUYS, I'M DOING A RECAP PAGE.
ANYWAY, I'M A MERCENARY. AND, UH...I TALK A LOT.
I SAID THAT ALREADY.
Tell them about your incredible healing factor.
OH, RIGHT! I HAVE AN INCREDIBLE HEALING FACTOR--WAY BETTER THAN ANY WOLF OR BADGER BASED HERO'S WOULD BE.
Except that it can't heal your horribly scarred face.
ALL RIGHT, I AM READY FOR YOU TO SHUT UP NOW.
SO, BACK IN ISSUE 33, I WAS HEADING OUT INTO SPACE TO REAFFIRM MY STATUS AS EL MERCENARIADOR NUMERO ONE-O.
BUT FOR THIS SPECIAL "POINT ONE" ISSUE, I'M CATCHING A RIDE BACK TO EARTH REAL QUICK. WHEN I RETURN FOR NEXT ISSUE, I'LL BE OUT IN SPACE DOING THAT THANG. YOU'LL NEVER EVEN KNOW I WAS GONE.
SO KICK BACK AND ENJOY--DEADPOOL ISSUE THIRTY-THREE POINT ONE!
WAIT...WHY IS IT CALLED "POINT ONE"?
Who cares? At least this issue there is a point.
CRAB NEBULA 6MIL LY
SIRIUS
ANDROMEDA 2MIL LY
CIGNUS X-1 8MIL LY
HOBOKEN, NJ 1MIL LY
RIGEL 9MIL LY
BABYLON 5
J. CALAFIORE '00
PETER PALMIOTTI 2/2000
Tom Chu

DEADPOOL #33.1 RECAP PAGE

Released between #33 and #34, issue #33.1 featured this recap to explain the break in the ongoing story.